Victorian Autobiography

Victorian Autobiography
The Tradition of Self-Interpretation

LINDA H. PETERSON

Yale University Press
New Haven and London

Designed by Susan P. Fillion and set in Garamond #3 type. Printed
in the United States of America by Vail-Ballou Press, Binghamton,
N.Y.

*The paper in this book meets the guidelines for permanence and durability
of the Committee on Production Guidelines for Book Longevity of the Council
on Library Resources.*

Library of Congress Cataloging-in-Publication Data

Peterson, Linda H.
    Victorian autobiography.

    Includes bibliographical references and index.
    1. Autobiography.   2. Great Britain—Biography.
I. Title.
CT25.P47   1986   820'.9'008   [B]   85—17964
ISBN 0—300—03563—2 (alk. paper)

10   9   8   7   6   5   4   3   2   1

For F.S.

CONTENTS

ACKNOWLEDGMENTS

y convention, the acknowledgments page records an author's intellectual debts and thus traces the stages of an intellectual career. Like many a Victorian autobiographer, I am resistant to conventions, but this is one to which I happily conform.

I owe particular thanks to George Landow, who introduced me to Victorian autobiography in all its complexities; to Dwight Culler and David DeLaura, who both challenged and supported my work at critical stages; to Leslie Moore, who read early drafts of my manuscript and helped hone its argument; and to Lynn Bloom, Ian Ker, George Levine, John Maynard, Hillis Miller, James Olney, Ronald Paulson, Thomas Vargish, and Thomas Whitaker, whose comments and suggestions improved individual chapters of this book.

Much of the research and writing was completed while I held a Morse Fellowship, for which I owe thanks to Yale University, and while I lived in England, for which I owe thanks to Sonia and Patricia Lindsay, who provided idyllic working conditions in Devon, Loch Laggan, and London. A version of chapter 4 was originally published in *PMLA* as "Newman's *Apologia* and the Traditions of the English Spiritual Autobiography," and I am grateful for permission to include it here. "But be his my special thanks," in Matthew Arnold's words, that "even-balanced soul" who, throughout the writing of this book, "saw life steadily and saw it whole." My thanks to Fred Strebeigh.

Introduction: The Hermeneutic Imperative

hen John Ruskin traveled abroad for the first time without his parents, his mother slipped a copy of *Grace Abounding to the Chief of Sinners* into his satchel. "What made you put that funny book of John Bunyan's in the bag," Ruskin wrote back. "You know it is not at all in my way." Bunyan's book—an autobiographical account of youthful depravity, conviction of sin, and dramatic conversion—was not to Ruskin's taste because, as he explained to his mother, it displayed a man who dwelt "painfully and exclusively on the relations of the Deity to his own little self," who puzzled over promptings he believed were of the devil and let biblical texts come "jingling into his head," who was "always looking to his own interests or his own state, loving or fearing or doubting, just as he happened to fancy God was dealing with him."[1] The book was, in other words, a classic version of the spiritual autobiography, and Ruskin's complaints against it virtually define the genre. From Bunyan's era to Ruskin's, the spiritual autobiography demanded an intense introspection and retrospection of the writer's life and a rigorous interpretation of his experience in terms of biblical texts or patterns of biblical history.

Ruskin put the matter to his mother in specific rather than generic terms, but when he decided to write his own autobiography in 1885, forty years after that European tour, he set out to produce a different sort of book. As if in answer to Bunyan's morbid fancies and self-lacerations, Ruskin decided, as he explained in the preface to *Praeterita*, that he would compose his autobiographical sketches "at ease," "speaking of what it gives me joy to remember" and "passing in total silence things which I have no pleasure in reviewing."[2] His autobiography was to reject Bunyan's mode of spiritual introspection, just as he had by then rejected his mother's religion. It was to be a memoir of past experience, an extroitive account of what he chose to recall and record.

Despite the disclaimer, Bunyan's funny little book stayed quite a bit "in the way" for Ruskin. For Bunyan's autobiographical mode was not easily avoided—either by Ruskin or by other Victorians who attempted to write autobiography, whether in its spiritual or newly secular form. Victorian autobiographers had to contend with a generic tradition that had developed from the spiritual autobiographies of the seventeenth and eighteenth centuries and with the methods of imagining and interpreting the self that that tradition had shaped. Their ways of contending, which comprise the chapters of this book, are diverse and fascinatingly complex, but for all of them the generic tradition presented a curious paradox: that autobiography, apparently the most personal and individual of literary genres, is in fact a highly conventional, even prescriptive form, and that its generic conventions shape our ways of thinking about the most private aspects of our lives.[3] If Ruskin responded, at least ostensibly, by attempting to reject the tradition and thus evade its influence, other Victorian autobiographers acknowledged the burden of the past and coped by manipulating or modifying the forms they had inherited from their generic predecessors.

Anyone who attempts to trace the history of a literary genre, especially one like autobiography which itself raises questions of historical method, recognizes soon that histories are created by interpreters and that interpretations depend upon chosen points of origin. For most literary historians, the history of autobiography as a genre begins with either a mirror or a book. Those who choose the mirror tend to see the genre as one of self-presentation; for them autobiography begins when Renaissance man learns to make mirrors and receives a reflection back from the glass he has created. Those literary histori-

but what are 'generic conventions'?

ans who, in contrast, choose the book tend to treat the genre as one of self-interpretation; autobiography begins for them in the act of reading, initially the book of Scripture but later other books of autobiography, and this act of reading provides the versions of history that autobiographers then use to interpret the lives they tell. My own study of Victorian autobiography is deliberately bookish, and it chooses to be so on both cultural and methodological grounds. The view of autobiography as self-presentation is essentially French, the qualities of the genre finding full expression in Rousseau's *Confessions*. The view of autobiography as self-interpretation is more typically English, the originating example being John Bunyan's *Grace Abounding*.[4] The decision to write literary history necessarily turns my attention to books, which were the sources that English autobiographers themselves turned to when contemplating their lives.

The line of descent from Bunyan to the Victorians, a line which this chapter traces, passes through a series of minor but popular practitioners of the spiritual autobiography in the eighteenth century— writers like William Cowper, John Newton, George Whitefield, and Thomas Scott. It bypasses more prestigious men like Edward Gibbon and Roger North who wrote in the public, *res gestae* mode. According to John N. Morris's account of this literary descent, the spiritual autobiographers transmitted a sensibility that "value[d] the private and the inward more highly than the public and the outward," a sensibility that we now call Romantic but that Morris argues is at root religious. The gradual ascendance of this sensibility in social and literary realms allowed the spiritual autobiography, rather than the *res gestae* form, to become the dominant mode of autobiography in the English tradition by the beginning of the nineteenth century. "Self," as Morris puts it, "became the modern word for soul."[5]

If a general shift in literary sensibility made possible the ascendance of the introspective spiritual autobiography by the end of the eighteenth century, we might focus more specifically on a continuity in method to explain the transmission of generic form from Bunyan to the Victorians. That method I shall call "hermeneutic"—hermeneutic first in the sense that it foregrounds self-interpretation rather

self-presentation: essentially French
self-interpretation: more typically English

than narration or self-expression, but hermeneutic also in the sense
that it appropriates its principles and strategies of interpretation from
biblical hermeneutics. The designation "hermeneutic" recognizes
that autobiography distinguishes itself as a genre by the act of
interpretation rather than the act of presentation, that its emphasis
lies in the understanding of events rather than in the art of narrating
them. In discussions of hermeneutic method since the early nineteenth century, theologians and philosophers have made this distinction, separating explication from interpretation or, to borrow
Schleiermacher's terminology, *Darstellen* (the art of presentation)
from *Verstehen* (the art of understanding). According to Schleiermacher, *Darstellen* is a necessary part of the hermeneutic enterprise,
but *Verstehen* is its focus, "ein Object der Hermeneutik."[6] A recent
commentator on hermeneutics since Schleiermacher phrases the distinction this way: "it is one operation to formulate something and
bring it to speech; it is quite another and distinct operation to
understand what is spoken."[7]

In autobiography, as in other hermeneutic forms, both presentation and interpretation play a part. The autobiographer must concern
himself with the presentation of his life, a concern he may execute
with the narrative skill of the novelist. But his ultimate goal lies
beyond such narration, beyond rhetorical formulation. In this goal
the autobiography differs from the novel, which has always valued
(re)presentation over other arts and which has, at least in some
periods, eschewed explicit interpretation. The autobiographer focuses less on narrative emplotment than on explicit interpretation.
This focus may help to explain why the finest practitioners of the
genre in the Victorian era were historians, philosophers, and critics
rather than novelists and why readers who value the autobiography
have been those who take special interest in the interpretative act.

The fact that autobiography includes both presentation and interpretation, however, creates a continual temptation to ignore or blur
the distinction. Indeed, many critics of the autobiography have
simply treated the genre as a variant of the novel, whether as a
sub-genre or as a prefigurative form that eventually merged with (or
transformed itself into) the novel. In a seminal study of the English
autobiography, for example, Wayne Shumaker classified examples

according to three modes: the expository, the narrative, and a "mixed" transitional mode that was common in the Victorian period and that suggested to him a gradual evolution throughout the nineteenth century from exposition to a "fully novelized form." In a subsequent study, *Design and Truth in Autobiography*, Roy Pascal implicitly adopted Shumaker's approach and raised what he defined as the related problem of narrative fiction versus historical truth. Because of his approach, Pascal had little praise for the classic Victorian autobiographies, but approved those, such as Brontë's *Villette* and Dickens' *David Copperfield*, that were already novelistic in form. Even an otherwise appealing treatment of the genre, William C. Spengemann's *The Forms of Autobiography*, only modifies Shumaker's original three modes with a more sophisticated taxonomy. Like Shumaker, Spengemann sees a formal modulation from the "historical" to the "philosophical" to the "poetic," a modulation that "rehears[es] the entire development of the genre from the Middle Ages to the modern era." Spengemann labels his final stage "poetic," but it is represented primarily by novels: *David Copperfield, The Scarlet Letter*, and (the one exception) *Sartor Resartus*.[8]

It may be true that there is a convergence of the novel and some forms of the autobiography at the end of the nineteenth century. But by describing an evolutionary progress from exposition to narrative or, alternatively, from the historical to the poetic, literary historians create a past that never was. Historically speaking, exposition and narrative did not develop as separate entities or emphases in the autobiography. Both were present from its beginning: the genre has always been, in Shumaker's phrase, a "mixed mode." Moreover, shifts in emphasis from the expositional to the narrative have often provided— from the beginning of autobiography as a genre—a pattern for novelists and storytellers to imitate in the writing of their fictional genres. As both G.A. Starr and J. Paul Hunter have shown in their studies of *Robinson Crusoe*, Defoe created his novel by adapting the materials of contemporary spiritual autobiography to a fictional purpose. Their descriptions of Defoe's adaptations are revealing: Defoe shifted his emphasis away from an exposition about the state of sin or gift of grace and concentrated instead on a narrative of the conversion process, rich with fascinating details. With a shift in the direction of intricate, fascinated and fascinating presentation, the autobiographical form becomes more like what we commonly call a novel.

Shifts of this sort have occurred frequently during the past two centuries and have occurred even within the spiritual autobiography itself. It may be a mistake to see in them, however, any significant generic trend. Readers of the autobiography from Bunyan to Ruskin have always noticed how different in structure and intention the autobiographical episode is from an episode in a short tale or a chapter of a contemporary novel: whereas the novelist takes primary delight in the telling of his tale, the spiritual autobiographer often summarizes or curtails his narrative, as if he wished the telling over so that he could get on to something else. This difference reflects the autobiographer's interest in interpretation rather than in narration or self-expression.

In short, the evolutionary metaphor, so comfortable to us in a post-Darwinian age, may be in some sense applicable to the development of the genre, but not in the sense that it sees the "novelized autobiography" or the "autobiography of poetic self-expression" as the product of an evolutionary process. If the metaphor applies, it works best to explain the demise of a species of spiritual autobiography, plentiful during much of the nineteenth century but nearly extinct at the beginning of the twentieth.

Before considering the causes of that demise, however, we need first to trace the ascendance of the spiritual autobiography as the primary form of autobiographical writing in the Victorian era and to understand its connection with a specific method of biblical hermeneutics, whose strategies for interpretation the autobiographer adapted almost directly in his attempt to discover the meaning of his life.[9] For by calling the autobiography "hermeneutic," I mean also to suggest that the genre depended upon—perhaps originated in—a particular system of biblical hermeneutics known as typology.

In its most orthodox form, biblical typology posited a system of interpretation in which characters, events, and sacred objects of the

Old Testament prefigured Christ or some aspect of Christian doctrine. In common practice, however, especially among Puritans and later among evangelicals, most of these Old Testament types were also applied to the lives of the individual Christians.[10] Samson destroying the Philistine temple, for example, might typify Christ destroying the forces of evil through his death on the cross, but he could also typify the Christian believer who, in battle with evil, triumphs but suffers greatly because of his ordeal. Moses leading the Israelites to the promised land might typify Christ leading his followers to spiritual redemption, but he could also typify a great, divinely ordained political leader or a humble, but also divinely ordained, spiritual pastor.

In the preface to *Grace Abounding* Bunyan uses Moses in just this way to justify the publication of his personal narrative: *"Moses* (Numb. 33. 1, 2) *writ of the Journeyings of the children of* Israel, *from* Egypt *to the Land of* Canaan; ... *Wherefore this I have endeavoured to do; and not onely so, but to publish it also; that, if God will, others may be put in remembrance of what he hath done for their Souls, by reading his work upon me."*[11] Bunyan also uses David's lyrical outpourings in the Psalms as a type of his own literary outpourings from the Bedford jail and Samson's struggle with the lion in Judges 14, from whose carcass was extracted a drop of honey, as a type of the spiritual benefit gained from struggle with the enemy. The possibilities for the personal application of types were almost infinite, limited only by the principles of typological hermeneutics and by the interpreter's imagination.

Because the spiritual autobiographer borrowed his fundamental interpretive strategy from biblical typology, the account he produced often resembled—in its formal features—a sermon or a segment of biblical commentary. Typically, a commentary that uses typology to interpret a biblical text includes three parts: (1) the pericope or quotation of the text itself, (2) a narrative redaction of the passage if it is episodic or an expositional restatement if it is not, and (3) the commentator's interpretation of the biblical material. Of the three, the last is most significant, the pericope and the narrative redaction preparing for and sometimes anticipating the interpretation that the commentator will propose. In spiritual autobiography, most episodes combine these same parts and with the same relative emphasis. The pericope may be present in the autobiographical text as a quotation from a diary, a letter, or even a previously published work. More likely it is absent, hidden from the reader's view, perhaps existing only in the autobiographer's memory. The narrative redaction corresponds to the text that the autobiographer creates from his past as he narrates what he remembers as significant or what he has recorded before as significant. This narrative, (re)created by the autobiographer, becomes the written text which he, like the biblical commentator, then interprets. As in biblical commentary, the autobiographer presents pericope and narrative redaction for the sake of interpretive commentary.

The *locus classicus* of this autobiographical structure—and of the hermeneutic imperative I describe—appear at the midpoint of Bunyan's *Grace Abounding*, that funny little book of which Ruskin so disapproved.[12] The episode is a crucial one, that of Bunyan's temptation to deny Christ. Recorded in sections 131 through 173, the temptation consumes Bunyan's attention for fully one-tenth of the autobiography. The episode is introduced with the general observation that "grievous and dreadful temptation" often strikes when the believer feels most secure, and it is followed by a straightforward narrative of Satan's prompting to sell Christ, "to exchange him for the things of this life; for any thing."[13] Despite his memory that the episode lasted for fully a year, without a day's respite, Bunyan allows very little narrative space to the temptation itself: only eight of the forty-three sections.

This brevity has nothing to do with narrative incapacity, for when Bunyan chooses to narrate, he renders his tale with remarkable skill. He suggests the scope of the temptation in a series of predicates—"I could neither eat my food, stoop for a pin, chop a stick, or cast mine eye to look on this or that, but still the temptation would come" (135)—that neatly encompass all of his experience; he uses similes—"as on a rack" (136) or "as a Bird that is shot from the top of a Tree" (140)—to convey the intensity of the temptation and the seriousness with which he struggled; and he describes the physiological effects of prolonged stress when he remembers his body, quite against his will, being "put into action or motion, by way of pushing or thrusting with my hands or elbows" (137). But although Bunyan can write powerful narrative and seems to take pleasure in doing so, his instinct as autobiographer is to limit the narrative's space. This one he cuts short with a "But to be brief," concluding with a three-sentence account of how he finally succumbed. His inclination, like that of the genre itself, is toward interpretation, toward a resolution of the hermeneutic dilemma that his actions once created and that his narrative now revives as a text.

For Bunyan, that dilemma has to do with meaning, with the spiritual significance of his actions, and it is at this point that hermeneutics in the second sense impinges upon autobiographical writing. For as Bunyan begins interpretation, the strategies of biblical typology consume his attention and shape his autobiographical account. Looking with a typologist's eye for an Old Testament figure whose predicament foreshadows (and thus explains) his own, he seizes upon Esau as a likely type. Just as Esau sold his birthright for a pottage of lentils, he believes that he has sold his spiritual inheritance for the perishables of this world and has doomed himself eternally to nothing "but damnation, and an expectation of damnation" (142). Bunyan's authority for this interpretation seems almost indisputable. Not only does the Old Testament narrative of Esau's sell-out seem parallel to his own, but the New Testament concurs that the story of Esau is a type of the Christian who loses his salvation through neglect or outright apostasy. Hebrews 12:16—17, which Bunyan quotes in its entirety, warns against such neglect or denial as the sin that may find no forgiveness: "*Or profane person, as Esau, who for one morsel of meat, sold his Birth-right; for you know how that afterwards when he would have inherited the blessing, he was rejected, for he found no place of repentance, though he sought it carefully with tears*" (141).

As Bunyan describes the hermeneutic situation, he as interpreter is quite passive, the interpretation coming to him rather than he coming upon the interpretation: "And withal, that Scripture did seize upon my Soul" (141). Surely this is a predicament that many an autobiographer finds himself in, unable to resist interpretation, uncomfortable with the results. Yet despite the proclamation of passivity, Bunyan works actively as interpreter for the next thirty sections, as if obsessed with the hermeneutic possibilities of his situation. The reason for his obsession is clear. If he accepts Esau as a correlative type, he also accepts his eternal damnation. This is a fate he quite literally cannot live with. Thus, for another thirty sections, he continues to interpret, surveying both Old and New Testament types who sinned grievously, weighing New Testament promises and threats one against another—in short, re-interpreting his original sin.

Like the initial interpretation, these subsequent re-interpretations follow the procedures of biblical typology: they attempt to discover parallels between the actions of a biblical character and those of the autobiographer. Bunyan tries out David because his "heinous crimes" were "committed after light and grace received" (151), Peter because he denied his Savior "after warning given him" (154), Solomon because he fell into idolatry, "doing this after light, in his old age, after great mercy received" (170), and a series of other biblical types, all of whom sinned after receiving the blessing of God. Ultimately, Bunyan rejects all of these types as inapplicable to his situation.

What is important for the reader of *Grace Abounding* as autobiography to recognize is that Bunyan has already devoted five times as much effort to interpretation as to narration and that he seems willing to continue such interpretation indefinitely—or at least until he finds a hermeneutic solution that releases him from damnation. Indeed, in sections 151–60 and again in 165–71, Bunyan runs through the list of possible biblical counterparts not once but twice. It is as if he hopes, in repetition, to stumble upon an example of mercy he missed the first time.

No doubt he might have run through the possibilities a third time or a fourth. What finally brings closure to the episode is not a solution, but another hermeneutic dilemma. Quite out of the blue, Bunyan feels "the noise of wind upon me" and hears "a Voice speaking, *Didst ever refuse to be justified by the Blood of Christ*" (174)? This new phenomenon demands interpretation, and the previous hermeneutic cycle ceases.

If one were to adopt Ruskin's view of the matter, Bunyan's obsession with interpretation signals the effects of ill training and an undisciplined imagination. "A man who has general knowledge," Ruskin insisted to his parents in the same letter home from the continent, "has always too many subjects of thought and interest to admit of his noticing every time that a text comes jingling into his head, and a man of disciplined mind would not suffer any such morbid fancies as Bunyan describes to take possession of him or occupy his attention for a moment."[14] Ruskin deliberately misrepresents Bunyan's relationship to biblical texts in *Grace Abounding*, which do not come jingling into his head willy-nilly but come to mind, quite appropriately, when he is puzzling out some problem. Yet even if Bunyan is guilty of what might be called "interpretive excess," he is guilty only because of the excess and not because of his insistence upon interpretation.

Autobiography requires the act of interpretation, a fact that literary historians have frequently noticed, if not always considered seriously as a generic trait. In his description of the religious literature that influenced Defoe, G. A. Starr has observed that in the typical spiritual autobiography of the seventeenth century

> little stress was laid on the actual recording of experience, although this obviously had to precede any interpretations instructive to oneself or others. The consistent ability to get beyond the merely documentary, however, was one distinctive feature of spiritual autobiography.... Undertaken as a religious exercise, such compositions were not to dwell on the narration of fact: fact was to serve purely as ground for reflection, and allowing it to become an end in itself would be a vain self-indulgence.

John N. Morris puts the case more emphatically in *Versions of the Self* when he argues that to neglect interpretation is "impious," for "it implies the acceptance of meaninglessness as a possibility, a notion incompatible with the fact that the data of experience are somehow God's dealings with us."[15] No doubt Ruskin was correct that *Grace Abounding* exhibits "morbid fancies," for Bunyan treats all the data of experience, including his games of cat and the muddy water in the rills of the lane he walks, as spiritually meaningful. But whether an autobiographer possesses an undisciplined imagination or an utterly rational mind, he will produce interpretation if he writes autobiography. And if he writes spiritual autobiography, his interpretation, because it seeks to discover divine purpose and order in everyday life, will tend toward excess.

A century after Bunyan, spiritual autobiographers of various sorts, from the highly fanciful to the eminently sober, continued to practice autobiography as a genre of self-interpretation, using the strategies derived from biblical typology that Bunyan had formulated. Their practice confirms this essential characteristic of the genre and its relation to a tradition of biblical hermeneutics. It represents, too, the link from Bunyan to the nineteenth century. As the immediate predecessors of the Victorians, these writers produced the prototypes from which the great literary autobiographies of the next century evolved.

At the fanciful extreme of the eighteenth century, the *Memoir of the Early Life of William Cowper* makes correct interpretation the measure of spiritual progress and faulty interpretation the mark of unpardonable sin. A man of unstable disposition from his youth, Cowper periodically went mad, convinced that he had sinned against the Holy Ghost. He wrote his autobiography in 1766 during a period of psychological calm, probably in an attempt to understand his obsession and thereby rid himself of it.

Most of Cowper's account narrates the sequence of events that led to his attempted suicide in 1764, beginning with his failure to stand for an examination for a clerkship in the House of Lords and ending with his terrible "conviction of sin." As Cowper views his life retrospectively, he concludes that much of his misfortune ensued from a willful misinterpretation of an experience that had occurred earlier in his life in the countryside near Freemantle. For months he had suffered from severe depression, seeking relief in prayer and spiritual meditation; then on a walk in the clear, calm morning air, in view of a sunlit sea, his depression lifted: "Here it was that on a sudden, as if another sun had been kindled that instant in the heavens on purpose to dispel my sorrow and vexation of spirit, I felt the weight of all my misery taken off; my heart became light and joyful in a moment; I could have wept with transport had I been alone."[16] As the pun on sun/Son and the insistence on heavenly purpose suggest, Cowper had at that moment accepted the experience as an "unexpected blessing," as an "answer to prayer." Unfortunately, he later persuaded himself against the legitimacy of such a providential interpretation: "But Satan, and my own wicked heart, quickly persuaded me that I was indebted, for my deliverance, to nothing but a change of scene, and the amusing varieties of the place."[17] In rejecting his original response, Cowper takes an anti-hermeneutic stance. He decides that there can be no spiritual meaning to the Freemantle experience, only the sensory pleasure of the walk itself.

For Cowper as autobiographer, this error creates the central dilemma of his life and of his memoir. Because he once took a stance against interpretation, he fears that he has rejected the Holy Spirit and thus committed the unpardonable sin. To a modern reader, accustomed to and even pleased by a multiplicity of interpretations on the one hand and the groundlessness of interpretation on the other, Cowper's fear seems illogical in the extreme: surely one act of misinterpretation is pardonable. But Cowper's conclusion results from a finely tuned evangelical sense of hermeneutic responsibility. According to the New Testament, the Holy Ghost himself is the original Interpreter. To reject the interpretation He provides, whether of one event or all experience, is to commit an unredeemable error. It is to sin against the Holy Ghost.

To the reader, the fact that Cowper can recognize his error suggests that he is not lost. But because he once sinned by rejecting interpretation, he now feels compelled to record and analyze every possible providential intervention in his life. Because he once failed to interpret correctly, he finds himself condemned to a Sisyphean form of interpretation: although he may *never* interpret correctly, yet he must continue to risk the attempt. This compulsion produces the same peculiar qualities in Cowper's *Memoir* that Ruskin complained of in *Grace Abounding*. Even Cowper's publisher, who insisted that he was bringing out the work posthumously to refute the "calumny" that

"Piety has a direct tendency to produce insanity," noticed some of these peculiarities: Cowper's conviction that he was favored by dreams, his "powerful applications of certain passages of Holy Writ, in cases of perplexity," and "his minute and confident explanations of the designs of Providence in the circumstances which happened to him."[18] Here, Ruskin might have said, is a man who lets biblical texts come jingling into his head and dwells all too painfully on the relations of Deity to his own little self. But these peculiarities—at least the latter two—describe essential characteristics of the genre and its hermeneutic mode. They reveal the spiritual autobiographer's confidence that he can discover design in his life by appropriating the patterns of biblical history.

As it turns out, Cowper's confidence was mistaken. His madness returned in 1773 and again, permanently, in 1794. For a moment as autobiographer, however, Cowper discovers both a method of inter-pretation and a confidence in his application. At the end of his *Memoir*, he manages to read the experiences of his life successfully—that is, redemptively. Writing of his removal to a new home with the Unwin family, he describes it as an entry into Canaan, to "a place of rest prepared for me by God's own hand, where he has blessed me with a thousand mercies, and instances of his fatherly protection."[19] This final Pisgah vision offers a classic combination of typological herme-neutics and autobiographical closure.

Although Cowper represents the fanciful extreme of spiritual autobiographers, he was certainly not the most fanciful nor all that extreme. The memoirs of an Edinburgh servant girl named Elizabeth West include some equally fanciful interpretations of the details of her everyday life—from the bleaching of mill webs she observes on her way to communion, which she reads as "the renewed soul on whom the Lord bestowed a great deal of pains before it changed its natural hue," to the ungodly acts of the family she is forced to serve, which seem to her "like going back to Egypt again."[20] More extreme than either Cowper or West was one of their evangelical contemporaries, a printer's corrector and self-designated "corrector" of morals who was incarcerated for taking divine vengeance into his own hands and swinging a shovel at swearers and blasphemers and who, in response, interpreted his life as "emblematical and typical" of the misfortunes of the Old Testament patriarch Joseph. His autobiography, *The Adventures of Alexander the Corrector*, is a justification of his actions, written in complete confidence "that God would be with him, bless him, and make him a prosperous man after his reproaches and troubles."[21]

In contrast to accounts like these, yet with the same hermeneutic focus, Thomas Scott's *The Force of Truth* (1779) is the product of an eminently sane, psychologically balanced autobiographer. A respectable Anglican clergyman, Scott worried that readers might take him for another frenzied convert to religious enthusiasm; hence, he begins his autobiography with a long description of his rationalistic training in philosophy and concludes with a summary of the reasons that none of his behavior could "reasonably be condemned as enthusiasm." "I never was taught any thing," he insists, "by impulses, impressions, visions, dreams, or revelations; except so far as the work of the Spirit, in enlightening the understanding for the reception of those truths contained in the Holy Scriptures, is sometimes styled revelation. Other revelation I never expected or experienced, nor ever taught others to expect."[22]

Over the course of five years, Scott had moved from Socinianism to an acceptance of evangelical doctrine, and he recounts this conversion as a gradual and carefully considered process, the result of extensive reading in the theological literature of his day. As a narrative, then, Scott's account is obviously different from Bunyan's or Cowper's, particularly in its lack of psychological laceration and dramatic tension. But the goal of his narrative is still interpretation. Hermeneutic dilemmas propel the narrative forward, just as they do in *Grace Abounding* and in Cowper's *Memoir*.

In Scott, these dilemmas are created not by dreams, celestial voices, or encounters with Nature, but by books. Generally, these books are theological, ranging in form from biblical criticism to sermons and devotional manuals to classic religious autobiography. All of them are in some primary way interpretations of a biblical text, interpretations which force Scott to re-examine and re-interpret his own theological assumptions and, ultimately, his life. The process of conversion begins, for example, when he reads Bishop Burnet's *History of His Own Times*, a didactic piece of ecclesiastical record which convinces him that his entrance into the ministry "had been the result of very wrong motives, was preceded with a very unsuitable preparation, and accompanied with a very improper conduct."[23] From Burnet, Scott continues with other texts—including Locke's *The Reasonableness of Christianity*, Burnet's *Pastoral Care*, sermons by Tillotson and Jortin, Soame Jennyn's *Treatise on the Internal Evidence of Christianity*, Clark's *Scripture Doctrine of the Trinity*, and Law's *A Serious Call*, to name only a few—until he gains conviction that the evangelical interpretation of doctrine represents the "true Anglican theology."[24] The autobiography becomes, in other words, the narrative of a series of encounters with written texts. These texts produce the autobiographical "events" that must, as in Bunyan and Cowper, be interpreted by the autobiographer.

With texts as events, the form of the episode in *The Force of Truth* remains remarkably similar to that in Bunyanesque autobiography, with its tripartite pericope, narrative redaction, and interpretation. Scott first describes a written text he encountered (the eighth article of the Athanasian Creed, for example) and reports his response ("No sooner therefore did I read the words, 'That it was to be thoroughly received, and believed; for that it might be proved by most certain warrants of holy scripture;' then my mind was greatly impressed, and affected").[25] Then he explains how the text instigated a re-interpretation of his theological beliefs at the time and how now, as autobiographer, he interprets the episode as a part of a providential pattern discernible in his life. As in Bunyan and Cowper, the narrative redaction occurs for the sake of the autobiographer's interpretation and the reader's instruction.

The autobiography of textual encounter, as Scott's work might be called, became common among educated Anglicans and Dissenters in the eighteenth century and, as we shall see, is put to clever use by Newman in the nineteenth. Modern readers who confront such works often disregard them as narratives that merely (and dully) incorporate extensive bibliographies into the text. One critic, mixing the language of psychoanalysis and religion, explains the practice as "in keeping with the habit of diagnosing one's own spiritual condition by comparing it with the case histories of others."[26] These references to other texts suggest more, however, than a bibliographic convention or characteristic mode of diagnosis. They testify to the increasing literariness of the genre and to a direction that at least one of its strains was tending.

Whereas in Bunyan or Cowper the autobiographical event might be initiated by something psychological (a demonic voice urging "Sell him") or natural (a walk in the countryside) or textual (a verse from the Scriptures or a printed sermon), in Scott it is almost exclusively textual. No doubt Scott felt psychological urges and responded to natural scenes,[27] but he deliberately restricts his autobiograpical episodes to matters of textual interpretation or re-interpretation. This restriction betrays, for one thing, a cultural assumption about the primacy of the written text: one proves to readers that one is a rational man by being a literate man. Rationality in this case has really very little to do with the absence of emotion, as the common lexical contrast of "rational" to "enthusiastic" would imply. Scott's responses to the texts he reads are sometimes quite emotional—as, for instance, when he reads Burnet's *History* and feels "some uneasiness . . . excited in my mind." What makes him a rational autobiographer is the graphocentricity of his experience and expression.[28] His emotions occur in response to written words (a matter of literary form) and are controlled by written words (a matter of literary style).

Scott's self-imposed restriction also suggests the tendency of the spiritual autobiography to become a genre of intertextuality. By the end of the eighteenth century, one composes an autobiography by re-interpreting other texts. This may seem peculiar to say of a literary form committed to understanding the individual self, but the genre can as easily inhibit self-understanding and self-expression as permit it—a result that may occur precisely because of a consciousness of prior autobiographical texts. Using Harold Bloom's terminology, we might say that an autobiographer can express or create an individual self only by committing textual misprision, by effecting a clinamen either from prior autobiographical texts or from the theological texts upon which those texts are based.[29] He can be individual, at least autobiographically, only by being different.

We need not adopt Bloom's theory of influence, however, to

understand the autobiographer's predicament. We can as readily trace the difficulty to the heuristic intention of the genre as originally written and as transmitted to the Victorians. In the spiritual autobiographer's determination to illumine the way for others (or at least point out a few guideposts), he contributes to a kind of generic continuity that is effective, but at the same time restrictive. Bunyan points the way, for example, in *Grace Abounding* and *The Pilgrim's Progress*. "My dear children, the milk and honey is beyond this wilderness," he tells his readers in the preface to the former. The problem is, there's no milk and honey unless you imitate the model and do what it prescribes.

The relationship of *The Force of Truth* to prior autobiographical and theological works is a much gentler one than a Bloomian theory of literary succession allows or than the heuristic insistence of the genre suggests. Committed to an Anglican ideal of progress, an ideal related to late eighteenth-century versions of typological history, Scott views himself not as a contestant, but as a beneficiary of the texts he inherits.[30] Their patrimony assures him that he is the legitimate offspring of Protestant Reformation theology, not a misguided enthusiast or heretical Socinian doomed to be excluded from the family of God.[31]

The continuity in autobiographical form and motive from Bunyan to Cowper and Scott resembles in many ways the continuity typical among works of the same literary genre, but this matter of *literary* continuity deserves a more complete exploration before we turn to that of *hermeneutic* continuity and change. Like Wordsworth preparing to write his epic poem, *The Recluse*, and calling upon Milton's muse Urania to help him "tread on shadowy ground" and "sink / Deep—and, aloft ascending, breathe in worlds / To which the heaven of heavens is but a veil,"[32] the autobiographer writes in dependence upon a literary past. The autobiographer calls not upon a muse, however, but upon his generic predecessors to guide the way as he explores the shadowy ground of his memory and searches for meaning in his past. That at least is the intention of Bunyan's heuristic, "My dear children, the milk and honey is beyond this wilderness." Not all spiritual autobiographers, of course, felt compelled to surpass their literary predecessors, to "pass them unalarmed" as Wordsworth did. The lesser of them were satisfied to demonstrate membership in a spiritual community by repeating the forms of narration and interpretation traditional in spiritual autobiography. Some of them, however, felt the need to create space within the form for individual differences. And the best, like Wordsworth, aspired to surpass their predecessors, though they did so not without alarm.

By the nineteenth century, the need to create space became greater, and the number of autobiographers who aspired successfully, greater too. For many Victorians, it was no longer crucial to be counted among the elect, at least not as defined by orthodox Protestant theology, and prior texts like Bunyan's, Cowper's, and Scott's became useful as means of showing differences from predecessors and a freedom from the past. By the nineteenth century, in order to create a *literary* autobiography, the writer needed to produce a work fully original rather than obviously dependent upon or imitative of other autobiographies. Thus, except for those popular evangelical authors who continued to churn out didactic autobiographical narratives for other believers, the Victorian autobiographer tended to subvert his literary heritage or hide it. At the least, he tried to insist that previous autobiographers had not got it quite right, that they had managed to misinterpret their biblical models.

This more contrary relationship to the past still produced generic continuity—but of a sort different from that in Scott. Like earlier autobiographers, Victorian writers described their lives as a passage from bondage to the promised land, albeit a promised land with a different topography. Unlike those autobiographers, however, they insisted upon finding the milk and honey without slavishly following Bunyan's model. They continued to write within the tradition of the genre by borrowing its conventions of episodic structure, narrative pattern, and interpretive method. But they also altered the tradition by rejecting conventions they considered restrictive and adapting others they found pliable.

Perhaps this has always been the means of writing autobiography, for the genre demands the contradictory act of interpreting within an established, authoritative framework and yet providing a fully individual life. Even in *Grace Abounding* there are hints of such contradiction. As William York Tindall points out, Bunyan comes early in the tradition of spiritual autobiography, but he is not an originator of the genre.[33] Rather, Bunyan imitates, modifies, and sometimes transforms narrative patterns common in contemporary accounts of spiritual crisis. One of these, *A Relation of the Fearful Estate of Francis Spira*, appears in the "selling" of Christ episode and suggests, I believe, an incipient version of the uneasiness vis-à-vis generic predecessors that will become characteristic in the Victorian period.

Francesco Spira was a Venetian lawyer whose story of apostasy and self-inflicted death circulated widely during the seventeenth century, sometimes on its own, often with similar accounts of apostasy and suicide.[34] Spira had converted to Lutheran doctrines and preached them to his neighbors, but under pressure from Rome he recanted, subsequently suffering immense psychological and physiological distress. Spira's narrative was actually a work of biography, assembled from contemporary documents and reports of conversations with friends, but it was presented as his own personal account of the fatal course of his life. Bunyan encountered the book while in despair over his own denial of Christ. It was, he says, "as salt, when rubbed into a fresh wound" (163).

Although Bunyan mentions only the psychological effect, Spira's book had a significant literary effect upon *Grace Abounding* as well. In the *Relation*, Spira examines the lives of various biblical characters to determine whether or not their examples assure him of forgiveness or damn him to eternal torment. Bunyan uses this same technique and the same biblical types in his denial episode, although he debates about the parallels with himself rather than with his friends. Like Spira, he is initially driven to interpretation by Hebrews 12, a chapter that warns against falling away from the faith. Like Spira, too, he compares his actions with the sins of many biblical characters: Cain, Saul, Judas, David, Solomon, Peter. What is most interesting about the text of *Grace Abounding* at this juncture, however, is that Bunyan begins to apply these types just as he remembers Spira's book.

Precisely at the moment of interpretive crisis, Bunyan's method and much of his content follow Spira's model.

Or seem to. For Spira's autobiography is a stumbling block as well as a signpost, and we can sense that Bunyan stumbles over this prior text as he repeats the list of biblical characters not once, but twice. Before reading Spira, Bunyan had compared himself typologically with David, Hezekiah, Solomon, Peter, Judas, and Esau (151—60). After reading Spira, he compares himself again to these and other biblical types: Cain, David, Solomon, Manasseh, Peter—and again, Esau (164—72). This is an unusual form of repetition, without narrative or rhetorical purpose. Why does Bunyan need to repeat the interpretive procedure? And why does he repeat it not only at the original occurrence, but again as he writes his autobiography?

One possibility might be that of historical accuracy: Bunyan intends to report what happened as it happened, and hence the necessity of repetition. While the account as Bunyan presents it may be true, we cannot say, however, that historical accuracy demands structural repetition. As we have seen, when he chooses, Bunyan can sum up his activities or impressions in a series of powerful predicates. Here he might have used a single catalogue to describe his search for an appropriate biblical type.

Perhaps he does not compress his interpretive activity because Spira's book so startles him that it makes him, even in retrospect, repeat the interpretive act and forget narrative structure. It startles him because its author had used the same hermeneutic method and biblical types that he had tried, but Spira reached no happy inter-pretation. After considering all the appropriate types, Spira con-cluded that he was damned. His suicide suggests the ultimate futility of self-interpretation. For Bunyan as autobiographer and interpreter, then, his predecessor's book represents an interpretation that must be countered—and countered with the same biblical types and herme-neutic method, although with a very different conclusion. This act of re-interpretation assumes such importance that Bunyan engages in the process obsessively, not only repeating it when he first reads Spira, but repeating it again as autobiographer. It is as if he hopes repetition will lead him to a more felicitous conclusion.

Bunyan's relationship to Spira represents, almost prefiguratively, the stance that Victorian autobiographers will adopt toward their predecessors. If Victorians did not literally repeat their predecessors' texts, they often repeated the conventional forms of self-interpretation and countered them with different conclusions. Or they countered with alternative hermeneutic systems. A few, like Carlyle, managed to reassess the tradition with a rare critical distance and renovate its hermeneutic method. Most Victorians developed far more tangled relationships with the genre. Ruskin's argument with *Grace Abounding* and the "morbid" forms of interpretation he thought it contained continued from 1845, when his mother stuffed the copy of the book into his satchel, until 1889, when he completed *Praeterita*, and it was death that ended the argument. Newman's discontent began early, too, when he systematically read conversion accounts of well-known evangelicals and found that their experiences had little in common with his own. These two, like Martineau, Butler, and Gosse after them, objected to the view of the self that the tradition forced upon them and to the method of self-interpretation that its religious practitioners had fostered. All five sought to dislodge the autobiography from the typological hermeneutics in which it had originated.

Finally, then, it was typology itself that ensured an intense continuity from Bunyan to the Victorians. So long as it remained the dominant method of biblical interpretation in England, writers had to contend with its influence upon forms of understanding and interpreting the self, whether those forms were primarily religious (the devotional manual, the moral allegory, the occasional sermon) or a combination of the religious and literary (the hymn, the diary, the autobiography). Indeed, the continuing emphasis upon interpretation and the persistence of hermeneutic self-consciousness in the spiritual autobiography can be explained as much by a continuity in this extra-literary tradition as it can by an account of generic continuity. From the seventeenth century through the middle of the nineteenth, as the essays in Earl Miner's *Literary Uses of Typology*

demonstrate, biblical typology was the most important hermeneutic method in England,[35] and even as more "scientific" approaches to biblical studies appeared in scholarly circles, typology continued to be the popular, familiar method. Any literary form even vaguely theological, as the autobiography was, felt the influence of typological practice.

It was a specific aspect of hermeneutic practice, however, that shaped the mode of autobiography and that contributed first to generic continuity, but ultimately to change—what was formally known as the *subtilitas applicandi* of the interpretive act, what in the eighteenth century came to be called "practical exposition" or "practical observation." Traditionally, *subtilitas applicandi* (the application of a text) differed in its purpose from *subtilitas explicandi* and *subtilitas intelligendi* (the explication and understanding of a text). The act of *subtilitas applicandi* encouraged every Christian believer, clergyman and layman alike, to apply his understanding of the Scriptures to his own life; moreover, it encouraged the hermeneutic writer to produce works of practical exposition in which he applied scholarly knowledge of the biblical text, gained from the two other aspects of hermeneutic activity, to the situation of contemporary Christians.[36]

The particular convergence of practical exposition and spiritual autobiography in England goes back to the state of hermeneutic practice in the late seventeenth century. At that time, during the incipient stages of the autobiography, most biblical commentators made no such careful distinctions between understanding, explication, and application, but wrote works of almost pure practical exposition. The seventeenth-century divine Richard Baxter assumes this approach—and quietly defends it—in his preface to *A Paraphrase on the New Testament, with Notes, Doctrinal and Practical*. "Where the text is plain itself," he explains, "I fill up the space by doctrinal or practical observations, seeing practice is the end of all, and to learners, this part is of great necessity."[37] For Baxter explication merges easily, seamlessly, into application. If he thinks it unnecessary to explain the grammatical-historical meaning of the words, he simply deals with their implications for Christian practice; he feels no obligation to make careful hermeneutic distinctions.

Baxter's attitude was typical in the late seventeenth century. In a study of the theological sources of *The Pilgrim's Progress*, for example, U. Milo Kaufmann cites commentary after commentary that fits this pattern, that produces Baxter's sort of practical application and considers it a primary responsibility of the theologian to do so. Richard Rogers, author of *A Commentary upon the Whole Book of Judges* (1615), introduces his study as a work with a practical end: "I intended...to benefit Students and Preachers...so they may learne how to use the historicall part of the Bible, and learne to draw doctrine and instruction out of the examples thereof, for the people." Similarly, William Perkins explains in *The Arte of Prophecying* (1612) that he takes the historical books of the Old Testament, from Genesis to Job, as "stories of things done, for the illustration and confirmation of that doctrine which is propounded in other bookes." And in *An Exposition of the Epistle to the Hebrews* (1668–74) John Owen discusses the account of Rahab the harlot, typically, in terms of its practical meaning for his contemporaries: "This Rahab was by nature a Gentile, an alien from the stock and covenant of Abraham. Wherefore, as her conversion unto God was an act of free grace and mercy in a peculiar manner, so it was a type and pledge of calling a church from among the Gentiles."[38] For these writers, as for evangelicals in the eighteenth and nineteenth centuries, such practical exposition was the primary activity—and ultimate goal—of hermeneutics.

With the advent of higher critical approaches to the Scriptures, the distinctions between *subtilitas applicandi* on the one hand and *subtilitas intelligendi* and *subtilitas explicandi* on the other became necessary, and the emphasis in hermeneutics shifted away from matters of application to problems of construal and meaning. Although this shift had a profound impact on the theoretical basis of biblical typology (and eventually on the form of Victorian autobiography), it had little effect upon the production of practical commentaries, which continued to be published in the same great quantities that manuals of popular psychology are today. The very fact that hermeneutics had become a scholarly enterprise, seemingly divorced from Christian faith and practice, inspired pious theologians to produce even more commentaries for the layman, books which would not, as one writer put it, be "useless and burdensome piece[s] of pedantry."[39]

When Hannah More decided to compose "An Essay on the Character and Practical Writings of St. Paul" (1815), then, the inclusion of the word *practical* in the title served as a ready indication of the work's hermeneutic intentions. More believed that, as a woman, practical application was the only hermeneutic activity legitimate for her to undertake, and in the preface she insists upon "her incompetency to the proper execution of such a work, on her deficiencies in ancient learning, Biblical criticism, and deep theological knowledge." Her justification to publish, however, relies upon the acknowledged distinction between critical and practical hermeneutics. "It may serve as some apology for the boldness of the present undertaking," she explains, "that these volumes are not of a critical, but of a practical nature."[40]

What More recognized as a standard distinction between critical and practical hermeneutics became, by the end of the eighteenth century, a visual distinction in the format of Thomas Scott's commentary on the Bible (1788—92) with its "Original Notes, Practical Observations, and Copious References." In his Socinian days Scott had immersed himself in the most radical critical studies of the Bible available in England, and although he later converted to a devout evangelical position, he did not banish from his commentary the insights that these earlier critical and grammatical-historical studies had taught him. He wanted to convey both critical insight and practical instruction, but he wanted to maintain the distinction, too. Thus he devised a special format, including both "Notes" and "Practical Observations" for each chapter of the Bible, but printing them in separate segments below the text itself. This separation of critical notes and practical application marks a century of hermeneutic change from Richard Baxter's *New Testament Paraphrase*, with its grammatical, critical, and practical matters mixed together, to Scott's commentary, with its visually divisive layout. (The hierarchy implicit in Scott's format, nevertheless, is significant. For him, as for Baxter, the biblical text itself is the beginning of all wisdom. The end of wisdom—and of all critical study—is the application of the text to the Christian life.)

The commentaries written by Baxter, More, Scott, and others like them and the hermeneutic distinctions they represent influenced the practice of clergymen and hence the assumptions of autobiographers. The Reverend Henry Melvill, to cite only one prominent Victorian example, was widely admired as an explicator of difficult biblical texts and as a skilled defender of typological hermeneutics in arguments of evangelical doctrine.[41] But Melvill also delivered what he called "Lectures on Practical Subjects," giving his most famous series at St. Margaret's, Lothbury, in the 1850s. These sermons were deliberate exercises in *subtilitas applicandi*, and the words *applied* and *application* appear repeatedly as Melvill wrests practical meaning from his text.[42] Melvill chooses his texts from all parts of the Bible— Numbers, Deuteronomy, Ruth, Isaiah, the Gospels, and the Epistles— and after a brief narrative redaction or explication of a difficult word or phrase, he concentrates his efforts on the text's relevance to his Victorian parishioners. The lectures were widely attended, then handsomely printed and distributed, copies making it into the libraries of the Ruskins, Brownings, and Gladstones, a testimony to the popularity of the preacher and his method.

The distance from Melvill's practical lectures to autobiographical forms of writing is quite short. In a journal, for example, an observation about a biblical character may be applied to the writer's own personality or actions; in a funeral sermon, the practical relevance of a biblical type may be extended to the life of the deceased. The same sort of application or extension occurs in the writing of spiritual autobiography. If, as Henry Melvill explained to his congregation, the history of the Israelites is "a typical or figurative history, sketching, as in parable, much that befalls the Christian Church in general, and its members in particular," then the spiritual autobiographer, quite apart from any knowledge of a literary tradition, need only turn to the story of the Exodus for an "account" of his life.[43] The transition from practical hermeneutics to autobiographical writing becomes simple and direct; what the autobiographer does is appropriate personally the *subtilitas applicandi*, making another application of the application.

Of course, the writing of autobiography is never this simple—and was not so for the Victorian autobiographers we still consider worth reading. As I have suggested, part of the challenge lay in the genre itself, which asked writers to interpret within established conventions and yet produce fully individual lives. As most Victorians understood it, however, the immediate challenge lay in the typological hermeneutics with which autobiographical interpretation had traditionally been carried out. For if the predominance of practical exposition and its relationship to autobiographical writing explain a continuity in generic form, there was also, during the seventeenth and eighteenth centuries, an increasing disjunction between the practical and critical aspects of hermeneutics, one made visible—if not articulated—by Scott's commentary.[44] This disjunction was consequently felt in a similar disjunction between the forms of autobiography and the theological and philosophical assumptions of Victorians who practiced the genre.

The major Victorian autobiographers were writers interested, in a theoretical sense, in such problems of interpretation: Carlyle in historical interpretation, Newman in theological hermeneutics, Ruskin in art and social criticism, Butler and Gosse in literary criticism and scientific theory. The one woman who succeeded in the genre, Harriet Martineau, was primarily a theologian and philosopher, although she made her name by writing practical tales that illustrated principles of political economy. These Victorian autobiographers were writers aware of the scholarly tradition in German and English biblical studies and of the implications for many varieties of interpretation. They chose to write autobiography in part because it was a genre concerned with the interpretive act and hence suited to their habits of thought. Some of them also chose autobiography, I think, because they sensed the disjunction between the inherited literary forms of self-interpretation and contemporary hermeneutic theory. By using theory to re-make form, they sought to re-vitalize the genre.

No doubt their motives were personal as well as literary. All of them came from intensely religious backgrounds. All had undergone experiences of conversion or de-conversion, and some felt compelled to recount them for therapeutic reasons. Most important, their experiences had occurred when inherited forms of faith confronted newer modes of thought, whether in biblical hermeneutics, science, or philosophy. Through personal experience, the major Victorian autobiographers both recognized and (re)presented the disjunction between inherited forms of self-interpretation and modern theories of hermeneutics. The genre provided the perfect melding of personal, literary, and theoretical interests.

In writing of these autobiographers, I have chosen to begin with two whose works most purely represent experiments in form: Carlyle's *Sartor Resartus*, which, as its title suggests, seeks a reconstruction of personality and literary form; and Ruskin's *Praeterita*, which, if we accept the terms of the preface, attempts a deconstruction of autobiography as genre. I continue with three works that establish new directions for autobiography: Newman's *Apologia Pro Vita Sua*, which reintroduces the model of Augustine's *Confessions* to the English tradition and reconsiders the relation of narrative to exposition in the autobiographical text; Harriet Martineau's *Autobiography*, which confronts the Victorian debate over feminine forms of self-interpretation; and Gosse's *Father and Son*, a work that both embodies and criticizes the attempts at "scientific" autobiography that emerged in the second half of the nineteenth century.

In all five cases, I have chosen to speak of the authors of these autobiographical texts as self-conscious literary writers, aware of generic precedents and deliberate in their intentions to adopt, revise, or circumvent them. I have done so not to revive a debate on the "intentional fallacy," but to suggest a sophistication on their parts about generic form. What I mean to argue by this critical choice, in short, is that the great Victorian autobiographies are not only examples of the genre, but critical reflections upon it as well.

Thus I am arguing that Victorian autobiography is hermeneutic in a third, modern sense. In a discussion of Gadamer's philosophical hermeneutics, D. C. Hoy distinguishes between the older sense of hermeneutics as an enterprise for formulating and applying rules of proper interpretation and the more modern sense of hermeneutics as an activity of self-conscious reflection upon the nature and process of interpretation itself.[45] Autobiography is intrinsically a hermeneutic genre in the older sense. It is such self-conscious reflection, however, that distinguishes Victorian autobiography from its generic predecessors and, in the nineteenth century, brings the genre to full literary status.

PART ONE

Two Approaches to Generic Form

2

Carlyle's *Sartor Resartus*: The Necessity of Reconstruction

reating *Sartor Resartus* as an autobiography rather than as a work with occasional autobiographical elements raises some difficult generic questions: What constitutes an autobiography? What characteristics define the genre? What conventions or topoi signal an author's intention to write within the genre? Despite a critical tradition that has used or implicitly sanctioned the modal adjective "autobiographical," *Sartor Resartus* is not by any conservative definition nor in its entirety an autobiography, that is, a professedly truthful record of Carlyle's life, composed as a single work and told from a consistent temporal point of view.[1] Even C. F. Harrold's modern edition, which implicitly treats *Sartor* as a form of autobiography and includes extensive footnotes to autobiographical allusions, acknowledges the problem in a discussion of the "plan" of the work: "*Sartor Resartus* is a collection," Harrold states, "of philosophic fragments, biographical narrative, and editorial comment."[2] As Carlyle himself explained, in a phrase that aptly describes the generic difficulty, the work is a kind of "Satirical Extravaganza on Things in General" (304). Nothing could be further from autobiography's demand for a life in particular than a work on "Things in General."

Most critics who call *Sartor Resartus* an autobiography mean, in fact, not the whole work but Book Second, and this chapter observes—at least initially—a similar distinction. Yet even if we evade the generic question of the entire work, limit ourselves to the second book, treat it as the autobiography of an imaginary German philosopher, Diogenes Teufelsdröckh, and then later equate Teufelsdröckh with Carlyle, the work still resists the label "autobiography." By definition, Teufelsdröckh, the subject of the book, must also be its author, but Teufelsdröckh does not write an autobiography. He rejects "these Autobiographical times of ours" (94). To his Editor's plea for autobiographical information and Hofrath Heuschrecke's promise of "an Autobiography" that will clarify "the whole Philosophy and Philosopher of Clothes," Teufelsdröckh responds with what can only be called an anti-autobiography: six paper bags filled with "miscellaneous masses of Sheets, and oftener Shreds and Snips, written in [a] scarce legible *cursiv-schrift*; and treating of all imaginable things under the Zodiac and above it, . . . and then in the most enigmatic manner" (78). In this chaotic mass the Editor discovers accounts of dreams, fragments of philosophical disquisitions, autobiographical delineations and anecdotes—all, as he notes with frustration, "without date of place or time," all "without connection, without recognisable coherence" (78). These bags testify to Teufelsdröckh's reluctance to engage in the most basic of autobiographical acts. He refuses to organize the data of his experience.

If Teufelsdröckh refuses to compose his life, his anti-autobiographical response nonetheless suggests the generic intention of *Sartor Resartus*. With his paper bags, "marked successively, in gilt China-ink, with the symbols of the Six southern Zodiacal Signs, beginning at Libra" (77−78), he alludes to the most famous of German autobiographies: Johann Wolfgang von Goethe's *Dichtung und Wahrheit*, which begins with Goethe's horoscope on 28 August 1749, the day of his birth.[3] And if Teufelsdröckh's refusal, like the work's uneasiness with the generic label, makes it problematic to call *Sartor Resartus* an autobiography, it paradoxically makes the work a model for the study of the genre and its conventions. For Teufelsdröckh's autobiography does get written—or, rather, constructed. Psychologically unable to accept the chaos of the paper bags, the British Editor assumes the task that Teufelsdröckh resists and produces the life we read in Book Second. As he constructs this life, moreover, the Editor assumes the role of Teufelsdröckh's alter ego, that half of the autobiographer who gives structure to what the other half holds in memory. As he continues in the role, the Editor becomes more and more like Teufelsdröckh himself. By the end of Book Second, as many readers of *Sartor* have remarked, it becomes impossible to distinguish between Teufelsdröckh and his Editor, between the subject of the autobiography and its narrator.

In the conscious division of Teufelsdröckh from his Editor, Carlyle embodies the formal problem of the autobiographer who is both the subject of his work and its author. In the tension between Teufelsdröckh and his Editor, the man who wants to leave his memories in chaotic formlessness and the man who feels compelled to decipher and interpret those "unimaginable Documents" of memory, Carlyle embodies the tension between what Roy Pascal has called "truth" versus "design."[4] And in the distance between the imaginary Teufelsdröckh and the real Thomas Carlyle, Carlyle calls attention to the writing of autobiography as a literary act, an act that interprets experience and thus creates a self by working within (and sometimes against) the formal conventions of the genre.

These tensions allow Carlyle to emphasize not so much the facts of his own or Teufelsdröckh's life, but the act of self-interpretation, and they urge us to read Book Second not so much as an account of Teufelsdröckh's experience or Carlyle's in disguise, but as an experiment in autobiographical form, one that is essentially hermeneutic. They point to generic intention as well. For the issues that concern Carlyle in *Sartor Resartus* have defined the "critical axes," as Avrom Fleishman calls them, along which autobiographical writing and generic criticism have run for the past two centuries: truth and fiction, memory and meaning, individual expression and literary convention.[5]

In *The Boundaries of Fiction* George Levine has suggested that we treat *Sartor Resartus* as a "confession-anatomy-romance," a combination that gives priority to these same critical axes and to the work's autobiographical basis, with its "introverted and personal" mode and "theoretical and intellectual interest" in religion, philosophy, and art.[6] Although I prefer the term "autobiography" to "confession," I think we might take Levine's suggestion seriously and explore its implications by emphasizing the autobiographical precedents of *Sartor*, while recognizing, too, the self-consciousness about method and form that "anatomy" implies and the impression of allegory fundamental to "romance" that Carlyle's frequent use of biblical typology produces. For if *Sartor Resartus* does not initially fit a conservative definition of autobiography, it is nonetheless a work of and about autobiography. It self-consciously uses the conventions of the genre to recount a version of a man's life. Its self-consciousness entails a critical examination of the autobiography and its hermeneutic demands. And this self-consciousness is no more evident than in the way that Carlyle, through the British Editor, manipulates the conventional pattern of autobiographical narrative and thus raises a larger question of autobiographical interpretation and its relation to biblical hermeneutics.

The pattern that the British Editor imposes upon Teufelsdröckh's life has its origin in the Old Testament account of the Exodus, but its more immediate origin lies in the Bunyanesque tradition of spiritual autobiography, a tradition to which we might turn first.[7] When John Bunyan wrote *Grace Abounding* in 1666, it was customary for new members of his Baptist sect to read or narrate accounts of their conversion before the entire congregation as an act of public witness. It was still uncommon, however, for members to publish such narratives: Anglicans considered the public exposure vulgar; Baptists and other sectarians thought it presumptuous. Bunyan chose to risk presumption in the service of evangelism. As a well-known convert and minister, he decided to present *Grace Abounding* in printed form to a public audience.

When Bunyan published, however, he felt obliged to attach an explanatory preface or, in his words, a "brief Account of the publishing of this Work." In it Bunyan justifies the publication of a personal history by summoning up Moses's example in the historical books of the Pentateuch:

> *Moses* (Num. 33.1, 2) *writ of the Journeyings of the children of* Israel, *from* Egypt *to the land of* Canaan; *and commanded also, that*

they did remember their forty years travel in the wilderness. Thou shalt
remember all the way which the Lord thy God led thee these
forty years in the wilderness, to humble thee, and to prove thee,
to know what was in thine heart, whether thou wouldst keep his
commandments, or no, *Deut.* 8. 2, 3. *Wherefore this I have
endeavoured to do; and not onely so, but to publish it also; that, if God
will, others may be put in remembrance of what he hath done for their
Souls, by reading his work upon me.*[8]

Bunyan's choice of scriptural texts, necessary for his own autobiographical act, had profound effect upon the tradition of spiritual
autobiography that followed from *Grace Abounding*. It linked the form
of autobiography to the Book of Exodus—both narratively, in that
spiritual accounts tended to repeat the order and episodes of Israel's
history, and also hermeneutically, in that interpretations of the
Exodus by Old Testament prophets and New Testament epistles and
later by Christian theologians tended to influence the interpretations
that autobiographers made of their own lives. Autobiographers who
wrote within the tradition wrote with the Exodus as a primary text.

Recent discussions of English autobiography have treated biblical
accounts other than the Exodus as originating or influencing patterns,
and indeed Bunyan used other biblical examples to justify his self-
narrative.[9] Later in the preface, for instance, he mentions Paul's
defense before Felix, the Roman governor, and David's commemorative psalms as examples of self-expression. For Bunyan, however, the
essential biblical text is the record of Israel's wandering and redemption, and the essential act, that of a spiritual leader writing the
history of his people and commemorating God's providence in the
writing.

The logical connection between Moses's history and *Grace Abounding* is not stated explicitly in Bunyan's self-justification, but is implicit in the transition, "Wherefore this have I endeavoured to do."
The phrase is worth considering, for it implies the terms on which
autobiography, Bunyan's and its successors, were to be written. The
connection depends upon at least two typological assumptions—one
commonplace, the other radical in the seventeenth century. It assumes, first, that the "Journeyings" of the Israelites prefigure the
experiences of Christians and, second, that Moses' *record* of these

journeyings in the narratives of the Pentateuch and the lyrical Song of
Moses (Deut. 32) is prefigurative also. Although I list it second, the
latter assumption was for Bunyan and other spiritual autobiographers
crucial: it sanctioned the publication of personal accounts and made
possible the development of the autobiography as a genre. By suggesting that Moses' act of writing history anticipates his own, Bunyan
in effect argues that the Old Testament, as a written and published
text, approves and even necessitates the kind of autobiographical
narrative that *Grace Abounding* represents: a history that demonstrates
the presence of providential design in man's activities or, as Bunyan
puts it, that "the Lord thy God led thee these forty years in the
wilderness."

Given Bunyan's choice of Mosaic history, it comes as no surprise
that *Grace Abounding* appropriates the pattern of the Exodus for its
narrative design—and here the initial typological assumption shows
its influence. In the preface, as in the text of the autobiography itself,
Bunyan makes his unrepentant ways correspond to the Egyptian
bondage; his dramatic conversion, to the flight from Pharaoh and the
crossing of the Red Sea; his confusion and backsliding, to the wilderness wandering; and his eventual redemption, to the entry into the
promised land of Canaan. When he speaks of conversion, for instance,
he notes that *"it is profitable for Christians to be calling to mind the very
beginnings of Grace with their Souls,"* and he quotes Exodus 12.42, the
Red Sea account, as his supporting text: "It is a night to be much
observed unto the Lord, for bringing them out from the land of *Egypt"*
(2). He cites Psalm 106 and Numbers 14 to reiterate the narrative
pattern and establish the importance of commemorative history,
observing that when God brought Israel through the Red Sea, *"they
must turn quite about thither again, to remember the drowning of their enemies
there"* (2). This turning about describes metonymically the autobiographer's act, which requires a retrospective glance, a looking
backward to understand the present and act wisely in the future.
Without the turning about, Bunyan suggests, one is likely to falter:
"for though they sang his praise before, yet they soon forgat his works, Psal.
106. 12, 13."

Even before we leave the preface, then, and begin the autobiography proper, we know that we will follow Bunyan typologically

through the wilderness and emerge at the border of the promised land. That we know the plot before we begin suggests the hermeneutic and heuristic (rather than narrative) emphases of autobiography. Our interest lies in Bunyan as reader of experiential data and in the dilemmas he confronts and resolves in his interpretations.

As the autobiographical narrative begins, Bunyan's assurance wanes as now, protagonist of the autobiography, he seems to find the role of typological interpreter bewildering. Esau as biblical type threatens with an alternative model for his life and prevents him from recognizing that he is, spiritually speaking, an Israelite. So, too, as we saw in the last chapter, other biblical characters menace, whose lives delineate different and less felicitous patterns of experience. But for Bunyan, the retrospective autobiographer, the Exodus as divinely ordained type continues to control the shape of the narrative, even when Bunyan, the protagonist, falters. At crucial junctures, it sums up segments of his history; it propels the narrative resolutely forward.

These points of summary or anticipation establish the Exodus as the dominant pattern in *Grace Abounding* and, because of its seminal influence, in the tradition of spiritual autobiography that follows. After a long bout of anxiety over his salvation, Bunyan receives assurance of election and expresses his joy in an allusion to the forty years' wandering: "Now was my heart filled full of comfort and hope,...wherefore I said in my Soul with much gladness, Well, I would I had a pen and ink here, I would write this down before I go any further, for surely I will not forget *this* forty years hence"(92). Although the elation soon collapses with the memory that "within less than forty days" he had begun "to question all again," at this juncture the experience of the Israelites provides Bunyan the protagonist with a means of understanding an otherwise chaotic period of his life. It also provides Bunyan the autobiographer with a means of imposing order upon the narrative, and it is significant that understanding and order, the perspective of the protagonist and that of the narrator, converge in this passage. Such convergence suggests that the protagonist's moment of understanding leads naturally to (and may be inseparable from) the autobiographical act of recording experience. At least this is the sort of convergence we typically find in the spiritual autobiography. When we as readers see the exodus pattern, we recognize it as a signal of the continuing control of the retrospective autobiographer (or of God through the autobiographer). We recognize it, too, as evidence of completion, as a step forward in the protagonist's self-understanding.

Such reassuring repetition is, however, only half of the reader's experience—and a half that had diminished significantly by the 1830s when Carlyle wrote *Sartor Resartus*. Even in *Grace Abounding*, typological allusions appear at moments of misunderstanding, when Bunyan the protagonist fails to see with clarity or Bunyan the autobiographer betrays his uneasiness about the act of interpretation itself. In the midst of confusion over his election, for instance, he expresses anxiety by linking his inward state to a troublesome episode in Exodus, saying that he fears his "heart would be unclean, the *Cananites* would dwell in the Land" (78). Later, as he worries more, he compares himself to the Israelites forbidden to enter Canaan because of their timidity and grumbling: "This the Devil urged, and set forth that in *Numbers*, which *Moses* said to the children of *Israel*, *That because they would not go up to possess the Land when God would have them, therefore for ever after he did bar them out from hence, though they prayed they might with tears*" (177). Both applications of the Exodus fit within the typological framework established by the preface, but they suggest hermeneutic misgivings. In the latter passage, Bunyan already knows that he is a spiritual Israelite, yet this recognition brings no assurance of peace. Perhaps the misgivings are those of the protagonist, the man who attempts to discover an appropriate type but cannot apply it fully to his life. But do not these allusions also testify, if unwittingly, to more subtle misgivings of the autobiographer?

Clearly, Bunyan sees his responsibility as autobiographer to lie in the beneficial application of typology of his life and, by extension, to the lives of others. His preface assures us that we may read his account as heuristic: "*My dear children*," Bunyan comforts, "the Milk and Honey is beyond this Wilderness. God be merciful to you, and grant that you be not slothful to go in to possess the land." Contrary to authorial intention, however, these passages suggest that the story of the Exodus—like other narratives—includes demonic elements that work against an optimistic interpretation. As Bunyan recalls in moments of doubt, the Israelites failed to purge Canaan of its pagan occupants, and some Israelites never set foot in the promised land at all. To put Bunyan's difficulty more generally, typology may have appropriated the Exodus as a prefiguration of the Christian's salvation from bondage and final attainment of heavenly bliss; nevertheless, some historical facts of the narrative speak against this unifocal appropriation.

These facts—or rather, the hermeneutic use of these facts—Bunyan consciously rejects. He labels them "devilish," in effect delimiting hermeneutic practice to a redemptive form of repetition.[10] Carlyle, like other Victorian writers, will treat such possibilities as the common dilemma of the autobiographer, as evidence that biblical types are humanly conceived rather than divinely ordained. Unlike other autobiographers, however, who will submit to the demonic or destructive aspect of the interpretative process that constantly unravels the autobiographer's carefully wrought achievement, Carlyle will keep his narrative pattern comic and its hermeneutic method redemptive.

Bunyan, his predecessor, could remain confident in the traditional method of biblical typology. Whatever the misgivings along the way, at the end of *Grace Abounding* both Bunyans, protagonist and autobiographer alike, accept the history of the Exodus as prefigurative of man's earthly experience. The autobiography closes with a final vision, shared by both, of "the city of the living God, the heavenly Jerusalem." The vision is a classic instance of autobiographical closure. Like Moses on Mount Nebo overlooking the promised land, Bunyan sees a "wonderful glory," which brings great refreshment to his spirit and ends his years of wandering.

Unlike Moses' vision, however, the glory Bunyan sees in *Grace Abounding* occurs not as a literal vision but as a typological envisioning. According to the account, the Spirit of God leads Bunyan again and again to specific words, those of the New Testament epistle to the Hebrews:

The words are these, *Ye are come to mount Zion, to the City of the living God, the heavenly Jerusalem, and to an innumerable company of Angels, to the general assembly and Church of the first-born, which are written in heaven, and to God the Judge of all, and to the spirits of just men made perfect, and to Jesus the Mediator of the New Testament, and to the blood of sprinkling, that speaketh better things than that of Abel.* (264)

This passage, which in the New Testament follows the one on Esau that plagued Bunyan for so long, resolves the dilemma of both protagonist and autobiographer. In its typological antitheses—between the sacrifice of Abel and the blood of Jesus, between Moses at Mount Sinai and the Christian at Mount Sion, between the law and the Gospel—it completes the pattern of wandering. It testifies to Bunyan the protagonist that he has traveled from damnation to salvation. Most important, it assures Bunyan the autobiographer that the New Testament validates his self-interpretation.

Carlyle's self-consciousness about autobiographical intention and generic form in *Sartor Resartus* expresses itself in the terms delineated by Bunyan's *Grace Abounding* and, less directly, *The Pilgrim's Progress*. This self-consciousness begins even before the narrative of Teufelsdröckh's life in Book Second. In the "Prospective" chapter of Book First, we find Hofrath Heuschrecke suggesting that some biographical facts relevant to Teufelsdröckh's intellectual development might help clear up the Editor's confusion over the philosophy of clothes. The biographical facts that Heuschrecke considers relevant— Had Teufelsdröckh also a father and mother? Has he fought duels? How did he comport himself when in Love?—turn out to be apparently irrelevant details. Heuschrecke's summary of the questions the Editor might ask, however, suggests that Carlyle is about to explore the act of writing autobiography under the guise of presenting Teufelsdröckh's life: "By what singular stair steps, [Heuschrecke queries], and subterranean passages, and sloughs of Despair, and steep Pisgah hills, has he reached this wonderful prophetic Hebron (a true Old-Clothes Jewry)

where he now dwells?" (76). The summary is a plan of organization, one that assumes the Exodus to be an appropriate pattern for understanding men's lives. More exactly, we might say that the summary uses the Exodus to organize Teufelsdröckh's life, but only as a biblical type that has been mediated by a tradition of spiritual autobiography. On the way to Pisgah hills and the land of Hebron lie sloughs of Despond from Bunyan's *Pilgrim's Progress*.

Like many another hack thinker, Heuschrecke is ready to apply a conventional pattern, accepting it as one the genre supplies for the (auto)biographer's ease. When the Editor himself sets to work on Teufelsdröckh's life, he follows Heuschrecke's tack, and the influence of exodus typology again appears, once again mediated by a generic tradition.[11] The Editor calls the first chapter "Genesis," but he counters the title with the qualification that "this Genesis of his can properly be nothing but an Exodus" (81). The opposition of Genesis and Exodus acknowledges a point of biographical fact: that Teufelsdröckh's origin is obscure, "the preliminary portion is nowhere forthcoming" (81) It also makes a philosophical point central to Carlyle's thinking: that physical origins are irrelevant to a man's life, his "true Beginning and Father is in Heaven" (86). In terms of generic precedents, however, the title acknowledges a matter of autobiographical form. In the conventions of the English spiritual autobiography, one's origin is Egypt, not Eden, and one's typological model is the Book of Exodus, not that of Genesis. Following convention, the Editor introduces Teufelsdröckh's life with what will become the basic pattern of his autobiographical account: the wilderness wandering.[12]

The Editor's decision to use this conventional pattern suggests Carlyle's interest in a fundamental dilemma of self-interpretation. The Editor's decision is neither so automatic nor so easy as Heuschrecke's, and he wavers between Genesis and Exodus as appropriate models for a life. According to the Puritan theology that influenced the spiritual autobiography, man is born in sin, in Egyptian bondage, and hence the Exodus, not the story of Genesis, is the applicable model. By the 1830s, however, there were other models for autobiography that allowed more idyllic origins: works of German Romanticism suitable to a foreign subject like Teufelsdröckh, including Goethe's *The Sorrows of Young Werther*, which Carlyle knew well. What should Teufelsdröckh's autobiographical models be? The Editor resolves the immediate dilemma by using the conventional pattern and at the same time acknowledging other forms. Writing to a British audience, he chooses the dominant pattern of its autobiographical tradition as his narrative basis. But he has it both ways, for he includes within the exodus pattern an alternate beginning.

Carlyle, too, has it both ways, for with the double allusion he can both write autobiography and explore problems that the genre creates for the author. There is first the problem that Pascal describes as "design" versus "truth." On the one hand, the autobiographer knows the conventions of the genre, conventions which encourage him and his audience to read experience in terms of familiar, predetermined patterns; on the other, he knows the truth of his experience, a truth which frequently belies the legitimacy of the patterns. Then there is the problem of memory. Even though the autobiographer may be conscious of the power of convention to distort the truth, he may still forget that memory itself distorts, making it difficult to recover the truth of the experience he intends to record and interpret accurately. The autobiographical act involves a pact between audience and autobiographer that, "whether or not what is reported can be discredited," the autobiographer "purports to believe in what he asserts."[13]

Both of these problems appear in "Genesis," suggesting that they are among Carlyle's specific concerns. Teufelsdröckh presents his father and mother, for example, as "the Andreas and Gretchen, or the Adam and Eve, who led [him] into Life, and for a time suckled and pap-fed [him] there" (86). He describes Gretchen in language reminiscent of Milton's Eve, a woman who created a paradise in their humble cottage, "embowered in fruit-trees and forest-trees, evergreens and honeysuckles, and flowers struggling-in through the very windows" (83). These are conventional descriptions of an edenic childhood, borrowed from German Romantic autobiography as well as from Milton. Despite this initial acquiescence to convention, however, Teufelsdröckh remembers the truth: life in Entepfuhl was no paradise. In a later chapter, ironically entitled "Idyllic," he describes his childhood again, this time in more detail:

My Active Power (*Thatkraft*) was unfavourably hemmed-in;...
In an orderly house, where the litter of children's sports is hate-
ful enough, your training is too stoical; rather to bear and
forbear than to make and do. I was forbid much: wishes in any
measure bold I had to renounce; everywhere a strait bond of
Obedience inflexibly held me down...so that my tears flowed,
and at seasons the Child itself might taste that root of bitterness,
wherewith the whole fruitage of our life is mingled and tempered. (98)

The description counteracts the earlier one, false to experience and
memory both. In the juxtaposition of convention and memory, one
interpretive possibility (childhood as Eden) is tried out and rejected
because of its inadequacy to organize the past satisfactorily.

In later Victorian autobiographies, this pattern of testing and
rejecting interpretive possibilities will become characteristic, and
autobiographers like Edmund Gosse will refuse to settle finally on any
single interpretive system. But *Sartor Resartus* comes early in the
century, and Carlyle is still concerned with reconstituting the traditional figures of interpretation for both private and public history.
Hence, even in the chapters "Genesis" and "Idyllic," the exodus
pattern of traditional autobiography dominates the account. As Teufelsdröckh recalls those early years, what he remembers with pleasure
and truth are the "glorious summer twilights" when the sun, like a
proud "imperial Taskmaster," turned its back so that "the tired
brickmakers of this clay Earth might steal a little frolic" (91–92).
The pleasure he recalls is not that of man in Eden, but that of the
children of Israel, released for a moment from the burdens of the
Egyptian bondage. Here narrative and interpretation, personal memory and biblical pattern, merge seamlessly.

As the Editor continues to collate the fragments of Teufelsdröckh's
life, the exodus pattern continues to shape both narrative and interpretation. The Israelite's bondage in Egypt becomes correlative to
Teufelsdröckh's years in the gymnasium and university and his preparation for a legal career. "For long years," the Editor explains,
quoting an autobiographical scrap, "had the poor Hebrew in this

Egypt of an Auscultatorship, painfully toiled, baking bricks without stubble, before ever the question once struck him with entire force: For what?—*Beym Himmel*! For Food and Warmth!" (131). Once the young philosopher recognizes the degradation of this bondage, the narrative modulates to a later phase of the exodus. In the middle chapters of Book Second, we see Teufelsdröckh, *Pilgerstab* in hand (147), setting off on a "world pilgrimage" which, like the wandering in the wilderness of Zin, seems more like a journey in a "dark labyrinth" than a journey with a destination (152). Teufelsdröckh appears not only as a contemporary Israelite on a worldwide exodus, but as several other types: as Ishmael in a desert "waste and howling with savage monsters" (114), as Cain or the Wandering Jew—"save only that he feels himself not guilty and but suffering the pains of guilt" (156), and even as a "young mettled colt" who "breaks-off his neck-halter" to try rich clover fields, only to find himself in "a certain bosky wilderness" (121).

All of these types modify or supplement the basic pattern of the exodus, and like the initial opposition of Genesis and Exodus, their inclusion focuses attention on the act of shaping an autobiography. They make visible the autobiographer's choice of narrative form, the representation of life as a wilderness wandering being a deliberate act of the Editor, one with which Teufelsdröckh's comments seem to concur.[14] Unlike the earlier opposition, however, these three variations on the pattern do not test it by the truth of experience. Instead, the validity of the experience is tested by the pattern. Or rather, the validity of Teufelsdröckh's interpretation of experience is tested— and, with it, the autobiographical act of self-interpretation is critically examined.

In one of these variations, the Editor repeats Teufelsdröckh's description of himself as a "young mettled colt" who "breaks-off-his neck-halter," jumps the fence hoping to find his way "into luxuriant and luxurious clover," but soon finds himself in a "bosky wilderness" (121). The description parallels the exodus account in several respects: the colt is kept in bondage, miraculously breaks free, but ends up in the wilderness. Appropriately, it appears in the chapter "Getting Under Way," moving the narrative along, carrying Teufelsdröckh from his Egyptian bondage to the next stage of his pilgrimage. Only the Editor realizes, however, that the next stage is the wilderness. To Teufelsdröckh, the young colt, it simply appears "bosky"— that is, sylvan.

That Teufelsdröckh misinterpreted the landscape at the time he saw it is confirmed by his explanation of what he felt when he broke off the neck-halter: "Then, in the words of Ancient Pistol, did the world generally become mine oyster, which I, by strength or cunning, was to open, as I would and could" (120). Obviously, Teufelsdröckh can't see the desert for the trees. He believes that one can go straight from Egypt to the promised land. But his Editor, with the foresight that typology provides, knows that the new landscape, however bosky it may appear, can only be a wilderness. With that knowledge, he re-interprets Teufelsdröckh's original passage: "He too must enact that stern Monodrama, *No Object and no Rest*; must front its successive destinies, work through to its catastrophe, and deduce therefrom what moral he can" (121). The revision suggests that without reliable systems of interpretation we will misread our experience, if indeed we can read it at all.

The next variation—Ishmael in a desert "waste and howling with savage monsters"—offers another perspective on the possibility of misreading. Here the Old Testament type is the Editor's choice, and it seems a perspicacious one. Like Ishmael cast out from Abraham's legitimate heirs, Teufelsdröckh discovers that he is an alien among the "eleven-hundred Christian youths" who attend the university with him. In this predicament the Editor depicts him beset by "fever-paroxysms of Doubt" about himself and his religion; like Hagar and Ishmael, he "cast[s] himself before the All-seeing" and "crie[s] vehemently for Light, for deliverance from Death and the Grave" (114). Though seemingly appropriate, the variation runs counter to the pattern of the Exodus in one crucial sense. Both Ishmael and the children of Israel descended from Abraham, both found themselves in a desert, but the Ishmaelites were not the elect of God. If Teufelsdröckh is an Ishmaelite, then he cannot expect to find his way out of the wilderness. To impose this pattern upon his experience will prevent the hoped-for resolution.

Unlike the analogy of the colt lost in a bosky wilderness, this correlative involves no mis-seeing of external reality: the Editor knows that a desert surrounds Teufelsdröckh. But he still misreads —or fears to read fully. Like Bunyan struggling with the possibility of Esau as his legitimate type, the Editor is plagued by the possibility that a pattern other than the Exodus may represent the key to Teufelsdröckh's life. Or, more skeptical than Bunyan, he may fear that he has no means of distinguishing a key that works from one that does not, a valid interpretation from an invalid one. The personal "fever-paroxysms of Doubt" are the product of a cultural "nightmare [of] Unbelief" (114), and the nightmare includes a loss of confidence in providential interpretation.

The third variation on the exodus pattern—the story of the Wandering Jew—is the most complex of the three and the most interesting for what it reveals about Carlyle's relationship to the conventions of the Romantic literary tradition. Carlyle's immediate source for the Wandering Jew as an autobiographical model was Goethe's *Sufferings of Young Werther*, but other Romantic wanderers had influenced his choice as well.[15] In Goethe's work the young hero loses his beloved and his position at court and sets off on a series of aimless travels: "True, I am but a wanderer, a rover on earth!" he writes in a letter. "Are you more than that?"[16] After being rejected by Blumine and the polite society of Towgoods and Zähdarms, Teufelsdröckh similarly sets off, "wend[ing] to and fro with aimless speed," covering "the whole surface of the earth (by footprints) [to] write his *Sorrows of Teufelsdröckh*" (156). Carlyle's repetition of this Romantic pattern intends to answer Werther's question—Are you more than that? —with a significant variation. Teufelsdröckh repeats Werther, but his repetition signals a difference.

At first glance, this Cain/Wandering Jew/Werther motif would seem merely to supplement the exodus typology of *Sartor*, allowing Carlyle to graft a continental and Romantic pattern onto an essentially English and Puritan form. But Carlyle does not introduce the motif to supplement or modify the biblical pattern. Rather, the Editor examines it critically and then rejects it as inferior to the traditional biblical type. He objects to the motif because it fails to fit at crucial points; he notes, for example, that Teufelsdröckh "feels himself not guilty and but suffering the pains of guilt" (156). But ultimately the Editor rejects the pattern because it offers a detrimental model: Cain remains an outcast, the Jew is condemned to wander until the Day of Judgment, and Werther commits suicide. Here the didactic-redemptive function of the spiritual autobiography dictates the narrative form. Just as Bunyan rejects Francis Spira, the Editor negates a possible autobiographical model not because it fails to fit experience, but because it may have the power to *create* experience. This is what the Editor means when he states that men would be happier if they wrote such matters not in books, but "on the insensible Earth, with [their] shoe-soles only." Men can "survive the writing thereof" (157), for the traces of their footprints disappear. Men could not survive words arranged in patterns and preserved in books.

By the time the Editor has reached the three central chapters of Book Second, which narrate Teufelsdröckh's conversion, the Exodus has become the authoritative pattern, and the Editor can invoke it both descriptively and prescriptively. As he explains the effects of Teufelsdröckh's "mad Pilgrimage" (158), he describes the philosopher's world as "all a grim Desert, this once-fair world of his; wherein is heard only the howling of wild-beasts, or the shrieks of despairing, hate-filled men; and no Pillar of Cloud by day, and no Pillar of Fire by night, any longer guides the Pilgrim" (161). Teufelsdröckh has lost the visible symbols of providence because he has succumbed to a rationalist (or post-rationalist) view of the universe; his world is "void of Life, of Purpose, of Volition, even of Hostility" (164). But his Editor continues to use the biblical patterns to describe his state rather than any others, because he now understands that the hermeneutics an autobiographer chooses has prefigurative power. It may determine his future state.

That Carlyle intends his readers to recognize the power of interpretive systems is clear from Teufelsdröckh's discussion of suicide. Unlike Goethe's Werther or Byron's Manfred, Teufelsdröckh does not wander unto death. He is prevented by what Carlyle calls the *Nachschein* of Christianity, an afterglow which prevents the young man *philosophically* from taking his life. The *Nachschein* also keeps him

literarily in the pattern he should follow. For, derived from the
biblical text and transmitted through a tradition of spiritual autobiography, exodus typology has the power to save the autobiographer
from death and release him from death-in-life.

The Editor's interpretive choice in the Cain/Wandering Jew passage has its predicted effect. By the next allusion to the Exodus,
Teufelsdröckh has moved through "The Everlasting No" and "The
Centre of Indifference" to "The Everlasting Yea." Significantly, the
young philosopher makes this allusion himself, linking the Old
Testament type with its New Testament fulfillment: " 'Temptations
in the Wilderness!' exclaims Teufelsdröckh: 'Have we not all to be
tried with such?...Our Wilderness is the wide World in an Atheistic
Century; our Forty Days are long years of suffering and fasting:
nevertheless, to these there also comes an end' " (183−84). The
comment is, in the Editor's phrase, an "ambitious figure" (184). It is
a figure not simply in the Coleridgean sense that, as metaphor, it
aspires to a metaphysical realm. It is an example of *figura* in the
theological sense: a record of a historical event that fulfills the
foreshadowing of an earlier biblical event and thus testifies to a
providential view of history. In this theological sense it is "ambitious"; it attempts to reassert the primacy of the Bible in a post-
rationalist interpretation of history.

Like the Israelites' experience in the wilderness and Christ's temptation in the desert, Teufelsdröckh's trials cease when he relies on the
biblical record—the authoritative "It is written"—and "work[s] out
[his] way into the higher sunlight slopes" (184). The autobiography
in Book Second ends with a description of its subject stationed "on the
high table-land," like Moses overlooking the promised land, contemplating "the nine Towns and Villages that lay round [his] mountain
seat," and watching a "blue pillar" of smoke ascend from each kitchen
fire (187). As Joseph Sigman has pointed out, the passage contains an
elaborate allusion to Moses' final vision of Canaan from Mount
Pisgah, the nine towns corresponding to the nine cities of Judah and
the blue smoke to the pillar of cloud that marks God's presence.[17]
The Pisgah vision comes as a reward for following the pattern of the
biblical text as transmitted by the tradition of Bunyan, a tradition

that made such visions the conventional method of closure. With Teufelsdröckh on the mountaintop, the exodus pattern is complete.

If Carlyle uses exodus typology to organize the (auto)biographical narrative of Book Second and simultaneously to foreground the complexities of self-interpretation, he also uses it to present an account of Teufelsdröckh's conversion and examine critically the hermeneutic implications of its conventions. As we have seen, spiritual autobiographies like *Grace Abounding* and Book Second of *Sartor Resartus* conventionally apply key events of the Exodus to the life of the individual Christian and thus derive both structure and content from biblical typology—the state of sinfulness corresponding to the Egyptian bondage; the dramatic conversion, to the flight from Pharaoh and the crossing of the Red Sea; the period of confusion or even backsliding, to the wilderness wandering; and the final peace, to the entry into Canaan. The details may vary or some aspect be diminished, but whatever the variation, at the center of the narrative is always the dramatic encounter.

By the nineteenth century, many conversion narratives had lost their specifically religious content, yet their writers still drew upon the traditional forms to recount secular experiences. John Stuart Mill described the crisis in his mental history, for example, as the state "in which converts to Methodism usually are, when smitten by their first 'conviction of sin,'" although his crisis had no overt religious component.[18] Even when autobiographers did not recognize the biblical origin of their narratives, most of them recounted experiences that followed the conventional pattern, always with a dramatic conversion, usually with a wilderness wandering. In Carlyle's case, however, the recognition of religious and literary sources is clear. The central chapters of Book Second deliberately invoke the pattern, "The Everlasting No" repeating the rebellion against Pharaoh; "The Centre of Indifference," the wilderness wandering; and "The Everlasting Yea," the entry into Canaan. At the center of Teufelsdröckh's experience is the dramatic conversion on the Rue St. Thomas de l'Enfer.

Despite such clear biblical patterns, the typological allusions in these chapters have become the focus of a small critical maelstrom in the past decade, with some critics attempting to diminish or deny the Christian elements of Teufelsdröckh's conversion. Walter L. Reed has argued, for instance, that there is "no clear Christian pattern behind Teufelsdröckh's conversion"; instead, the structure of the autobiographical narrative derives from German Romantic philosophy, particularly from Goethe's belief "that all action was the effect of the juxtaposition of positive and negative poles."[19] While German philosophy certainly influenced Carlyle, a fact no critic would deny, this argument represents a misunderstanding of what constitutes a Christian pattern of conversion. Certainly, it ignores the generic tradition in which Teufelsdröckh's autobiography participates and misses Carlyle's use of radical biblical hermeneutics in Book Second. For even if Carlyle divests the exodus pattern in *Sartor Resartus* of its orthodox Protestant meaning, he does not efface its Christian origins; indeed, he exposes them.

Such misunderstandings do not originate with Reed, who was attempting to correct what he considered a mistaken emphasis in Carlylean scholarship. From the beginning, readers of *Sartor Resartus* have discussed the orthodox Christian and German Romantic influences upon Carlyle, but it was C. F. Harrold in *Carlyle and German Thought* and then in his edition of *Sartos Resartus* who, more than anyone else, formulated the questions that later scholars would ask of the text. In Harrold's view Carlyle was a "Calvinist without the theology," one who sought "in German thought and elsewhere, an acceptable intellectual restatement of these beliefs"; *Sartor Resartus* was a specific instance of "a brilliant metaphorical adaptation of German idealism, in its terms and concepts, to the surviving intellectual design bequeathed by Calvinism when shorn of its dogmas."[20] Harrold's reading initiated a critical tradition that has attempted to explain the details of the Carlylean adaptation, and subsequent critics have felt obliged either to disagree with his stance or accept it with modifications. Reed represents the former attitude; a critic like G. B. Tennyson in *Sartor Called Resartus*, the latter.[21]

Much of this critical debate has confused philosophical ideas and narrative patterns, theological commitment and generic intention.[22] Yet it may perhaps remind us here of the careful relationship between theology and narrative that Carlyle intends. There are too many biblical allusions, particularly those associated with typological hermeneutics, to ignore the influence of the English spiritual autobiography. And there are too many allusions to German literary and philosophical sources to ignore their contribution either.[23] Whatever relationship we formulate between Christian and Romantic sources in *Sartor Resartus*, we must credit both, distinguishing between narrative patterns and philosophical/theological content, but also connecting narrative and exposition in terms of autobiography's concern with both.

In Carlyle's case, the disjunction between traditional narrative form and philosophical content suggests the place to begin. The disjunction is deliberate, I think. Carlyle adopts the traditional form of the English spiritual autobiography for the structure of Book Second and for Teufelsdröckh's conversion in its central three chapters. As we have seen, his literary predecessor, John Bunyan, was able to derive this autobiographical structure directly from biblical typology by applying the events of the Exodus to the experiences of his spiritual life. In Bunyan the movement from biblical hermeneutics to literary form is uncomplicated: the account of the Exodus, divinely inspired and hence authoritative, needs no modification, only personal application. In Carlyle, however, this movement cannot be so simple. Mediated by a century and a half of literary tradition and by radical methods of German biblical criticism as well, the movement from biblical hermeneutics to literary creation becomes a complicated autobiographical act.

The differences between Bunyan and Carlyle and the distance that English autobiography has traveled are no more obvious than in the treatments of standard Old Testament types in *Grace Abounding* and *Sartor Resartus*. When Bunyan introduces the Exodus as the pattern for autobiographical writing, he acknowledges virtually no separation between the Old Testament narrative and his own life. He writes of *Grace Abounding* as "a Relation of the work of God upon my own Soul," using the language of Scripture:

[In it] *you may perceive my castings down, and raisings up; for he woundeth, and his hands make whole. It is written in the Scripture (Isai.* 38.19), The father to the children shall make known the truth of God. *Yea, it was for this reason I lay so long at* Sinai (Deut. 4.10,11), *to see the fire, and the cloud, and the darkness,* that I might fear the Lord all the days of my life upon earth, and tell of his wondrous works to my children, *Psal.* 78.3,4,5.

At first glance, we might conclude that typographical distinctions separate the biblical language from Bunyan's own, italics indicating a direct quotation of scripture. But this is not so, for the clause "he woundeth, and his hands make whole" quotes Job 5.18 exactly, as does the unitalicized sentence from Isaiah that follows. In Bunyan's autobiography the language of the Bible merges imperceptibly with his own so that one cannot separate its text from his, Moses from John Bunyan, the "I" of Deuteronomy from the "I" of *Grace Abounding.* In such matters of scriptural interpretation and literary creation, Bunyan is thoroughly Protestant. He allows nothing to intervene between himself and the biblical text nor between the text and his autobiography; he needs no other models to tell his story, no special literary language. "God *did not play in convincing of me,*" he explains: *"The* Devil *did not play in tempting of me; neither did I play when I sunk as into a bottomless pit, when* the pangs of hell caught hold upon me: *wherefore I may not play in my relating of them, but be plain and simple, and lay down the thing as it was"* (3−4). For Bunyan, "the thing as it was" is the thing as it is in the biblical text. That text grounds his language and provides his reality.

In contrast, when Carlyle introduces exodus typology into *Sartor Resartus,* he does so with an understanding of the distance between the type and his subject Teufelsdröckh, a distance created by a tradition in generic form and a revolution in biblical hermeneutics. Hofrath Heuschrecke's question demonstrates the contrast: "By what singular stair-steps, in short, and subterranean passages, and sloughs of Despair, and steep Pisgah hills, has he reached this wonderful prophetic Hebron (a true Old-Clothes Jewry) where he now dwells?" (76). The question suggests an autobiographical form: a man's life as a spiritual exodus. It does not, however, suggest a direct typological application. Between the biblical text and Teufelsdröckh's autobiography a literary tradition intervenes, alluded to in the "sloughs of Despair" from Bunyan. Also intervening are the autobiographer as literary artist, who adds his own "singular stair-steps" and "subterranean passages" to the biblical place names, and the autobiographer as contemporary historian, who acknowledges in the allusion to a London ghetto, the "true Old-Clothes Jewry," a difference between the Old Testament milieu and his own.

What Carlyle demonstrates in Heuschrecke's question is that autobiographers "accommodate" prior literary texts as they create their own. I use the term *accommodation* here as it was used by rationalist and mythological biblical critics in nineteenth-century Germany and England, but the term in fact appears in the writings of both orthodox theologians and the Higher Critics, as they were called. According to orthodox theology, God has accommodated divine truth to man's limited understanding throughout history; he revealed his truth partially to the Israelites in the "shadowy types" of the Old Testament, then more fully to Christian believers in the New. According to the Higher Critics, "accommodation" refers not to the beneficent action of God but to the literary activities of the writers of Scripture, particularly the writers of the Gospels and Epistles. These writers accommodated (that is, adapted) Old Testament materials to their own narrative and doctrinal purposes. As Patrick Fairbairn explained the issue in an attack on the Higher Critics and in defense of traditional biblical typology,

> The rationalistic spirit, in the progress of its antichristian tendencies...discarded the ...types of the elder divines; and the convenient principles of *accommodation*, which was at the same time introduced, furnished an easy solution for those passages in the New Testament Scripture which seemed to indicate a typical relationship between the past and the future. It was regarded only as an adaptation, originating in Jewish prejudice or conceit, of the facts and institutions of an earlier age to things essentially different under the gospel.[24]

Fairbairn presents the introduction of the concept of accommodation as a new critical laxity, making an almost *ad hominem* argument against rationalist hermeneuticians. But the disagreement between orthodox theologians and the Higher Critics was fundamentally theoretical. It centered, as Fairbairn knew all too well, on the issues of who (or Who) made the accommodation and why.

In practice, the disagreement often came down to a matter of types and prophecies. According to the Higher Critics, accommodation might take place in either of two ways: a New Testament writer might adapt the *words* of the Old Testament (what orthodox theologians would consider prophecy) or he might adapt a narrative *pattern* (what the orthodox would call a type). The apostle Matthew's account of the star of the Magi and the flight into Egypt illustrates the different approaches and suggests the literary adaptations possible in a work like *Sartor Resartus*, where the author understands both older and newer hermeneutic modes.

In the evangelical interpretation of Thomas Scott, the star of Bethlehem represents a divine sign and typological fulfillment, a "luminous appearance" which "looked like a star, and which was formed by God...to mark out a single house in the midst of the city; as the cloudy pillar pointed out the spot, where Israel was to encamp in the wilderness."[25] In *The Life of Jesus Critically Examined*, David Friedrich Strauss analyzes the assumptions of such orthodox criticism, including the older notion of accommodation: "The most obvious explanation, from the orthodox point of view, is an appeal to the supernatural intervention of God; who, in this particular instance, in order to bring the distant magi unto Jesus, accommodated himself to their astrological notions, and caused the anticipated star to appear."[26] To a mythological critic like Strauss, the narrative of the star represents not a revelation from God, but rather an adaptation of prior biblical, rabbinical, and secular literary texts. Synthesizing the work of a century of Higher Criticism, Strauss points to the origin of the story in Balaam's prophecy: "A star shall come out of Jacob" (Numbers 24.17). He traces the prophecy through rabbinical tradition to show its gradual association with the Messiah. He then documents the belief in astrology "prevalent in the time of Jesus" and cites

extra-biblical stories in which stars, comets, and other stellar distur-
bances mark the appearance of great leaders (the comets appearing at
the birth of Mithridates and the death of Julius Caesar, Jewish legends
claiming "that a remarkable star appeared at the birth of Abraham,"
and so on). All of these elements—the biblical prophecy, the contemporary belief in astrology, the rabbinical and secular narratives—
contribute to the mythus of the star in Matthew's Gospel. According
to Strauss,

> The early converted Jewish Christians could confirm their faith
> in Jesus, and justify it in the eyes of others, only by labouring to
> prove that in him were realized all the attributes lent to the
> Messiah by Jewish notions of their age.... Hence it soon ceased
> to be a matter of doubt that the anticipated appearance of a star
> was really coincident with the birth of Jesus. This being once
> presupposed, it followed as a matter of course that the observers
> of this appearance were eastern magi; first, because none could
> better interpret the sign than astrologers, and the east was
> supposed to be the native region of their science; and secondly,
> because it must have seemed fitting that the Messianic star
> which had been seen by the spiritual eye of the ancient magus
> Balaam, should, on its actual appearance be first recognized by
> the bodily eyes of the later magi.[27]

This complicated web of sources hardly corresponds to the "con-
venient" hermeneutics that Fairbairn describes as typical of the Higher Critics. In Strauss's criticism the Gospel narrative becomes a
complex example of literary influence and intertextuality. Having
removed God as the divine author of the text, the biblical critic
assumes the task of tracing the multiple human authors who contributed to it.

Carlyle could not have known Strauss's analysis of the star passage
in 1830 when he was writing *Sartor Resartus*, for the first German
edition of *Das Leben Jesu* did not appear until 1835. But the principles
of mythological analysis, as E. S. Shaffer has demonstrated, had
already been formulated by 1795. They were introduced to English
audiences by Herbert Marsh, a student of Michaelis, in the first and

second decades of the nineteenth century, and they were present in the
works of many German critics whom Carlyle read in the 1820s,
including Lessing and Schleiermacher.[28] In Book Second Carlyle
appropriates these principles of textual influence as he (or, rather, his
Editor) accommodates the narrative of the Exodus to compose the
autobiography of Diogenes Teufelsdröckh. Unlike an orthodox typologist or a Puritan autobiographer, the Editor does not apply types
directly to Teufelsdröckh's life. For him they are not immediate
revelations from God, unmediated by human concerns or cultural
assumptions. Such revelations are not possible—at least, not possible
to comprehend. Even in Heuschrecke's initial allusion to the Exodus,
the application of the sacred pattern includes an acknowledgment of a
tradition of biblical hermeneutics as well as of traditional and contemporary literary forms.

"Communion of Saints," "cloud of witnesses," and simply "Tradition" are terms Carlyle gives to this web of multiple authorship and
intertextual influence.[29] "Who printed thee, for example, this un-
pretending Volume on the Philosophy of Clothes?" Teufelsdröckh
asks. "Not the Herren Stillschweigen and Company; but Cadmus of
Thebes, Faust of Mentz, and innumerable others whom thou knowest
not" (246). The answer recognizes the dependence of contemporary
writers on the man who invented movable type, on the earlier man
(real or imaginary) who introduced the Phoenician alphabet of sixteen
letters into Greece, and on all the other contributers to written
language. The dependence is not simply mechanical, not a matter of
reproduction. It is literally a matter of production. The type and the
letters give form to man's thought: they provide the forms through
and in which man expresses himself. Like the prior biblical and
secular texts which (in)form the Gospel of Matthew, the written and
printed texts prior to Teufelsdröckh's inform his *Die Kleider, ihr
Werden und Wirken* and his autobiography. One might even say that
those prior texts compose—that is, "make by putting together parts
or elements," a term appropriate to both writing and printing—the
works, and not Teufelsdröckh himself. "It is thus," his Editor says,
"that the heroic heart, the seeing eye of the first times, still feels and
sees in us of the latest; that the Wise Man stands ever encompassed,

and spiritually embraced, by a cloud of witnesses and brothers; and there is a living, literal *Communion of Saints*, wide as the World itself, and as the History of the World" (247).

Such a view of autobiographical writing explains why critics have discovered so many narrative patterns in *Sartor Resartus*, why they are right to see them but misled to debate the priority (or final authority) of any single pattern. By invoking the exodus initially, Carlye acknowledges the origin of his Editor's autobiographical form and places Book Second within a generic tradition. But the original form, like Balaam's prophecy of the star, is modified by other biblical and secular texts. Narratives of other wanderers and outcasts complicate the exodus pattern and, like the rabbinical and pagan stories of astrological wonders, supplement and even alter its meaning. Similarly, contemporary autobiographical forms, especially those of German literature, influence the content of Teufelsdröckh's narrative. So, too, do stories from classical mythology, which are abundant in the *Sartor Resartus* but rarely discussed.

All of these modifications and variations suggest that a debate over whether *Sartor Resartus* and especially Book Second represent an Augustinian, a Calvinistic, or a Goethean pattern of conversion is unresolvable. G. B. Tennyson is probably correct to see in *Sartor* an Augustinian point of crisis, the "spiritual nadir from which the soul arises to salvation," and Walter Reed is probably correct, too, that Goethe's influence adds to the crisis "a time and space of indifference." But the issue should not be one of exclusivity or doctrinal purity or philosophical allegiance. For Carlyle in *Sartor Resartus*, the key issues are those of intertextual relationships: of generic conventions shaping texts and of texts modifying the genre.

In using the new biblical hermeneutics as his model for literary creation, Carlyle revises our conventional definitions of autobiographical writing. The autobiographer does not, as we usually say, begin with the raw facts of his experience and then create or discover an order from within. Instead, he constructs a life from the models of prior autobiographical texts, the facts of his life being accessible only indirectly, given in part by the practice of the autobiographers before him. Just as the Gospel narrative of the star, the Magi, and the flight into Egypt depends less upon historical events than upon Old Testament and apocryphal models, so Teufelsdröckh's autobiography (like all autobiographies) depends less on the facts than on textual models, biblical and secular, that explain and thus *create* man's experience. As both Strauss and Carlyle understood, the historical facts are irrecoverable anyway.

Strauss makes this point implicitly in the title of his *The Christ of Faith and the Jesus of History*.[30] Carlyle makes the point explicitly at the end of Book Second when the Editor admits that "these Autobiographical Documents are partly a mystification" (202). As the Editor despairs that all his labor may be for naught, fearing "What if many a so-called Fact were little better than a Fiction," the answer comes back "on a small slip, formerly thrown aside as blank, the ink being all-but invisible": " 'What are your historical Facts; still more your biographical? Wilt thou know a Man, above all a Mankind, by stringing-together beadrolls of what thou namest Facts? The Man is the spirit he worked in; not what he did, but what he became. Facts are engraved Hierograms' " (203). Teufelsdröckh's answer can be read simply as an acknowledgment that the autobiographer ought not merely to record the historical facts of his life, but instead should discover the shape, "the spirit he worked in." This reading would confirm the traditional delineation of fact to form in autobiography argued by Roy Pascal: "the autobiographer is not relating facts, but experiences—i.e. the interaction of a man and facts or events. By experience we mean something with meaning."[31]

But might not Carlyle be suggesting here a more radical notion of autobiographical writing? In Book Second, historical facts or events are never really a part of the autobiographical process. In the six paper bags, Teufelsdröckh sends fragments of his life that are not raw materials, but already responses to (interpretations of) autobiographical, theological, and philosophical texts. The Editor's question defines the issue: "What if many a so-called Fact were little better than a Fiction?" *Sartor Resartus* suggests an answer: the fiction is inseparable from the fact, the symbolic history from the personal life, the generic models from the individual autobiography.

On the grounds of its fictionality and lack of real facts *Sartor Resartus* is usually excluded from serious accounts of the English autobiography. Carlyle admitted, as we know, that the account of Teufelsdröckh's life was "symbolical myth all," and its densely allusive texture seems to corroborate his description. Yet he qualified his admission with an exception: "the incident in the Rue St. Thomas de L'Enfer, which occurred quite literally to myself in Leith Walk [Edinburgh], during three weeks of total sleeplessness, in which my one solace was that of a daily bathe on the sands between Leith and Portobello."[32] Carlyle's acknowledgment of the truth of this central incident suggests an essential, personal connection with the narrative of Book Second. Might not this single, literal incident form the basis of a genuine Carlylean self-interpretation, an autobiography of reconstruction through literary convention?[33]

That *Sartor Resartus* is an autobiography of reconstruction its title affirms: sartor resartus, the tailor re-tailored. In the work, the British Editor reconstructs Teufelsdröckh's life and Philosophy of Clothes, and thus Carlyle reconstructs the worn-out philosophy of a post-rationalist age and with it the lives of his British readers. But Carlyle also reconstructs himself. Around the central episode of conversion in Leith Walk, he composes an interpretation of his experience that takes form specifically through generic conventions. This, as *Sartor Resartus* teaches us, is what all autobiographers do. If in his reconstruction Carlyle relies more completely upon literary predecessors than most autobiographers do, that is compatible with his sense of *Sartor Resartus* as a literary "extravaganza" (302). It is compatible, too, with his understanding of autobiography as a fundamentally hermeneutic literary form.

❧ 3 ❧

Ruskin's *Praeterita*:
The Attempt at Deconstruction

Even as a middle-aged adult, John Ruskin referred to Carlyle as his "master," writing almost daily letters to "Papa" Carlyle with a reverence he had never felt for his own father.[1] Late in life, in an appendix to *Modern Painters*, Ruskin recorded his great intellectual debt to Carlyle: "I read [Carlyle] so constantly," he confessed, "that, without wilfully setting myself to imitate him, I find myself perpetually falling into his modes of expression."[2] Carlyle may have been Ruskin's intellectual master, and indeed John Rosenberg has traced the literary debt that political works like *Unto This Last* and *Munera Pulveris* owe to *Past and Present*.[3] But in *Praeterita* the Carylean modes of expression are noticeably absent—as are the modes of interpretation that Carlyle applied to his personal experience in *Sartor Resartus*.

Perhaps the difference between the two autobiographers was one of experience. Unlike Carlyle, John Ruskin had no single, dramatic conversion to record, only a gradual loss of faith and a quiet decision in 1858 that he would "put away" his evangelical beliefs, "to be debated of no more."[4] But perhaps the difference is more fundamentally one of intention. Had he desired, Ruskin might have transformed this religious falling away into a variant of the spiritual autobiography—not into a revision of the form like Carlyle's, but into a secular account of vocational conversion or into a parodic inversion of the traditional spiritual narrative, one taking his rejection of evangelical faith as its central incident. He might have used, in other words, the conventional forms of the spiritual autobiography for different, but still personal, ends.

When Ruskin began *Praeterita*, however, he seems to have had little desire to work with the conventions of a genre he found emotionally and intellectually distasteful. As his 1845 criticism of Bunyan's *Grace Abounding* suggests, he considered much spiritual autobiography to be nothing more than "a particular phase of indigestion, coupled with a good imagination and a bad conscience," and if his language forty years later was less extreme, it is still clear from the preface to *Praeterita* that he found intensive concentration on "the relations of the Deity to his own little self" to be a "painful" and "morbid" enterprise.[5] Indeed, the prefatory comments suggest that he intended to take a radically different approach to autobiography, one that avoided the dominant generic tradition and the religious modes of introspection and interpretation characteristic of it. *Praeterita* was to be a collection of "sketches of effort and incident," an informal assemblage of memories written "frankly, garrulously, and at ease."[6] The principle for selecting the memories (if memory could be subjected to principle at all) was to be a highly personal application of *dulce et utile*. "I have written," Ruskin states, "of what it gives me joy to remember at any length I like—sometimes very carefully of what I think it may be useful for others to know; and passing in total silence things which I have no pleasure in reviewing, and which the reader would find no help in the account of."

However congenial its tone, this preface firmly rejects the traditional generic demands of the spiritual autobiography. The emphasis upon incidents "it gives me joy to remember" avoids the introspective and often painful method of the genre; the insistence on "total silence" about matters that yield "no pleasure in reviewing" excludes many of the episodes crucial to the form, those which recall the autobiographer erring and then struggling to regain his way; and the decision to write of individual incidents "at any length I like" resists the conventional proportions of the genre, which dictate that narration should occur for the sake of interpretation and interpretation continue until providential design has been discovered and accepted.

In general, the preface denies the hermeneutic imperative of autobiographical writing—the imperative that had motivated Bunyan to search repeatedly through the Old and New Testaments for a biblical type who, like himself, had "sinned grievously" yet been forgiven, and that motivated Victorian autobiographers like Carlyle, when they found typology inadequate as a method, either to revitalize it or search for hermeneutic alternatives.

Praeterita attempts neither to revitalize nor to substitute. Rather, Ruskin attempts to dissociate his work from the tradition of English autobiography and from its distinctive hermeneutic method. Dissociation from a literary tradition is no simple matter, and much of the literary (as opposed to biographical) interest of *Praeterita* lies in the distance between intention and achievement. For, Ruskin's statements to the contrary, the autobiography is not simply a collection of pleasant sketches, nor is it a memoir of external events and forces— "of what my life has taught me, or made of me," as he puts it in one version of the preface.[7] It is a record of Ruskin's personal struggle with evangelical modes of thought and thus an example of a major literary writer's struggle with generic conventions and the hermeneutic issues that autobiography as a genre entails. As such, *Praeterita* is one of the most significant instances of the self-conscious literary autobiography in the Victorian period.

For Ruskin, the hermeneutic issues were difficult to avoid. The methods of interpretation that spiritual autobiographers had appropriated and then modified from biblical typology had been fundamental to his own religious training and later to the development of his aesthetic and critical theories. As a child, he had learned biblical typology from the sermons of the Reverend Henry Melvill, dutifully writing on Sunday afternoons abstracts of the sermons he had heard on Sunday mornings.[8] As a young author, he had adapted typological principles for his work in *Modern Painters* and *The Stones of Venice*, using them, as George P. Landow has explained, not only to defend the achievement of Turner and "convince Evangelicals to build costly Gothic houses of worship," but more significantly, to develop his "theories of imagination and imaginative conception of truth" and his "notion of the artist-poet as prophet.'"[9] Naturally, then, Ruskin might have turned to typological methods of self-interpretation in his autobiography. Typology had been part of his past experience as well as of his interpretive practice; it might have provided both substance and method for *Praeterita*. Ruskin chose, however, the more difficult task of generic dissociation, a choice which reflects his increasingly complex understanding of hermeneutic issues.

The formal difficulties that this choice poses become apparent, in microcosm, in the second half of the preface. There, as Ruskin explains the occasion for publishing the first volume (and just after he denies the traditional demands of autobiography), he succumbs to conventions of the genre he has just rejected:

> I write these few prefatory words on my father's birthday, in what was once my nursery in his old house.... What would otherwise in the following pages have been little more than an old man's recreation in gathering visionary flowers in fields of youth, has taken, as I wrote, the nobler aspect of a dutiful offering at the grave of parents who trained my childhood to all the good it could attain, and whose memory makes declining life cheerful in the hope of being soon again with them.

A life trained "to all the good it could attain" suggests the teleological arrangement of episodes conventional in spiritual autobiography, whether the force guiding the arrangement be God or God acting through his parents. The final "hope of being soon again with them" repeats the traditional closure of the spiritual narrative, with its vision of future bliss, like Bunyan's vision of the milk and honey beyond this wilderness. If the preface has no religious conversion to offer, there is a metaphorical substitute: the conversion of sensual, mortal flowers into an everlasting tribute to his parents. Such language testifies to the power of generic precedent over private desire.

Yet even as Ruskin succumbs, he manages a dissociation from the autobiography's hermeneutic mode. It is difficult to identify, for example, the agent of the conversion. Ruskin says that "a delight in visionary flowers" has "taken on" a "nobler aspect," but he does not say from what or from whom. The metaphor suggests that *Praeterita* was transformed naturally into a filial tribute—as if interpretations grow on trees or in fields. There is no acknowledgment of the autobiographer's conscious arrangement of narrative or of any hermeneutic act, nor is there acknowledgment of a system of hermeneutics, biblical or otherwise, within which such arrangements and acts occur. Moreover, the conversion is presented within (or as) a metaphor. The effect is to efface its theological origin and the basis upon which the arrangement of much autobiography, including Ruskin's own, depends. Bunyan had been able to arrange his life "to all the good it could attain" because he applied the patterns of biblical typology: he may have bemoaned periods of bondage in Egypt and wandering in the wilderness, it is true, but he knew also that the biblical types promised redemption and a final entry into Canaan. Ruskin's language dissociates *Praeterita* from these origins.[10] This choice is made despite the fact that his parents had "trained" their son's life "to all the good it could attain" by applying biblical types—by devoting him to God's service before he was born, by forcing him "to learn long chapters of the Bible by heart," by giving him *Robinson Crusoe* and *The Pilgrim's Progress* to read in order "to make an evangelical clergyman of [him]" (I. i. 1).

The fact is, the only dutiful offering Ruskin could have given his parents was a full-fledged spiritual autobiography. And therein lies the source of Ruskin's difficulty as autobiographer and the conflict within the preface. Put biographically, the conflict was one between a need to satisfy his parent's expectations and a desire to write his own form of autobiography. Put generically, it was one between a decision to avoid the literary tradition of spiritual autobiography and a seemingly inevitable submission, in the act of writing, to conventions of the genre. The personal and generic were not separate issues. Ruskin faced a powerful alignment of parental with generic authority.

It is one of the ironies of literary history that modern readers have aligned themselves with Ruskin's parents, identifying in *Praeterita* those narrative patterns that place it within the tradition of spiritual autobiography. Pierre Fontenay unwittingly started the critical trend when he identified patterns of quest, purifying trial, and lost Edens regained in "The Simplon" chapter; then, George P. Landow pointed out the numerous Paradises Lost and Pisgah Visions in the work, linking them to the practice of biblical typology; and Elizabeth Helsinger discussed the repetition of the emblematic scenes of the book's beginning, scenes that allude to or reproduce Ruskin's infant paradise and that culminate in the final passage of "Joanna's Care," with its "Elysian walks with Joanie, and Paradisiacal with Rosie." Most recently, the critical trend has been continued by Heather Henderson, who suggests that the "Rome" and "Cumae" chapters use "the Exodus account to describe a period of physical and spiritual crisis and re-emergence," and by Avrom Fleishman, who argues that *Praeterita* is dominated by "figures of the garden and the Fall."[11] Summing up the critical tradition, Fleishman concludes that "what appears to be locally significant motif and metaphor achieves a wider resonance when related to the fund of biblical language and iconography, which writers of Ruskin's culture assimilated early and harbored long."[12]

These biblical patterns—of lost Edens, wilderness wanderings, and paradises regained—are certainly present in *Praeterita*, and they represent common biblical types that autobiographers have used to understand their experience. Yet in Ruskin's hands, this "fund of biblical language and iconography," as Fleishman calls it, creates as much dissonance from, as resonance with the tradition. *Praeterita* challenges the hermeneutic imperative of autobiography and its traditional hermeneutic mode.

The personal motives for this challenge appear early in *Praeterita*. In the first paragraph of "The Springs of Wandel," Ruskin denies that evangelical writers and their practices had any lasting effect upon the course of his life, even though his parents intended to model his life after biblical patterns, both those traditionally recognized as Old Testament *figurae* and those transmitted through the popular forms of the spiritual autobiography. John James and Margaret Ruskin may have allowed their son to read Walter Scott's novels and Pope's translation of the Iliad on weekdays, but "on Sunday their effect was tempered by Robinson Crusoe and the Pilgrim's Progress"—those two classics of spiritual bondage, struggle, and redemption. To the young boy, the parental strategy was clear: "my mother [had] it deeply in her heart to make an evangelical clergyman of me" (I.i.1).

Ruskin insists that the two books were about as palatable as the cold mutton his evangelical aunt served him for Sunday dinner. But his wit in this opening passage, the wit of the retrospective autobiographer, betrays a real anxiety. These spiritual classics threaten to shape his life in a more insidious way. Despite the fact that he has not become an evangelical clergyman and has even renounced his evangelical faith, the books continue to influence the way he recollects his past; they threaten now to predetermine the design of his autobiography.

The opening of "The Springs of Wandel" sounds the dissonance that resounds throughout the book. Later in the chapter, Ruskin recalls that his mother had solemnly devoted him to God before he was born, "in imitation of Hannah." "Very good women," he comments, once again attempting to deflect parental influence with wit, "are remarkably apt to make away with their children prematurely, in this manner" (I.i.19). Imitation of Old Testament types defines precisely what Ruskin rejected in his life and resists still as autobiographer. His wit turns on the disparity of a good woman committing a bad deed and provides him with a seemingly gentle way of negating his mother's typological habits. But the effect is not gentle at all. The point is that typological thinking results in death— death first to the child, for it takes away his ability to live his life as he chooses, but death also to the autobiographer, for typological patterns prematurely make away with his life, the life that he as author should have within his power to create.

Claudette Kemper Columbus has written tellingly of *Praeterita* as a work in which the recurrent pattern is one of "negation of any positive value" and of its silences as a revelation of Ruskin's "repressive ways of not coming alive." She wonders, as many readers have, about Ruskin's awareness of his repression and especially about his self-consciousness in *Praeterita* of his depiction of that repression. [13] In terms of modern psychoanalytic theory, Ruskin was of course unaware of what he revealed. In theological and literary terms, however, Ruskin was acute. The comment about pious mothers making away with their sons suggests that he understood the theological source of the repression, as well as its literary consequences.

Ruskin's acuteness reveals itself in more than witty exposures of parental maneuvers. It appears in direct criticism of typology as an interpretive mode, whether for autobiography or such didactic forms as the sermon and spiritual "progress." Commenting in "Christ Church Choir" on his spiritual state while at Oxford, Ruskin notes that it "had never entered into [his] head to doubt a word of the Bible," although he realized that "its words were to be understood otherwise" than as he had been taught:

> [T]he more I believed [the Bible], the less it did me any good. It was all very well for Abraham to do what angels bid him,—so would I if any angels bid me. . . . Also, though I felt myself somehow called to imitate Christian in the Pilgrim's Progress, I couldn't see that either Billiter Street and the Tower Wharf, where my father had his cellars, or the cherry-blossomed garden at Herne Hill, where my mother potted her flowers, could be places I was bound to fly from as the City of Destruction. Without much reasoning on the matter, I had virtually concluded from my general Bible reading that, never having meant or done any harm that I knew of, I could not be in danger of hell. (I.xi.216—17)

As these comments imply, young Ruskin understood perfectly well the interpretive assumptions of the evangelical religion in which he had been raised. The Bible was first to be read literally for the truth it contained. Then, the Old Testament was to be read typologically and its lessons applied correlatively to events in contemporary life. Moreover, spiritual allegories like *The Pilgrim's Progress* were to be read as models for Christian behavior and their narratives transposed onto the everyday activities of the individual believer.

If Ruskin understood all this, his comments also suggest why and how he resisted. He not so much ignores the literal truth of the Bible (as he claims he did), as he declares it irrelevant to his own situation: angels no longer visit men, and Christ no longer walks the earth. Ruskin's literalmindedness involves a fine irony that nicely undermines the typological applicability of the biblical text. Since evangelicals argued that typology (unlike allegory) proceeded from and, indeed, depended upon the literal meaning of the Bible, typology could not legitimately provide a means of self-interpretation for Ruskin, whose life failed to supply the necessary data of experience at the literal level. In effect, Ruskin separates one tenet of typological hermeneutics from the other, and here makes literal truth exclude typological application.

Such tactics, with their claims of disregard and irrelevance, are similar to those of the preface, and they are as problematic in the text itself as there. Even if Ruskin had successfully ignored biblical and didactic texts as a boy, he could not ignore them as an autobiographer, for typology supplied the episodic structure, narrative patterns, and interpretive framework of the genre as Ruskin and the Victorians knew it. In the end, Ruskin finally succumbed to parental and generic pressure. But he did so only after he had resisted at every important point, revising the generic materials and using that resonant "fund of biblical language and iconography" to undo the typological basis upon which the spiritual autobiography rests.[14]

If Ruskin attempts to resist the forms of spiritual autobiography in *Praeterita* and signals his intention in the preface and early chapters, he also employs more comprehensive strategies to avoid or resist the traditional forms, the first of which is his treatment of the autobiographical episode. As we saw earlier, the conventional structure of the episode, one developed by Bunyan in *Grace Abounding* and revitalized by Carlyle in *Sartor Resartus*, originated in the practice of biblical hermeneutics. It placed an unremitting emphasis upon interpretation, each episode beginning with narration as a prelude to self-conscious and systematic interpretation.

For Ruskin, the strongest form of resistance to this conventional structure would have been a refusal to interpret at all—or, given the impossibility of such an extreme, a refusal to interpret systematically. In a sense, Ruskin came close to the extreme. As he wrote the initial draft of *Praeterita*, he carried out the plan of the preface, "speaking of what it gives me joy to remember at any length I like" and "passing in total silence things which I have no pleasure in reviewing." He composed the draft as daily entries in his diary for 1885, each day recalling some segment of his past, the next day continuing that segment or beginning another as he chose. Only later did he combine the diary segments and add the chapter endings so famous for their "felt" summarizing effect. The original entries, what now comprises volume I and the first four chapters of volume II, were as free from interpretive summary as any autobiographical account can be.

In the final version of *Praeterita*, Ruskin chose a form of resistance less extreme. For most episodes, at least in volumes I and II, Ruskin offers some sort of interpretation, whether in terms of his vocational development or of his social or emotional state. His interpretations, however, avoid typological hermeneutics—as, indeed, they resist any hermeneutic mode that presents itself as systematic and authoritative. We can see this avoidance in three key episodes, all of them suggestive of the direction in which Ruskin revises the episodic structure, each of them dissociating *Praeterita* further and further from any specifically biblical frame of reference.

In the Schaffhausen segment of Volume I, for instance, Ruskin describes a series of scenes: his first dreamy midnight entry into the medieval city, his delight the next morning in the quaint houses with their "bow-windows projecting into the clean streets," and then his view of the countryside from "high above the Rhine"—"Infinitely beyond all that we had ever thought or dreamed,—the seen walls of Lost Eden could not have been more beautiful" (II.vi.132−34). Although the description includes an allusion to Eden, it is given for the record, for the clarity of the description itself. This allusion does not introduce a section of typological interpretation; instead, the comments that follow focus on the facts of this world, not the possibilities of the next.

Ruskin's interest in the episode is overtly historical. How could he have found delight in the mountains and their inhabitants, he wonders, when less than a century before, "no child would have been born to care for mountains, or for the men that lived among them, in that way" (II.vi.134)? His speculations cite the influence of Rousseau and Scott upon the modern consciousness, upon modern man's love of nature and "all sorts and conditions of men." Implicitly, they deny the possibility of discovering spiritual meaning in nature—at least in the nineteenth century. Centuries ago, Ruskin notes, St. Bernard of La Fontaine saw "above Mont Blanc the Madonna" and St. Bernard of Talloires, "not the Lake of Annecy, but the dead between Martigny and Aosta" (II.vi.134). In the Alps, Ruskin sees only what a nineteenth-century man can see: "snow" and "their humanity." His explanation of why he can see only these things binds the autobiographical episode to historical circumstance, not to a realm of spiritual meaning which is the traditional goal of biblical hermeneutics.

If in the Schaffhausen episode Ruskin interprets within a purely historical context, in the Abbeville segment (I.ix) he again reports a natural and historical scene without reference to a biblical or transcendent realm. The segment includes a brief history of the town, followed by a description of its social organization in 1600 and then in 1835, the year he first visited. In Ruskin's analysis, Abbeville represents "the preface and interpretation of Rouen"—by which he means that there he first saw "art,...religion, and present human life" existing "in perfect harmony," just as he would later observe them working together in Rouen. He also means that in Abbeville he found the praxis of his later aesthetic and critical theories, there embodied in the daily activity of the town, with its Gothic churches, bustling commercial square, quiet courtyards and "richly trellised" gardens in family dwellings.

As in the Schaffhausen episode, Ruskin extracts meaning from this scene, and one might say that this very extraction betrays the characteristic hermeneutic impulse of the genre. For Ruskin, however, meaning is not found within a typological framework. His interpretation includes a religious component, but religion offers no special key to understanding; rather, it is an ordinary, unprivileged mode: "For here I saw that art (of its local kind), religion, and present human life, were yet in perfect harmony. There were no dead six days and dismal seventh in those sculptured churches" (II.ix.181). Moreover, as Ruskin articulates this meaning, he does so within a narrative framework that avoids biblical patterns. Abbeville is another stage of an earthly journey, not of an exodus. It is preface to Rouen, not to a celestial city.

Like other episodes in the first half of *Praeterita*, the Schaffhausen and Abbeville passages reverse the traditional method of interpreting experience. Instead of using a biblical framework to discover meaning in nature or human events, Ruskin speaks only "of what he had seen, and known" (I.viii.173), thereby giving priority to his own experience and judging even the Scriptures by the witness of historical fact. Such a reversal of priorities, as Hans Frei has argued, is primary evidence for the demise of biblical typology as a viable hermeneutic system. [15] By the nineteenth century, Frei explains, "the real events of history" began to constitute "an autonomous temporal framework of their own": "Instead of rendering them accessible, the [biblical] narratives, heretofore indispensible as a means of access to the events, now simply verify them, thus affirming their autonomy and the fact that they are in principle accessible through any kind of description than can manage to be accurate either predictively or after the event." [16]

That the meaning of experience is accessible through channels other than the biblical text is nowhere more subtly illustrated than in the Fontainebleau episode (II.iv). On the face of it, the episode belies any reversal of interpretive method or conventional structure, for it begins with a brief narrative that ends in a biblical allusion. After a languorous walk along a cartroad, Ruskin recalls that he stopped to rest among some young trees, "and the branches against the blue sky began to interest me, motionless as the branches of a tree of Jesse on a painted window" (II.75). The allusion seems to promise an interpretation that will connect the iconographical tree with the natural trees—perhaps one that, as in Hopkins' poem "The Windhover," reveals figurations of Christ in all natural objects. The narrative avoids such interpretive speculation, however, and continues with an account of Ruskin's drawing of a "small aspen tree against the blue sky" and his discovery of the natural composition of the branches, "by finer laws than any known of men." Finally, the episode closes, now using a biblical text to interpret the experience: "'He hath made everything beautiful, in his time' became for me thenceforth the interpretation of the bond between the human mind and all visible things; and I returned along the wood-road feeling it had led me far" (II.iv.77).

The parts of this episode repeat those traditional in the spiritual autobiography: an event, a moment of insight, an illuminating text. The arrangement, moreover, with its frame of biblical allusions, gives the appearance an episode that follows the conventional pattern. But Ruskin has altered the pattern, just as he has done in the more obvious examples of Schaffhausen and Abbeville. At Fountainebleau, the biblical text is not the key to his self-understanding, nor is it the authority upon which his interpretation depends. What is most crucial at Fountainebleau is the act of drawing itself: as Ruskin traces the lines of the aspen trees, "More and more beautiful they became, as each rose out of the rest, and took its place in the air. With wonder increasing every instant, I saw that they 'composed' themselves, by laws finer than any known of men" (II.iv.77). The biblical quotation that closes the episode is an afterthought; it merely illustrates an interpretation that Ruskin has already conceived through his own experience and observation.

In this sense, the Fountainebleau episode reverses the formula. The biblical text is interpreted by experience, not vice versa. Viewed historically, this reversal in the form of the autobiographical episode from Bunyan to Ruskin parallels the shift in biblical hermeneutics from the seventeenth to the nineteenth century. Like Ruskin, the rationalist and mythological critics who succeeded the older typologists found their authority not in divine revelation, but in what reason and experience taught. To explain *Praeterita* using Frei's argument that the biblical narratives, once "indispensible as a means of access to [historical] events, now simply verify them," we might say that Ruskin treats biblical texts not as a means of access to his life, but merely as a verification of his interpretation. If it happens, as in this episode, that the Bible contains the appropriate description, that fact might be evidence of providential design. But it might also be evidence of authorial creation—or of neither or both. Ruskin's text makes no judgment on the matter. [17]

One can explain Ruskin's treatment of the autobiographical episode historically, as I have done, as evidence of the eclipse of biblical narrative. Ruskin himself, however, understood his authorial stance as the result of a literary influence—specifically, a Byronic one. Ruskin was peculiarly preoccupied with Byron as he composed the first volume of *Praeterita*. In the draft of the autobiography, he included long segments about his youthful decision to take Byron "as his master in verse, just as Turner was in colour"; about his adolescent attempts at verse writing, much of it in a Byronic mode; and about a poetic diary, written during a Swiss journey in 1835 and done "in style of Don Juan, artfully combined with that of Childe Harold."[18] The preoccupation has an obvious personal source: years before, his father had desired that he should become a poet like Byron, "only pious," and that desire must have been on his mind as he wrote the account of his early years and then the prefatory tribute to the parents who had "trained [his] childhood to all the good it could attain."[19]

Little of this Byronic material survives in *Praeterita*. Ruskin concluded the diary draft on 21 April 1885 with an analysis of his lack of poetic gifts and with a realization that he "never could be Rubens, or Roubilliac, or even (by this time I knew so much) Byron."[20] Rereading his diaries and thinking again about his poetic failures seem to have brought on depression: in his diary on 22 March 1885 he notes, "I desperately sad, after two days of headache, and sorting and destroying"; on 4 April 1885, "Tore up some old diary—pas[sed] a bad night." Still, the Byronic influence had been significant in his formative years. And the need to acknowledge Byron's influence coincided with a more immediate need to explain—whether to his parents, himself, or his readers—his motives in avoiding the traditional forms of autobiography.

This explanation is embedded, I believe, in the discussion of Byron's "essential qualities" (I.viii)—so deeply embedded, in fact, that it is easy to miss Ruskin's intention. At some point in 1885, Ruskin substituted the "Vester, Camenae" chapter for the Byronic segment of his life, in it providing an analysis of Byron's literary achievement rather than the account of his own poetic failure that appears in the draft.[21] The "essential qualities" that he associates with Byron are creditable enough: sense, learning, effect, imagina-

tion, passion, and invention.[22] But what is significant is less the
catalogue of Byronic traits than Ruskin's identification of other texts
that lack these "essential qualities."

The texts Ruskin cites are "the stories of Pallas and Venus, of
Achilles and Æneas, of Elijah and St. John." Such classical and
biblical texts, indeed "the whole world as it was described to me
either by poetry or theology," he dismisses as "shadowy and impossible" (I.viii.172), whereas he praises Byron as a poet "who spoke only
of what he had seen, and known; and spoke without exaggeration,
without mystery, without enmity, and without mercy." Byron "felt
the facts, and discerned the natures with accurate justice." When
Byron reports on man or nature, Ruskin insists, he tells no more than
what "he was and knew": not "the Alps voided their rheum on the
valleys," but "the glacier's cold and restless mass moved onward day
by day" (I.viii.173).

That Ruskin can write of theology as "shadowy and impossible"
and Byron's poetry as real and "accurate" testifies to the hermeneutic
revolution that the nineteenth century witnessed. Ruskin presents
the case in *Praeterita*, however, as simply an imitation of Byron's
method in *Childe Harold* and *Don Juan*, a late tribute to the poet he
had once made "his master in verse." Typically in *Childe Harold*, at
least as Ruskin might have read it, Byron has his protagonist descend
upon a new scene, observe the natural or social milieu, and draw from
it "fresh lessons to the thinking bosom."[23] In the opening episode,
Childe Harold confronts the squalor of Lisbon, where "hut and palace
show like filthily" (I.17); he then sees, in immediate geographical
contrast, the "glorious Eden" of Cintra with its "horrid crags," mountain torrents, moss and cork trees, "mix'd in one mighty scene, with
varied beauty glow" (I.18—19). The contrast prods him to consider
the lack of influence that the natural landscape exerts upon the men
living within it, a lack that belies the Wordsworthian doctrine of
Nature's ennobling power. In a similar episode at the end of the
poem, Harold approaches Venice from the water and sees "a sea-
Cybele fresh from Ocean / Rising with her tiara of proud towers / At
airy distance, with majestic motion" (IV.2). Once on land, he finds a
less delightful city:

In Venice, Tasso's echoes are no more,
And silent rows the songless gondolier;
Her Palaces are crumbling to the shore,
And music meets not always now the ear. (IV.3)

The contrast between what he sees from afar and what he sees in place comes to stand for a contrast between a Venice created by the literary imagination, the Venice of "Shylock and the Moor, / And Pierra," and the Venice of historical reality. What puzzles Harold is that written texts seem to have little power to shape the reality. With its rich literary and historical heritage, Venice should be virile and free, but it is not, having failed "to cut the knot" which ties it to tyrants.

In Ruskin's view, such scenes from *Childe Harold* and *Don Juan* deal with "felt facts": " 'That *is* so—make what you will of it,' " Byron seems to say (I.viii.172). Nature, contra Wordsworth, does not necessarily ennoble man; cultural achievement does not necessarily ensure political wisdom. The key to these episodes, according to Ruskin, lies in their commitment to "fresh lessons." Byron refuses to repeat the conventional wisdom, reporting "only of what he ha[s] seen, and known."

Ruskin must have realized that Byron's "fresh lessons" often contradict the teaching of theology and poetry: in the Lisbon episode, for example, Byron questions the poetical claim for moral influence at the same time he undermines the theological view of Nature as a second revelation. Yet under Byron's influence, these traditional sources of illumination came to represent "the words of Peter to the shut up disciples—'as idle tales; and they believed them not' " (I.viii.172). The quotation, expressive of the disciples' disbelief in the resurrection of Christ (Luke 24.11), shows how far Ruskin's own skepticism about religious systems of meaning had taken him as early as the 1830s.

Yet even if Byron's "fresh lessons" had not contradicted the teachings of Scripture, the influence of Byron's method would still have altered Ruskin's mode of self-interpretation in *Praeterita*. Byron does not present his lessons as authoritative; the key word in *Childe Harold* is "piecemeal" (IV.157). As Jerome G. McGann has argued, the technique of *Childe Harold* suggests "the necessity of a 'piecemeal' apprehension of a life which we can never fully comprehend precisely because it involves us in constant passage and possibility. Human life is not something that can be 'gained' or 'concluded' or 'fulfilled,' but must simply be 'kept' in our experience of consecutive vital particularities."[24] Thus the lessons Byron offers are transitory and partial, only pieces of a frame and only useful for a brief time. They teach a poetic method that has, in Michael Cooke's phrase, "the insistence of experience or evidence, rather than of dogma."[25]

Throughout "Vester, Camenae" Ruskin repeatedly insists that it was his parents who gave him Byron to read and that the poetry never caused "the slightest harm" (I.viii.164). When he refers specifically to such sexually charged tales as "Juan and Haidee," we can scarcely disagree. Yet judging from the perspective of his evangelical mother, who had tucked a copy of *Grace Abounding* into his traveling bag, we can only conclude that Byron's influence did great harm. If it did not lead him into sexual sin, it lead him into hermeneutic ambivalence. The evidence lies in the combination of admiration that Ruskin expresses and guilt that the chapter betrays. It lies also in the structure of Ruskin's episodes and the narrative pattern of *Praeterita* as a whole.

If the individual episodes of *Praeterita*, under the influence of Byron, show a self-conscious deviation from the traditional forms of autobiography, the narrative structure of the work suggests a similar strategy of resistance, particularly in the second volume. Again a key influence was Byron. Ruskin had once intended to write an autobiographical account of his European tours in the combined style of *Don Juan* and *Childe Harold*, and as he wrote the draft of *Praeterita* in 1885, he reread his European diaries and the two cantos from 1835, letting the shape of the earlier works suggest a narrative form for the autobiography. More particularly, Ruskin used the pattern of the Byronic tour to avoid the pattern of the exodus conventional in spiritual accounts. To understand the extent of this avoidance, we need only consider how he might have shaped the material in volume II.

Had Ruskin intended, he might have transformed the second volume of *Praeterita* into a classic reversal of the conversion narrative, beginning with his position of narrow Protestantism in 1839 and ending with his decision in 1858 to put away his evangelical beliefs, "to be debated of no more" (III.i.23). The raw data of Ruskin's life certainly fit the pattern: his European tours suggest a parallel to the wilderness wandering; the episodes, like those of the Exodus, are associated with geographical places and represent points of discovery; and the series ends with a vision in Turin from the upper windows of an art gallery—not exactly Mount Pisgah, but elevated nonetheless. Moreover, the time scheme takes Ruskin up to 1859, the fortieth year of his life. The critic who looks for evidence of the traditional pattern will find it, for the pieces are there. Indeed, in the opening chapters of volume II, Ruskin seems himself to have decided to tell a classic, if inverted conversion story.

In the first chapter, "Of Age," he begins by depicting himself, at age twenty, as a violent anti-Papist, "as zealous, pugnacious, and self-sure a Protestant as you please" (II.i.8). Two chapters later, he notes the modifications that exposure to Catholicism, medieval and modern, made in his convictions. Describing his experience in Rome, he recalls that there he learned to take pleasure in a combination of natural beauty and religious splendor:

> The weather was fine at Easter, and I saw the Benediction, and sate in the open air of twilight opposite the castle of St. Angelo, and saw the dome-lines kindle on St. Peter's, and the castle veil the sky with flying fire. Bearing with me from that last sight in Rome many thoughts that ripened slowly afterwards, chiefly convincing me how guiltily and meanly dead the Protestant mind was to the whole meaning and end of mediaeval Church splendour; and how meanly and guiltily dead the existing Catholic mind was, to the course by which to reach the Italian soul, instead of its eyes. (II.iii.53)

The criticism of Catholicism still persists, but balanced by an admission of Protestant failures and a pleasing awareness of his own capacity for intellectual development.

Significantly, the autobiography connects this awareness with a new understanding of vocational responsibility. As Ruskin describes the Roman experiences, where he first encountered "mediaeval Church splendour," he uses an image of new birth: "the chrysalid envelope began to tear itself open here and there to some purpose" (II.iii.51). A few paragraphs later, he narrates an episode of vocational crisis. At Lans-le-bourg "at six of the summer morning," with "the red aiguilles on the north relieved against pure blue" and "the great pyramid of snow down the valley in one sheet of eastern light," his self-doubts seem to dissolve in a moment of illumination: "I had found my life again;—all the best of it. What good of religion, love, admiration or hope, had ever been taught me, or felt by my best nature, rekindled at once; and my line of work, both by my own will and the aid granted to it by fate in the future, determined for me" (II.iii.57). The discovery of a true "line of work" follows as the result of (and compensation for) a change in religious beliefs. This, at least, is the interpretation that Ruskin suggests as retrospective autobiographer.

After the opening chapters, however, Ruskin finds it increasingly difficult to continue this interpretation. Instead of describing his loss of evangelical faith and the simultaneous development of a vocational commitment, Ruskin becomes increasingly obscure. Midway through the second volume, as many readers have noticed, *Praeterita* loses its coherence, and by the end Ruskin refuses to interpret at all.

Usually, biographers explain the loss of coherence as the effect of recurrent and increasingly severe bouts of insanity that plagued Ruskin from 1885 onward: Rosenberg states, for example, that by the end of volume II "the life of the book and of Ruskin's mind were failing."[26] Undoubtedly, the bouts of insanity made the task of organizing the notes and drafts of the autobiography more difficult. During a particularly troublesome period, as Ruskin pored over the materials for the "Otterburn" chapter (II.xii), he recorded in his diary his utter frustration: "Have had a weary sick time all February—'gone to water.' Could do neither Otter nor Potterburn."[27] Yet the incoherence of volume II originates in afflictions more than physiological. It suggests the same convergence of personal desires and generic demands that we saw earlier in the preface.

As before, Ruskin wants both to honor the memory of his parents and narrate his experience freely, avoiding those things that give "no pleasure in reviewing." For the events of volume II, these needs are not easily fulfilled. The experience involves a process of de-conversion, the details of which had caused his parents much grief. Moreover, even to think of the experience as a process of de-conversion means to impose the conventions of the spiritual autobiography upon it and thus to begin an account of what it gave Ruskin no joy to remember.

Evidence that Ruskin cannot resolve the conflict begins to appear in chapters like "The Campo Santo" (II.vi), where he defines the essence of Christianity and reports that he was prepared for its new lessons, but fails to continue with an explanation of the effects of these lessons upon his religion and his work. The "total meaning" of Christianity, Ruskin writes,

> was, and is, that the God who made earth and its creatures, took at a certain time upon the earth, the flesh and form of man; in that flesh sustained the pain and died the death of the creature He made; rose again after death into glorious human life, and when the date of the human race is ended, will return in visible human form, and render to every man according to his work. (II.vi.117)

His definition has the clarity and concision of the Apostles' Creed, two characteristics that the account itself lacks. Although he writes that he was "prepared at this time for the teaching of the Campo Santo," that his study "put into direct and inevitable light the questions I had to deal with," and that these questions were "clearly not to be all settled in that fortnight" (II.vi.119), he never measures his own faith by the clear definition he has given. Instead, he continues the narrative with an evasion, "Meantime, my own first business was evidently to read what these Pisans had said of it," substituting what he calls *reading* for what he knows should be *interpreting* (II.vi.120).

Ruskin's rationalization for this substitution indicates the larger confusion he faces as autobiographer. He explains that his mind was not yet ready to interpret: "I had to read its lessons before I could interpret them." (II.vi.124). While this distinction may explain his inability to interpret at the time, it does not explain his inability (or refusal) to interpret as autobiographer in 1886. In retrospect, surely he knew how to judge his experience by the lessons of the Campo Santo. "Anything less than this, the mere acceptance of the sayings of Christ, or assertion of any less than divine power in His Being," will "not make people Christians" (II.vi.117), he observed after his definition of the "total meaning" of Christianity. Surely he knew that, while studying in Pisa, his commitment to orthodox Christianity was "less"—and his commitment to art, more.

The reluctance to admit that, during the middle two decades of his life, he was losing his orthodox Christian faith grows worse in the final chapters of volume II, and eventually Ruskin refuses to ask the meaning of his experience in any terms—Christian or otherwise. This refusal is expressed in a variety of ways. In "Crossmount," for instance, he tries to postpone the account of what he calls "this trial," saying only "All that I had been taught had to be questioned; all that I had trusted, proved" (II.x.201). Instead of an account of de-conversion, he offers a fragment from his 1847 diary that is supposed to substitute, in some sense, for what he will not tell. The fragment itself interprets nothing. But it is revealing as a substitute, for in structure and content, it prefigures the episode at Turin which Ruskin knows must be the final scene, the *telos*, of his autobiography.

The "Crossmount" fragment (II.x.202) records an encounter with a poor cottager and her mother in which the narrowness of the women's religion becomes painfully clear. It continues with a walk home in the freshness after a storm, during which "a bright bar of streaky sky in the west, seen over the glittering hedges...made my heart leap again" (II.x.202). Here is the story of a pious mother, like his own, who limits the household reading to serious books of religion and who entreats him to participate in her mode of worship, a participation he is characteristically unable to resist. Here, too, is the contrast between the drabness of evangelicalism and the brilliance of nature that will become, in the Turin episode, the final evidence for Ruskin's rejection of evangelical faith. What is absent from the diary fragment, however, is any admission of a diminution of his own faith. Similarly absent from the "Crossmount" chapter is any attempt at interpretation. The fragments are not, in essence, true autobiographical episodes. They are old diary entries. Thus the chapter closes with the words of the 1847 diarist, not the insight of the 1886 autobiographer.

One would expect interpretation to come easier after this prefigurative fragment. In "L' Hotel Du Mont Blanc" (II.xi), however, Ruskin finds it even more difficult to impose the perspective of the retrospective autobiographer, and the chapter becomes an even more confusing pastiche of old diary fragments. Once again, the fragments allude to a growing tolerance for a variety of religious beliefs, as in the sketch of the "undisturbed Catholicism" at Sallenches (II.xi.220). They also refer to Ruskin's own irreversible loss of faith: "many signs [of the coming Apocalypse] seem to multiply around us, and yet my unbelief yields no more than when all the horizon was clear" (II.xi.222). Yet connections among these fragments are not offered, and the episodes receive little commentary that could be called interpretation.

It is possible for the reader of *Praeterita* to supply a connection among these episodes and Ruskin's motives in quoting them. One possibility is that many, perhaps all, of the diary fragments involve Mont Blanc, and as we know from the poem that introduces volume III, Mont Blanc represents the last point at which Ruskin attempted to express an orthodox religious faith. In 1845 he had sought there "Such thoughts as holy men of old / Amid the desert found." There again in 1849, the year of the diary entries, he sought no such holy thoughts (or, at least, he found no such thoughts). Implicitly, then, the fragments signify another stage in the process of de-conversion, another episode in the undoing of his faith. Yet to suggest such a signification of the Mont Blanc entries is to move closer to interpretation than Ruskin himself was willing to go. At this stage, he merely repeats the entries, avoiding or obfuscating their meaning for his readers and perhaps also for himself.

Eventually, Ruskin ceases such obfuscation, and in "The Grande Chartreuse" (III.i) provides a forthright account of his loss of faith at

Turin in 1858. What must perplex the reader of *Praeterita* at this
point is the utter confusion of "Otterburn," the final chapter of
volume II, in contrast to the utter lucidity of "The Grande Chartreuse." Chronologically, the Turin episode belongs in the "Otterburn" chapter: it occurred in 1858, precisely at the end of the
twenty-year period covered in volume II and at the end of the process
of de-conversion the volume records. But Ruskin does not record the
experience there with any coherence, and instead seems to attempt
something else.

What he attempts is imperceptible to the reader of the "Otterburn" chapter in its published form—unless, perhaps, one can
guess from the opening lines which speak of a "want of affection to
other people" and a "wonder that ever anybody had any affection for
me" (II.xii.225). The proof sheets for the chapter make sense of these
remarks, however, and suggest what it is Ruskin needed to achieve
and why his need resulted in such incoherence. At the end of the
proofs, as part of the original text as planned in 1887, Ruskin
transcribed two letters: one from his father, the other from his
mother. The first, dated 8 February 1850, was written on Ruskin's
thirty-first birthday:

> My dearest JOHN—
>   You see by the date, I write on your birthday, and you are,
> I hope, as happy in it as your mamma and I are. I can truly say
> that with all that remains of illness and weakness left, I never
> felt my heart more rejoicing in the unmingled blessings heaped
> upon my undeserving head, unmingled with a single sorrow or a
> single want; and the completion of this happiness, owing to that
> son who, during thirty-one years, has scarcely given his father a
> single pang beyond the anxieties for his safety, and these en-
> gendered only by that parent's own mistrusting and impatient
> temperament.

The second, dated 23 August 1869, was written by his mother when
Ruskin was fifty:

> My Dearest—
>   I should be thankful to pay you with double interest the
> more than comfort and pleasure I have had, and I think latterly

more than at any former times, I have had from your letters. . . .

    I am, my dearest, with a thousand thanks for all the pains you have taken to give me pleasure and save me anxiety, always,

Your affectionate Mother,
Margaret Ruskin

The letters include much more information, all of it irrelevant to the material in "Otterburn," some of it jarringly out of place. (There is, for instance, an allusion to a "beautifully written" letter from Effie Gray, then still Ruskin's wife. Effie is nowhere else named in *Praeterita*.)

Ruskin must have had an unusually compelling motive for including these letters and giving them the authority of closure in volume II. In the proof sheets he explains his fear that he will be unable to carry on the story of those he cares for—an explanation that complements the introductory remarks about his failures to express and receive affection. Similarly, in an alternate draft of the chapter's conclusion, he refers to his inability to carry on, "being disturbed by instant troubles which take away my powers of tranquil thought, whether of the Dead or Living who have been and are yet dear to me."[28] And we can extend Ruskin's explanations to make them account for certain formal difficulties in the chapter, particularly the queer transitions between episodes. Perhaps the discussion of Scott's novels and of Scottish types reminded him of his parents, who read Scott to him as a child and who were themselves Scottish types. Afraid that he might be forced to abandon *Praeterita* before he could reach (logically or chronologically) his parents, Ruskin may have decided to abandon order and transcribe the letters as substitutes for the account he could not give. His book, begun as "an offering" to his mother and father, would thus close with a memory of—and a tribute to—them both.

However satisfactory this explanation may appear, factually or even formally, it still fails to account for the narrative lapse. Instead of family letters, the closing chapter of the second volume should have included the Turin episode and interpreted it in terms of Ruskin's loss of faith or new vocational commitment. Despite his apologies, I suspect that Ruskin could not himself account for the lapse, even in the unpublished proofs, because for him it was an unintended, if un-avoidable act.

The transcribed letters represent, then, an emotional prelude to an episode demanded both by the facts and by convention, but which Ruskin would have preferred to avoid. Perhaps the literary craftsman in him decided, by 1887, that it was easier to let his life conform to the conventions of the genre than it was to resist its narrative patterns at every point. Perhaps he realized that, far from being possible to narrate his life "frankly, garrulously, and at ease," the act of autobiography inevitably involved concealment and pain. Before facing the pain, however, he published the letters first. The letters offer assurance: despite his loss of faith, he need not fear loss of love. In 1849, in the midst of Ruskin's religious crisis, his father had written that much of his happiness was "owing to that son who . . . ha[d] scarcely given his father a single pang"; in 1869, when the crisis was over, his mother had thanked him for words that brought "comfort and pleasure" and had praised him for seeking always to spare her anxiety. Armed with these assurances, Ruskin had the evidence that he could proceed with the Turin episode and still satisfy both the generic demands and his own emotional desires.

On 26 April 1887, Ruskin sent "Otterburn" to the printer, complete with transcriptions of the letters from his father and mother. Between April and October, when the chapter was in galleys, he revised its ending, substituting for the letters a description of a sea horizon at sunset whose clouds he had attempted to draw fifty-five years earlier and whose skies, to his amazement, "were still bright above the foulness of smoke-cloud or the flight of plague-cloud" (II.xii.235). It was as if in the interval the plague-cloud had disappeared for Ruskin, too. By January, 1888, he was working on the new volume of *Praeterita*, thinking over the "Turin bit," as he called it, and writing the episode he had postponed for so long.[29]

The opening chapter of the new volume, "The Grande Chartreuse," handles the Turin episode and the events leading up to it with a clarity and sureness of purpose unimaginable in "Otterburn." I have already intimated the emotional factors contributing to this shift from confusion to clarity. Another factor was that of repetition: Ruskin had narrated the episode before in *Fors Clavigera*, and once the emotional blocks were cleared away, he had only to re-interpret the story within the context of a spiritual autobiography. The most important factor, however, was Ruskin's solution to another formal problem: how to be faithful to his experience, which ended in an episode of de-conversion, without merely imitating the patterns of spiritual narrative in which he no longer believed.

The solution is a chapter formed on the principle of de(con)struction. What Ruskin gives the reader in "The Grande Chartreuse" is, I believe, first the text of a conversion experience—or, rather, a text written at the time of a conversion experience. This text is "Mont Blanc Revisited," the poem written at Nyon in 1845 and reproduced as the epigraph to the chapter. Then, Ruskin deconstructs the text by undoing it, by "depriving it" (as the OED tells us the prefix *de-* will do) "of the thing or character therein expressed." The "thing therein expressed" is not only the spiritual experience, but also the typological hermeneutics which Ruskin used in 1845 to invest the experience with meaning. Finally, the de(con)structive process accomplished, he narrates his "Turin bit," the episode we label his de-conversion but he treats as the result of an undoing.

"Mont Blanc Revisited" is an autobiographical poem, a record of conversion which makes Ruskin's choice of it as an epigraph to a chapter about de-conversion itself significant. Midway through *Praeterita*, Ruskin refers to the poem as the "last serious exertions of my poetical powers" (II.vi.109). When he composed the verses in 1845, however, he had thought himself at the beginning of a new line of vocational work: "I had rhymed to his snows in such hope and delight, and assurance of doing everything I wanted, this year at last" (II.vii.146). His optimism was in part created by a solution to a familial dilemma: he had left for the Continent alone for the first time, and removed from daily contact with his parents, he could manage their demands at a distance.[30] The optimism was created in greater part by a solution to a vocational dilemma: Ruskin discovered how to re-channel his religious training and spiritual impulses into the service of beauty and morality.

That solution came at Nyon, after he had been reading John Bunyan and George Herbert. In Bunyan, as we have seen, he found little to commend. *Grace Abounding* he thought "a most dangerous book," for it suggested "a most false impression of God's dealings" and gave the skeptical ammunition against religion.[31] Herbert's *The Temple* he found, in contrast, a model of man's "communings with God." Equally as "immediate" as Bunyan's, they were nevertheless the communings of "a well bridled and disciplined mine." Ruskin in fact disapproved of Bunyan because the man, in true Calvinistic fashion, found God by gazing at himself. Too literal an application of Calvin's tenet, "Without the knowledge of self there is no knowledge of God," would not work for the sort of poetry he intended to write.[32] In 1845 Ruskin wanted a model, poetic and religious both, who found God by gazing at the external world.

What Ruskin thought he had discovered in 1845 was a species of poetry that answered his requirements. Romantic and religious both, it found God by gazing at nature, and thus allowed him to write as successor to the Romantics, fulfilling his parents' desire that he become a second, but pious Byron. He experienced this discovery as a moment of conversion. According to his diary, "all the way to Nyon," where he composed the poem, he felt a "strange spiritual government of the conscience": "I began to wonder how God should give me so much reward for so little self-denial, and to make all sorts of resolves relating to future conduct...In the state of mind in which I then was it seemed a lesson given by my own favourite mountain—a revelation of nature intended only for me."[33]

"Mont Blanc Revisited" thus embodies what Ruskin experienced in the mid-1840s—that is, the poem is both autobiographical and exemplary of the poetry Ruskin intended to write. As such, it is fitting that Ruskin should make it an epigraph, a piece of writing that has marked and still makes its mark upon his life. It is also, however, an epigraph whose experience the remainder of "The Grande Chartreuse" will undo and whose hermeneutic assumptions the chapter will challenge and finally deprive of authority.

The experience itself is readily deprived of its autobiographical significance. To begin, Ruskin suppresses a crucial stanza of the poem, one in which he had asserted his vocational calling by comparing himself to Moses and Elijah:[34]

> Yet let me not, like him who trod
> In wrath, of old, the mount of God,
>   Forget the thousands left
> Lest haply, when I seek His face,
> The whirlwind of the cave replace
>   The glory of the cleft.

This stanza simply does not appear in the epigraph to "The Grande Chartreuse," as if the experience itself had never included a call to become a poet-prophet. Then, the chapter denies the worth of the literary work that Ruskin produced subsequent to the calling: "The events of the ten years 1850–1860," he writes in perhaps the most startling statement of *Praeterita*, were "for the most part wasted in useless work" (III.i.10). These "wasted years" are those that saw the publication of *Modern Painters*, III–V, and *The Stones of Venice*.

If Ruskin deprives the experience of the significance he once assigned, he further denies the validity of the hermeneutic system that led him to it. Like traditional spiritual autobiography, "Mont Blanc Revisited" draws upon biblical typology for its method of self-interpretation. The poet understands his state in terms of the Exodus and the Psalms, making himself a typological correlative of the Israelites receiving manna and of the wild hart in Psalm 42:

> Ah, happy, if His will were so,
> To give me manna here for snow,
>   And by the torrent side
> To lead me as He leads His flocks
> Of wild deer through the lonely rocks
>   In peace, unterrified.

He understands his calling, too, in terms of the prophets Moses and Elijah, who serve as types of the poet-prophet's stance in the modern world. Such uses of typology are doubly autobiographical: the poem not only applies types as patterns of moral behavior; it also uses them to confirm providential design in the experiences of Ruskin's life and to assert a poetic calling.[35]

Lest Ruskin fall into the hermeneutic extremities of *Grace Abounding*, he restricts the method of self-interpretation: there is to be no "unreigned state of a strong imagination," as in Bunyan, but as in George Herbert, only "the communings of a well bridled and disciplined mind." Thus the poet seeks the "frontier waste" with "religious haste / And reverent desire," but once there, he becomes passive as observer and interpreter. Interpretation is grounded outside of the self in an objective source, and thoughts are attributed not to the self but to the mountain:

> They meet me, 'midst thy shadows cold,—
> Such thoughts as holy men of old
>   Amid the desert found.

The interpretive act is self-consciously passive throughout: the mountain initiates the thoughts; the thoughts come to meet the poet, not vice versa; and they teach the poet to be "more resigned," to imitate the "trustful rest" of the animals.

The hermeneutic assumptions that "Mont Blanc Revisited" embodies are, like the experience itself, put through a process of deconversion in the text that follows, so that the chapter is not only *about* de-conversion but assumes the *form* of a de-conversion. Despite their diverse settings, the episodes of "The Grande Chartreuse" all concern themselves with hermeneutics and hermeneutic practices that challenge Ruskin's own in 1845.

The first episode records an encounter with a monk who "rebukes" Ruskin for assuming that men receive special revelations in the shadows of mountains: "We do not come here," says the monk, "to look at the mountains." In narrating the episode, Ruskin stresses the aesthetic disappointments of his visit to the Carthusian monastery: "the building was meanly designed and confusedly grouped," the mountains surrounding "were simplest commonplace of Savoy cliff," the monks were "ungraciously dull" and "without sagacity" (III.i.2). But the crux of the visit lies in the monks' failure to respond to the natural beauty around them, as Ruskin assumed all religious minds would, and in their challenge to his own hermeneutic assumptions. To the monk's rebuke, the young Ruskin makes no reply: "I bent my head silently, thinking however all the same, 'What, then, by all that's stupid, do you come here at all for?'"

Critics have argued that Ruskin's silence betokens his inability to take command of his autobiography, that it reveals the "near extinction" of "the inner magnitude which was the source of value in the forties."[36] Although there may be an extinction of earlier values, this argument mistakes, I think, the function of the episode. The silence is that of Ruskin at age thirty, not the silence of Ruskin the autobiographer. In the monastery the young man's assumptions about mountain scenery as a source of religious revelation are challenged sharply. The mature Ruskin uses the episode to acknowledge, in retrospect, his youthful error: at Mont Blanc the lessons came from the self, not from the mountain. Narrow and unappealing though it may have been, the monk's rebuke nonetheless raises crucial questions about the source of revelation and hermeneutic authority.

The next episodes add to the questions by describing the hermeneutic practices of Ruskin's contemporaries and thus raising the issue of objectivity and certainty in interpretation. In the first, F. D. Maurice reads the story of Jael's slaying of Sisera as an instance of "dreadful deeds" done "in the Dark Biblical ages," implicitly denying that Old Testament characters can be read typologically as patterns for the modern Christian (III.i.13–15). In the second, set at a "fashionable seance" in Belgravia, an evangelical named Molyneux discourses on "the beautiful parable of the Prodigal Son." Molyneux ignores the implications of the elder son to his affluent audience and, when questioned, denies that a character in a New Testament parable need have meaning to be interpreted or significance to be applied personally (III.i.16). For both episodes, Ruskin notes the error the interpreter makes: Maurice forgets that the Bible, through the song of Deborah the prophetess, "declared of Jael, 'Blessed above women shall the wife of Heber the Kenite be'"; Molyneux forgets that Jesus included the elder sibling as a warning to the selfish and the self-righteous. The function of these episodes, however, is less hermeneutic correction than a recognition of lack of grounding. They suggest that one will find in the Bible, as in nature, what one goes looking for—or what one has been taught to look for.

This recognition sets the stage for the final episode in the de(con)-structive process. In the episode, an old preacher of the Waldensian faith, taking Genesis 14 as his text, discourses on "the wickedness of the wide world" while assuring his congregation of their "exclusive favour with God," though they live "in the streets of Admah and Zeboim" (III.i.23). His sermon is a sincere but parodic application of biblical typology, yet another example of self-assured or self-interested interpretation, another example that challenges the authority of typological hermeneutics. This time Ruskin, "neither cheered nor greatly alarmed" as he tells us, attempts no correction. He simply abandons the scene, the process of de-conversion complete, his evangelical beliefs "to be debated of no more."[37]

All of these episodes in "The Grande Chartreuse" call into question the hermeneutic assumptions of its autobiographical epigraph: that the interpreter can be a passive recipient of divine revelation; that interpretations can be authoritatively grounded outside the self, whether in a biblical or natural text; that typology can confirm providential design or poetic calling. And they mark the distance that Ruskin as self-interpreter traveled over the course of forty years. In 1845 he may have believed that "a well bridled and disciplined mind" could proceed confidently upon solid hermeneutic principles, and he may have written autobiographical poems based upon that belief. But as the writer of *Praeterita*, he had come to recognize the perils of self-interpretation. It is no wonder, then, that in 1885 Ruskin avoided the traditional forms of the autobiography, with their demands that the autobiographer interpret his experience and discover within it a providential design. If *Praeterita* was to be a dutiful offering, it had to be dutiful first to Ruskin himself and to the complexity of his experience.

PART TWO

Three Versions of
Generic Revision

Newman's *Apologia pro vita sua:*
The Dilemma of the
Catholic Autobiographer

hen John Henry Newman revised the *Apologia pro vita sua* in 1865 for publication as a book, he replaced the original parts I and II of his text, "Mr. Kingsley's Method of Disputation" and "True Mode of Meeting Mr. Kingsley," with a brief summary of the events that had occasioned the work. In his original response to Kingsley, published serially from 21 April to 2 June 1864, Newman had begun by confronting the charges against him, referring directly to the accusation that he had denied truth to be a virtue for its own sake and refuting as well the implicit charge that he had acted with deceit during his years as an Anglican priest. In his revision, however, he chose to omit specific details of the controversy and emphasize instead his intellectual and spiritual development. "He [Kingsley] asks what I *mean*," Newman generalized, "not about my words, not about my arguments, not about my actions, as his ultimate point, but about that living intelligence, by which I write, and argue, and act."[1] Accordingly, Newman decided that the *Apologia* should give the "true key" to his life, in order to "show what I am, that it may be seen what I am not"; "I mean to be simply personal and historical: I am not expounding Catholic doctrine" (11–13).

Given this emphasis upon the "personal" and "historical" nature of the account, this desire to interpret a "living intelligence" to a public audience, one could hardly ask for a more explicit declaration of autobiographical intention. The alteration of the title, moreover, from the original *Apologia pro vita sua* to the *History of My Religious Opinions* suggests an attempt to make the work's intention as a spiritual autobiography clear, the combination of "history" and "religious opinions" signaling two fundamental elements of the genre.[2] Yet in critical discussions of the *Apologia* the misconception still lingers that, in some fundamental way, the work is not a true autobiography. This assumption may be stated explicitly, as in Robert A. Colby's comment that the *Apologia* is generically a "fusion of theological disputation, epic, and biography" or in Martin A. Svaglic's that the work, lacking details of Newman's family life, student activities, and intellectual interests, is thus neither "the autobiography of Newman from 1801 to 1845," nor "even a spiritual autobiography of those years except in a limited sense."[3] More frequently, the assumption remains implicit, nonetheless controlling critical analyses of the work that rely on the terminology of other literary genres, including the epic, the drama, or the novel.[4]

The circumstances under which the *Apologia* was published certainly add to the suspicion that the work is not an autobiography in the usual sense: rather than the calm, retrospective account of the traditional autobiographer, Newman's work was dashed off in seven weekly installments to counter a public attack. Yet despite the generic misconceptions of its readers, and despite the circumstantial evidence of publication, the *Apologia* is a classic example of the spiritual autobiography—indeed, the culminating English example. Newman's motivation for composing the work, and hence his rationale for handling his materials, are characteristic of autobiography as a genre; as he states in the 1865 preface, he intends not only to "draw out, as far as may be, the history of my mind," but also to "give the true key to my whole life" (12). More important, the works to which Newman responds consciously as he shapes his personal history are models of the spiritual autobiography in not one tradition, but two: the first, a Protestant tradition that informs English autobiography generally; the other, an Augustinian and Catholic tradition that Newman re-introduced to the Victorians.

Newman's goal as autobiographer is to negotiate successfully between these two traditions. And he uses the conventions of both to shape his argument, as well as to define the specific problem he faced as a Catholic autobiographer writing within an English generic tradition that was inseparable from its Protestant theological origins and that imposed its conventions upon his process of self-composition and self-interpretation.

When Newman wrote the *Apologia*, the dominant form of self-writing in England was the spiritual autobiography, descended, as we have seen, from accounts such as John Bunyan's *Grace Abounding to the Chief of Sinners* and continued by Methodists and evangelicals such as George Whitefield, John Newton, William Cowper, and Thomas Scott. Newman was familiar with this tradition of spiritual autobiography, particularly in its evangelical manifestations. In the opening pages of the *Apologia*, he refers to Thomas Scott as "the writer who made a deeper impression on my mind than any other, and the man to whom (humanly speaking) I almost owe my soul," and he cites Scott's autobiography, *The Force of Truth*, not simply as a book he possessed, but as a book he "had been possessed of" since his boyhood (17). Moreover, in an autobiographical memoir written in 1874 to supplement the *Apologia*, and thus to supply the details of his evangelical phase at Oxford, Newman refers specifically to Scott's *The Force of Truth*, Beveridge's *Private Thoughts*, and Doddridge's *The Rise and Progress of Religion in the Soul* as crucial influences. These seminal works of English evangelical thought, he notes, "had sheltered and protected him in his most dangerous years" and "brought him on in habits of devotion till the time came when he was to dedicate himself to the Christian ministry."[5]

If Newman was familiar with the standard works of English Protestant spiritual autobiography, he also knew intimately the pattern of conversion they represented. In the supplementary memoir of 1874, Newman tells of a private memorandum written years before, in 1821, in which he used these standard autobiographies, along with scriptural texts, to draw up "an account of the evangelical process of conversion."[6] His description of the stages in the process—"conviction of sin, terror, despair, news of the free and full salvation, apprehension of Christ, sense of pardon, assurance of salvation, joy and peace, and so on to final perseverance"—reads like an outline for a classic spiritual autobiography. Indeed, it might have been taken directly from Philip Doddridge's *The Rise and Progress* which, although not an autobiographical work per se, attempts to describe the stages in a Christian's journey from sin to salvation.[7]

Although Newman was familiar with this tradition of spiritual autobiography, he was not experimentally knowledgeable (to use an evangelical phrase) of the intense, often violent process of conversion it described. In a footnote to the private memorandum, he observed that his own experience had not been characteristically evangelical: "I speak of conversion with great diffidence, being obliged to adopt the language of books. For my feelings, as far as I remember, were so far different from any account I have ever read, that I dare not go by what may be an individual case." Five years later, he noted more emphatically on the same memorandum: "I wrote *juxta praescriptum*. In the matter in question, viz. conversion, my own feelings were *not* violent, but a returning to, a renewing of, principles, under the power of the Holy Spirit, which I had already felt, and in a measure acted on, when young." Finally, when he wrote the autobiographical memoir in 1874, thirty years after his conversion to Catholicism and ten years after the publication of the *Apologia*, he stressed again that he "had ever been wanting in those special evangelical experiences, which, like the grip of the hand or other prescribed signs of a secret society, are the sure token of a member."[8] The added footnotes suggest the power which "the language of books," the written tradition of spiritual autobiography, had upon Newman's way of thinking and writing about his life. He felt compelled to record three times that the evangelical pattern of experience did not represent his own, a denial of "experimental knowledge" that could scarcely have been more insistent.

Newman in fact exaggerates the exclusivity of the pattern. In the preface to *The Rise and Progress*, Philip Doddridge states quite clearly that the dramatic process frequently described in spiritual autobiographies is not the only possible form of conversion. The renewing of principles acquired in youth, which Newman describes as his own experience, resembles an alternative Doddridge explicitly suggests:

> I would by no means be thought to insinuate, that every one who is brought to that happy resolution, arrives at it through those particular steps, or feels agitations of mind equal in degree to those I have described.... God is pleased sometimes to begin the work of his grace on the heart almost from the first dawning of reason, and to carry it on by such gentle and insensible degrees that very excellent persons, who have made the most eminent attainments in the divine life, have been unable to recount any remarkable history of their conversion.[9]

But to cite Doddridge as counterevidence is to miss Newman's motive, for it was more than a lack of personal experience that prevented Newman from writing an autobiography in the standard English mode. His Catholic theology inclined him against using literary forms, however popular, that held the stain of Protestant dogma, and the English spiritual autobiography certainly had been shaped, if not stained, by its Protestant theological origins.

The *Apologia* does nevertheless respond to the dominant tradition of English autobiography, both by imitating and diverging from it. Newman's model in the first two chapters is, I suggest, Thomas Scott's *The Force of Truth*, the autobiography of the writer who, according to Newman's testimony in the opening pages of the *Apologia*, "followed truth wherever it led him" and thus "planted deep in my mind that fundamental truth of religion" (17). Scott's emphasis upon truth and truth-seeking appealed in a crucial way to Newman, who had been accused of condoning falsehood in theological teaching and thus might be suspected of practicing falsehood in his autobiography. Kingsley's attack, as Newman realized, had attempted "to cut the ground from under my feet;—to poison by anticipation the public mind against me, John Henry Newman, and to infuse into the imagination of my readers, suspicion and mistrust of everything that I may say in reply to him" (6). But equally important was Scott's variation on the pattern of conversion. Rhetorically, Newman needed a model that his readers would recognize as a legitimate form of spiritual autobiography, but not one they would associate with the common evangelical pattern of conversion.

Scott's autobiography, *The Force of Truth*, is a modest, carefully documented account of conversion from Socinianism to evangelical Christianity. Unlike the autobiographies of Bunyan and later of Cowper, Newton, and Whitefield, all painfully introspective tales that dwell upon conviction of sin and despair of salvation, this is an eminently rational work. Scott stresses his wrestling with biblical and ecclesiastical texts, not with angelic messengers or demonic voices. "I never was taught any thing," he insists, "by impulses, impressions, visions, dreams, or revelations; except so far as the work of the Spirit, in enlightening the understanding for the reception of those truths contained in the Holy Scriptures, is sometimes styled revelation."[10] Instead, as we saw in Chapter 1, Scott presents his conversion as the outcome of extensive reading in the Anglican divines, begun in 1775 to shore up his defenses of Socinianism and continued until 1777, when the old theology he had "proposed to repair, was pulled down to the ground, and the foundation of the new building of God laid aright."[11]

Scott organizes his account in terms of books read and doctrines derived. An episode typically begins with a statement of what he read ("In January, 1777, I met with a very high commendation of Mr. Hooker's works"); includes a doctrine or passage that troubled him ("I had no sooner read this passage, than I acquired such an insight into the strictness and spirituality of the divine law, . . . that my whole life appeared to be one continued series of transgressions"); and concludes with an alteration he made in his religious beliefs ("Thus was I effectually convinced, that if ever I was saved, it must be in some way of unmerited mercy and grace").[12] Typically, too, Scott insists upon the orthodoxy of the doctrine he has discovered. Conscious of the prejudice of Churchmen against Methodists and Dissenters, he is careful to point out that he avoided sources not purely Anglican: "Had I at this time met with such passages in the writings of Dissenters, or any of those modern publications, which under the brand of methodistical publications, are condemned without reading, or perused with invincible prejudice, I should not have thought them worth regard, but should have rejected them as wild enthusiasm. But I knew that Hooker was deemed perfectly orthodox."[13]

Given this extreme (inter)textuality, it seems odd that *The Force of Truth* should have become one of the most popular conversion narratives of the late eighteenth and early nineteenth centuries: the book is literally a debate among theological texts. But the conversion of Socinians to a more orthodox understanding of Christian tenets, especially the doctrine of the Trinity, was a major preoccupation of evangelicals, and Scott himself, as the author of an influential commentary on the Bible, exerted a special attraction in evangelical circles like those Newman mixed with during his early days at Oxford.[14] When Newman wrote the *Apologia*, however, *The Force of Truth* was attractive not only for its author's sake, but for the solution it provided to the problem of generic form. Scott's model allowed Newman to write within the English autobiographical tradition without acquiescing, in narrative pattern, to radical Protestant notions of conversion.

In the first two chapters of the *Apologia*, Newman makes his account almost exclusively a series of encounters with theological texts. Like Scott, Newman chronicles the sources of his beliefs in "The History of My Religious Opinions to the Year 1833," beginning with those he acquired from evangelical associates or writers: the need for conversion and "a definite Creed" from the Rev. Walter Mayers, one of his masters at Ealing (16); an informed belief in the Holy Trinity from the essays of Thomas Scott and Jones of Nayland (17); the doctrine of the final perseverance from the works of William Romaine (16); and a zealous anti-Romanism from Joseph Milner's *History of the Church of Christ* (18). He continues with the more general Anglican tenets that he learned at Oxford from tutors and friends: that of baptismal regeneration from Richard Whately (20), of tradition from Dr. Hawkins (20), of apostolical succession from the

Reverend William James (21), of analogy and probability from Butler's *The Analogy of Religion* (21—22), and so on throughout the first
chapter. "I am all along engaged," Newman writes in explanation of
his method, "with matters of belief and opinion, and am introducing
others into my narrative, not for their own sake, or because I love or
have loved them, so much as because, and so far as, they have
influenced my theological views" (31—32).

Newman's emphasis on the sources of his religious opinions, to the
omission of details of family and student life, has led some literary
critics to exclude the *Apologia* from the canon of English autobiography. But it is precisely the work's omission of secular concerns
and its consistent attention to the development of Newman's theological beliefs that provide the most conclusive evidence of its generic
intention. In *Grace Abounding*, for instance, Bunyan mentions his wife
and her father only to explain his familiarity with *The Plain Man's
Pathway to Heaven* and *The Practice of Piety*. Similarly, John Newton
tells of his courtship and its effect upon his life only to satisy the
queries of one of his patrons.[15] Scott, Newman's immediate model,
mentions his "increasing family" and his lack of "private fortune" in
an appendix, but only to argue that his situation in life rendered a
conversion to evangelicalism for personal gain improbable. The generic precedent, in other words, inclined against the mention of
personal details superfluous to the development of the autobiographer's soul or intellect.

Just as Newman's method of constructing his autobiography follows Scott's model, the motives informing the method are Scott's as
well: he intends to demonstrate that his religious opinions derive
exclusively from orthodox Anglican theology. To *The Force of Truth*
Scott had appended some "Observations on the Foregoing Narrative," in which he argued the validity of his conversion to evangelical
Christianity on the grounds that, first, as a Socinian, he was "a most
unlikely person to embrace this [evangelical] system of doctrine" and
that, further, he had changed his religious beliefs "without any teaching from the persons, to whose sentiments I have now acceded." [16]
Like other evangelicals, Scott believed that anyone who disinter-
estedly studied the Scriptures and Anglican theology would adopt,

sooner or later, the evangelical position. Newman uses the same sort of argument implicitly throughout the *Apologia* to counter the prejudices of his anti-Catholic readers, on whom the allusions to Scott's autobiography and its principle of truth would not be lost. Late in his account, Newman explicitly repeats the point made in Scott's "Observations": "My opinions in religion were not gained, as the world [has] said, from Roman sources, but were, on the contrary, the birth of my own mind and of the circumstances in which I had been placed" (82). This combination of a divinely endowed mind and divinely ordained circumstances is Newman's adaptation of Scott's argument and, indeed, a revision of the evangelical formula for conversion.

Whether or not contemporary readers of the *Apologia* recognized the allusions to *The Force of Truth*, the deliberate repetition of Scott's method and argument suggests that Newman himself felt the need to engage the dominant English tradition of autobiography and shape it to his own ends. Newman records, as we have seen, that he "had been possessed of" Scott's essays and autobiography "from a boy" (17). This way of phrasing the matter suggests that Scott's work had somehow possessed the young Newman—possessed, if not his very self, at least his self-conception.

In the autobiographical tradition, prior works of the genre do somehow possess each new autobiographer's self: they determine how he views his experience, how he understands the self, how he orders the contours of his personal history. Yet if the autobiographer cannot escape the power of the generic conventions to shape his self-conception, it is equally impossible to imagine an autobiography (that is, a history of an individual self) that merely repeats the conventions. In order to write an autobiography, the autobiographer must in some way violate the generic tradition or deviate from it—and, in so doing, discover the self.

For Newman the violation of generic predecessors is a self-conscious literary act, one that extends to autobiography a technique he had used before in arguing against evangelical critics. Newman explains it this way:

> "Two can play at that," was often in my mouth, when men of Protestant sentiments appealed to the Articles, Homilies, or Reformers; in the sense that, if they had a right to speak loud, I had the liberty to speak out as well as they, and had the means, by the same or parallel appeals, of giving them tit for tat.... I aimed at bringing into effect the promise contained in the motto to the Lyra, "They shall know the difference now." (82)

Newman calls his means in religious controversy "by the same or parallel appeals," and it describes as well his use of *The Force of Truth*. Even as he adopts Scott's model to present his own history, his method is tit for tat: a repetition of its major structural patterns (what the repetition of the consonantal *t's* in Newman's metaphor suggests), but with the intended effect of difference (what the variation between the vocalic *i* and *a* creates). The models and methods of the evangelicals are, in Newman's hands, to be turned to different ends.

Newman creates this difference in the *Apologia* by maintaining Scott's narrative structure, while replacing Scott's fundamental principle of interpretation with one of his own. In the closing "Observations," Scott had designated the crucial factor in his conversion as "the great influence which the study of Scriptures had in producing [the] change."[17] Men were too apt, he complained, to borrow their "schemes of divinity from other authors" or to think they possessed sufficient proof of their doctrines if they could "produce the sanction of some great name."[18] Given his conversion to evangelicalism, Scott is thoroughly predictable in the principle he enunciates: evangelicals believed the Bible, not any ecclesiastical interpretation, to be the ultimate authority in matters of faith and practice. In contrast, Newman makes his principle as thoroughly Catholic as Scott's is Protestant. In the final exposition of his religious beliefs, "Position of My Mind since 1845," Newman assigns to the Church "the means of maintaining religious truth in this anarchical world": its judgment "must be extended even to Scripture, though Scripture be divine." The Bible itself, he allows in acknowledgment of testimonies like

Scott's, "may be accidentally the means of the conversion of individuals," but by attempting to ground religious interpretation solely in the Bible, Protestants make it "answer a purpose for which it was never intended" (188).

Newman's divergence from Scott may seem to be merely the doctrinal divergence of a Catholic from an evangelical Protestant. But it involves much more than a rejection of an evangelical tenet that Newman had earlier held. The "purpose for which it was never intended" includes a purpose to which English evangelicals put the biblical text in the writing of spiritual autobiography; their commitment to the Bible as the authority in matters of interpretation directly influenced the form and method of the autobiographies they composed. In diverging from Scott in principle, then, Newman had also to diverge in autobiographical method.[19]

In writing spiritual autobiography, English Protestants from Bunyan through Newton, Cowper, and Scott had depended upon the hermeneutic method of biblical typology. Bunyan justified the publication of *Grace Abounding*, as we have seen, by treating the wanderings of the Israelites as prefigurative of his own experiences and Moses' record of these events as prefigurative also. His use of scriptural texts had been necessary for his own autobiographical act: as Sacvan Bercovitch has observed for American Puritan writers, without the biblical model the writing of autobiography would have been impossible, its goal being not to proclaim the self but, as for Bunyan, to efface it, to "dissolve [it] into the timeless pattern of spiritual biography."[20] Bunyan's use of the Exodus had, in turn, a profound effect upon the tradition of spiritual autobiography that followed. As history made literary classics of *Grace Abounding* and *The Pilgrim's Progress*, and as the latter became what might be called a prospectus for anyman's autobiography, subsequent autobiographers came to follow the narrative patterns and system of interpretation that Bunyan had introduced.

A generation after Bunyan, the Quaker Alice Hayes described her spiritual experiences just as Bunyan had—as a repetition of "the Mistery [of] what Israel of old passed through, while in Egypt's land, and by the Red Sea; and their Travels through the Deeps with their coming up on the Banks of Deliverance."[21] Nearly a century later, John Newton began his "Authentic Narrative" with "reflections upon that promise made to the Israelites in Deuteronomy viii,2": "Thou shalt remember all the way, by which the Lord thy God led thee through this wilderness." Like Hayes, Newton interpreted this text "in a spiritual sense," as "addressed to all who are passing through the wilderness of this world to a heavenly Canaan,"[22] and like Bunyan, he used it and a variety of other biblical types to interpret his spiritual predicament. While enumerating the disasters he faced on board a foundering slave ship, for instance, Newton viewed himself not only as an Israelite, but as a Jonah, reproached by the captain as "the cause of the present calamity."[23] And Newton's sometimes mad contemporary Alexander Cruden interpreted his life using an even greater variety of types, ranging from Joseph (whose life he believed was "emblematical and typical" of his own) to Alexander the Great (after whom he titled his autobiography, *The Adventures of Alexander the Corrector*).[24]

The possibilities for such acts of self-interpretation were numerous, limited only by loosely defined principles of typological hermeneutics and by the interpreter's imagination. It was probably the excessiveness of the evangelical imagination, displayed so frequently in spiritual accounts like Cruden's, that made Newman shun typology as his mode of interpretation in the *Apologia*—that and its cause, the Protestant dependence on private judgment and on what was known in matters of biblical interpretation as "the inspiration of the Holy Spirit."

Newman did not object to typological interpretation in itself. As an Anglican priest, he had used biblical typology in his *Plain and Parochial Sermons*, applying types to both individual experiences and historical events.[25] As a Catholic autobiographer, he might legitimately have continued a method that had originated in Patristic hermeneutics, one that even Augustine had used in the *Confessions*. In the nineteenth century, however, typology was so intricately bound to the tradition of the evangelical conversion narrative that Newman could not have used it without seeming to acquiesce in the theology with which it was associated. Newman had once spoken of his evangelical years at Oxford as "a type of Protestantism": "zeal, earnestness, resolution, without a guide; effort without a result." They were "a pattern instance of private judgment and its characteristics."[26] Surely he had no desire to propagate in the *Apologia* a pattern of private interpretation he had rejected as insufficient for his life.

Biblical allusions, then, because of their associations with evangelical spiritual autobiography, do not dominate the text of the *Apologia*, and those that do appear are not typological in intention. When Newman compares his indecision before his conversion to Catholicism with the uncertainty Samuel felt "before 'he knew the word of the Lord,'" he uses the Old Testament character to explain a psychological state, not to establish a typological link between the prophet's life and his own. So, too, when he discusses the difficulty of keeping young disciples under control and remarks that "a mixed multitude went out of Egypt with the Israelites" (86), he intends to illustrate his predicament as leader, not to provide a pattern for the history of the Oxford Movement. Such biblical allusions (and they are few) focus upon the audience's understanding, not the autobiographer's, and in this focus they resemble Newman's allusions to classical myths or historical events. When Newman echoes Achilles' words on returning to battle, "You shall know the difference, now that I am back again" (40), or repeats Dido's cry on her funeral pyre, "Exoriare aliquis!" he is using a classical echo to explain a predicament or to illustrate a state of mind, here his emotional state on the return from his Sicilian journey. These allusions, like the biblical ones, do not represent a mode of self-scrutiny or a method of autobiographical interpretation. To put it another way, the purpose of both kinds of allusions is primarily rhetorical, not hermeneutic: they involve neither a systematic approach to interpretation nor a self-conscious stance toward the interpretive act.

The most telling evidence of Newman's rejection of evangelical patterns of autobiography, however, is the absence of a specific set of allusions: allusions to the Exodus, the biblical type fundamental to the genre. Newman had used the Exodus frequently in the verse of the *Lyra Apostolica*, especially in his best-known autobiographical poem, "Lead, Kindly Light." In the *Apologia*, however, he does not cast his account as a spiritual pilgrimage, despite the fact that he wandered for years before finding his peace in the Catholic church. Quite distinctly, he avoids allusions to exile, exodus, or wilderness wandering,[27] and substitutes an alternative method of interpretation. Newman bases this new hermeneutic on the analogy of ecclesiastical history rather than on the more characteristically evangelical correlations of biblical typology.

Because the argument of the *Apologia* depends upon the Anglican origin of his religious knowledge, Newman links his hermeneutic method to standard Anglican divines. In chapter I, he points out that he learned from Bishop Bull "to consider that Antiquity was the true exponent of the doctrines of Christianity" (33) and this belief, coupled with the principle of analogy that he learned from Butler, prepares for the view of ecclesiastical history that eventually leads to Rome. In chapter I, too, Newman emphasizes the "doctrine of Tradition": both Hawkins and Froude taught him, he notes, to view Tradition as the teacher and Scripture as the verifier of truth (20, 33). Moreover, as Newman describes his participation in the Tractarian Movement, he again points out that he found his arguments in the writings of the early Church: "my stronghold was Antiquity" (96).

Newman was, of course, as deeply influenced by Catholic sources, including Augustine, as he was by the Anglican divines he cites. But whether the influences were Anglican or Roman Catholic, the effect on the course of his life is well known. It was in reading a segment of early Church history, the fifth-century controversy between the Monophysites of Alexandria and the Chalcedonian Catholics, that Newman came to understand the impossibility of holding the Anglican position of the *Via Media*. In that fifth-century controversy, he found the doctrinal and ecclesiastical issues of the sixteenth and nineteenth centuries foreshadowed: "I saw my face in that mirror, and I was a Monophysite. The Church of the *Via Media* was in the position of the Oriental communion; Rome was, where she now is; and the Protestants were the Eutychians" (96).

Not all readers of the *Apologia* can understand how Newman reached the conclusion he did or, to continue his metaphor, how he received anything but an extremely distorted reflection from the mirror of church history. As Henry Chadwick has explained, both the Roman Chalcedonians and the African Monophysites adhered to legitimate doctrines, both positing reasonable definitions of the nature of Christ and both articulating formulae about the union of the human and divine (the Chalcedonian, "in two natures," and the Monophysite, "out of two natures" or sometimes "one nature of the incarnate Word") that were "fully orthodox in intention and fact."[28] But this is to ignore Newman's perspective. For if his face and not our own reflects from the mirror of history, that is as it should be in the *Apologia*. For Newman, the essential issue was not one of doctrine, but of attitude and action. In the refusal of the African Church to honor the decree of the Council of Chaldedon, in its acquittal of the heretic Eutyches, and in its defiance of Leo, the Bishop of Rome—in all these acts, Newman found parallels to the acts of the Anglican Church in the modern period.

In the middle chapters of the *Apologia*, then, Newman introduces a new hermeneutic principle, one derived from Anglican and Patristic sources and formulated specifically for the autobiographical situation he feels compelled to understand. According to the interpretation this principle generates, it is the Anglican Church, not the Roman, that has fostered heresy and dissension, and his own participation in the Anglican-Roman controversy, however well-intentioned, has contributed to the dissension:

> What was the use of continuing the controversy, or defending my position, if, after all, I was forging arguments for Arius or Eutyches, and turning devil's advocate against the much-enduring Athanasius and the majestic Leo? Be my soul with the Saints! and shall I lift up my hand against them? Sooner may my right hand forget her cunning, and wither outright, as his who once stretched it out against a prophet of God! (97)

The basis of self-interpretation here is ecclesiastical rather than biblical. Newman equates himself with religious sects, the Arians and

Eutychians: "I was forging arguments" and "turning devil's advocate." The biblical parallels—from Psalm 137, which laments Israel's exile in Babylon, and I Kings 13, which narrates Jereboam's paralysis for opposing God's prophet—become secondary, following as rhetorical emphasis, as elaboration and verification of the truth that Tradition has authoritatively taught.

By replacing biblical with what might be termed "ecclesiastical hermeneutics," Newman moves the *Apologia* away from the tradition of Bunyan and nearer that of Augustine. This movement will not be complete—nor, indeed, even figurally obvious—until the opening lines of chapter IV in which Newman invokes the Augustinian topos of the medical crisis. Before he can turn to a specifically Augustinian topos, however, Newman must undergo a generic crisis. For the movement from one tradition to another represents a matter of both uneasiness and desire—the uneasiness of a convert from Protestantism about an autobiographical method tainted by old patterns, the desire of an advocate of Catholicism for an account thoroughly orthodox in principle and method.

The uneasiness appears as Newman draws the analogy between Christendom in the fifth and nineteenth centuries. He admits surprise (even in retrospect) that the Monophysite controversy should have instigated his conversion:

> Of all passages of history, since history has been, who would have thought of going to the sayings and doings of old Eutyches, that *delirus senex*, as (I think) Petavius calls him, and to the enormities of the unprincipled Dioscorus, in order to be converted to Rome! (97)

In this admission Newman virtually undermines the validity of his self-interpretation by drawing attention to inconsistencies within the original analogy: not only is Eutyches, the prefiguration of Protestantism, a "crazy old man," but Dioscorus, the man whose position is analogous to his own, is a leader "unprincipled" in the extreme—

the very charge the *Apologia* seeks to refute. And if the analogy creates uneasiness, Newman seems doubly uneasy as he insists that he is not writing "controversially," but is merely telling his story, narrating the events "with the one object of relating things as they happened to me in the course of my conversion" (97). With this statement he tries to deny that he has made any interpretation at all, at least any for which he is accountable. He claims his object to be narration—something controlled by chronology, not by autobiographical intention.[29]

Why should Newman write with such uneasiness? In one sense, his response typifies the uneasiness of all spiritual autobiographers who formulate interpretations upon which their souls depend. As Bunyan searches for an appropriate type in *Grace Abounding*, for instance, he runs through the list of possible Old Testament precursors not once, but twice, each time trying desperately to find one who, like himself, having sinned greatly after receiving God's grace, has yet been forgiven. In his *Memoir* William Cowper, too, is riddled with guilt about faulty interpretations he has made in the past; central to his account, as the sin that led to attempted suicide, is a failure in hermeneutics, a failure to believe in the possibility of providential interpretation. Some of Newman's uneasiness is of this general sort. Newman admits that "on occasion," when he reached new interpretations of ecclesiastical material, he felt "a positive doubt" whether "the suggestion did not come from below" (100), the same fearful thought that plagues Bunyan and Cowper.[30]

If Newman's uneasiness is typical of the genre, however, it is also particular to the *Apologia*—that is, to the *Apologia* as a Catholic autobiography in the English tradition. Protestant autobiographers had extended typological hermeneutics, after all, to correlate the events of biblical history with episodes in their own lives, and Newman perhaps feared that his method would simply seem a modification of theirs, one that drew on post-biblical history rather than on biblical narrative. As Martin J. Svaglic has pointed out, among the readers whom Newman felt he must reach were "his fellow Catholics," so many of whom "had begun to have doubts about him."[31] It is one thing for Newman to declare that it does not matter to him "if any Catholic says...that I have been converted in a wrong way, I cannot help that now" (157). It is another for him to demonstrate, as he composes his autobiography with a new hermeneutic method, that it does not matter. What he needs as a Catholic autobiographer is a validation of his method.

This validation Newman finds in the Augustinian sentence, "Securus judicat orbis terrarum" (98). The words themselves derive from the *Contra epistolam Parmeniani* (III.iv.24), a minor polemical work in which Augustine urges the Donatists, a separatist sect, to rejoin their Catholic brethren and create a unified Christian community in Africa: "The world judges with assurance that they are not good men who, in whatever part of the world, separate themselves from the rest of the world."[32] But Newman's immediate source is an 1839 essay in the *Dublin Review*, in which Nicholas Wiseman quotes Augustine in order to argue against contemporary Anglican claims of apostolical succession. According to Wiseman, it does not matter whether the case between contemporary Catholics and Protestants is precisely the same or "so simple as that of Donatists and the Catholics of their times." Augustine's words represent "an axiom," "a golden sentence," for the Church in all ages.[33]

Newman calls these words "palmary" (98), associating them with a key Catholic principle of interpretation and then with Augustinian autobiography itself, and his motives suggest a desire for assurance that his uneasiness has provoked. Obviously, Newman calls the words "palmary" because he finds in them a superior interpretation of the Donatist and Anglican controversies—and of his own situation in 1839. But he also calls them "palmary," I suspect, because they remove the necessity of self-interpretation altogether. "Securus judicat orbis terrarum": with their initial stress upon "securus," the words signal Newman's primary need for assurance, for certain judgment, for reliable interpretation. The Augustinian principle avoids the ambiguity of historical circumstances and the uneasiness of the interpreter, ecclesiastical or autobiographical, who must understand them. The simplicity appeals. Newman concludes that the words "decided ecclesiastical questions *on a simpler rule* than than of Antiquity; nay, St. Augustine himself was one of the prime oracles of

Antiquity.... What a light was hereby thrown upon every controversy in the Church!" (98, italics mine).

In this principle, articulated by the great Catholic divine of
antiquity and repeated by a leading English Catholic of the nineteenth century, Newman finds validation for his use of eccesiastical
history in the *Apologia*. He recalls that Augustine's words struck him
"with a power which I never had felt from any words before." They
were "like the 'Tolle, lege,—Tolle, lege,' of the child, which converted St. Augustine himself" (98—99). The allusion to the unprece-
dented power of the Augustinian sentence revokes the power that
Scott's text once had over Newman: he is no longer "possessed of" *The
Force of Truth*. And the association of the Augustinian principle with
the *Confessions* itself is crucial, for it supplies the autobiographical
authority that Newman otherwise lacks. In this passage Newman
effectively transfers the *Apologia* from an English Protestant tradition
to a Catholic literary form, distinct from that tradition and chronologically prior to it. By the end of the third chapter he has prepared
the way for an Augustinian version of the spiritual autobiography.

Augustine's *Confessions* has frequently been cited as a seminal work
in the tradition of spiritual autobiography, but in the English tradition before Newman its formal influence was, in fact, negligible.
English autobiographers might have read the *Confessions* in the original Latin or in a seventeenth-century translation by Tobias Matthew
or William Watts, but they made little attempt, as Karl J. Weintraub has argued, to imitate its figural motifs or larger formal
structure.[34] It was Newman who re-introduced the *Confessions* to the
English reading public through the editions of the Church Fathers he
sponsored,[35] and it was Newman, too, who through the *Apologia*
reminded English autobiographers of the Augustinian figures and
form they might use as alternatives to Bunyanesque patterns. Newman's version of an Augustinian autobiography takes shape in chapters IV and V through a repetition of two characteristic Augustinian
figures—the deathbed motif of chapter IV and the elegiac closure of

chapter V—and, more generally, through an adaptation of the multiple forms of confession that organize Augustine's work and inform Newman's final statement of faith.

Chapter IV of the *Apologia* opens with Newman, as he puts it, "on my death-bed, as regards my membership with the Anglican Church" (121). This scene repeats the *Confessions*, book VI, which begins with Augustine bodily in Milan, under the tutelage of St. Ambrose, but spiritually still in Africa, in a state of "grievous peril, through despair of ever finding truth."[36] To describe this state, Augustine introduces two figures: that of a dead man on his bier and that of a sick man on his deathbed. My mother "bewailed me as one dead," he begins, "carrying me forth upon the bier of her thoughts, that Thou mightest say to the son of the widow, Young man, I say unto thee, Arise." A few sentences later, the figure alters: "she anticipated most confidently that I should pass from sickness unto health, after the access, as it were, or a sharper fit, which physicians call 'the crisis.'"[37] The figures originate in Luke 7:11−18, where Christ comes upon a funeral procession from the city of Nain and raises a dead man, "the only son of his mother," from his bier. For Augustine, the biblical account of a bodily resurrection has come to stand for the spiritual regeneration of all Christians and, here, of himself as autobiographer. Augustine the protagonist may seen to be on his deathbed-cum-bier, but Augustine the autobiographer knows that his state is one of crisis-cum-conversion.

For Newman, the figures of deathbed and bier provide a crucial strategy: they reveal and they avoid. The figures explain why his actions seemed so erratic during the period 1841−45, wavering between Anglicanism and Roman Catholicism and going in both directions (and no direction) at once: "A death-bed has scarcely a history; it is a tedious decline, with seasons of rallying and seasons of falling back;...it is a season when doors are closed and curtains drawn, and when the sick man neither cares nor is able to record the stages of his malady. I was in these circumstances, except so far as I was not allowed to die in peace" (121). But the figures also avoid the stain of evangelicalism, the language of the Protestant conversion experience. As images of disease and debilitation, they provide an alternative to the trope of wandering in the wilderness, and except for them, Newman's account might sound at this point like countless other evangelical conversion narratives. Instead of "seasons of rallying and seasons of falling back," the text might have read, for example, "periods of forging ahead and periods of losing my way"—as, indeed, out of habit, I used the more traditional spatial metaphor of wandering, adopting it implicitly in the phrase "going in both directions (and in no direction) at once."

The figures of deathbed and bier are crucial in another way: they allow Newman to interpret his Anglican past with both truth and tact. As Newman understood very well, the moment of "crisis" described in the *Confessions* was the moment of transition from Manicheanism to Roman Catholicism. As a Manichee, Augustine had been a heretic; as neither Manichee nor Catholic, his state was one of spiritual death. Once rescued from death, Augustine recognized the errors of the Manichean doctrines and the soundness of Catholic teaching; "with joy I blushed," he confesses, "at having so many years barked not against the Catholic faith, but against the fictions of carnal imaginations."[38] By adopting the Augustinian figures, Newman passes judgment on his defense of the *Via Media* and on many of the doctrines he held previously, recognizing them in retrospect as heresy, as a source of spiritual death. But of course the word *heresy* is never invoked.

What follows in chapter IV of the *Apologia* is modeled on books VI and VII of *Confessions*. For Newman, as for Augustine, the transition from death to life involves a recognition of error and a confession of Catholic truth. The first half of the chapter (1841–43) describes the recognition, with the shattering of the *Via Media* as a tenable system. Like Augustine in book VI, Newman cannot yet embrace Roman Catholicism; he quotes a letter in which he had explained to a Catholic acquaintance, "That my *sympathies* have grown towards the religion of Rome I do not deny; that my *reasons* for *shunning* her communion have lessened or altered it would be difficult perhaps to prove" (150). The second half of the chapter (1843–45) makes the confession, beginning with a formal retraction "of all the hard things which I had said against the Church of Rome" (158). Again like Augustine, who had condemned the Catholic faith for what were in fact his own misconceptions, Newman traces the steps that led him to accept all the Church's teachings, including those on the Blessed Virgin and the saints that had initially been a stumbling block: "this I know full well now, and did not know then, that the Catholic Church allows no image of any sort, material or immaterial, no dogmatic symbol, no rite, no sacrament, no Saint, not even the Blessed Virgin herself, to come between the soul and its Creator. It is face to face, 'solus cum solo,' in all matters between man and his God" (154). With this confession, the dead man has been raised from his bier, an Augustinian pattern has replaced a Protestant one, and Newman is free to complete his autobiography in a Catholic mode.

This completion involves a second repetition of the *Confessions* in the elegiac inscription that closes the *Apologia*. Instead of concluding with a Pisgah vision, the traditional form of closure in Bunyanesque autobiography, Newman writes what he calls a "memorial of affection and gratitude" to his brother priests of the Birmingham Oratory. Just as Augustine's text in book IX creates a substitute for the burial marker that his mother, who died in Ostia, was never to have in her Numidian homeland, so the text of the *Apologia* carves the priests' names on the page in upper-case letters and their deeds beneath them in epitaphic clauses:

> AMBROSE ST. JOHN, HENRY AUSTIN MILLS,
> HENRY BITTLESTON, EDWARD CASWALL,
> WILLIAM PAINE NEVILLE, and HENRY IGNATIUS DUDLEY RYDER [:]
> who have been so faithful to me;
> who have been so sensitive of my needs;
> who have been so indulgent of my failings;
> who have carried me through so many trials;
> who have grudged no sacrifice, if I asked for it;
> who have been so cheerful under discouragements of my causing;
> who have done so many good works, and let me have the credit of them;
> —with whom I have lived so long, with whom I hope to die.

Newman intends to pay tribute to the priests as examples of Christian charity, just as Augustine commends his mother as an example of

Christian piety, but the choice of the elegiac here has a more complex Augustinian purpose, redemptive as well as nostalgic and rhetorical.[39] Augustine closes book IX of the *Confessions*, the biographical account of his mother, with a hope that his readers might in prayer "remember my parents in this transitory light, my brethren under Thee our Father in our Catholic Mother, and my fellow-citizens in that eternal Jerusalem which Thy pilgrim people sigheth after from their Exodus, even unto their return thither."[40] Newman closes the *Apologia* with a similar prayer for redemption and reunion: "And I earnestly pray for this whole company, with a hope against hope, that all of us, who once were so united, and so happy in our union, may even now be brought at length, by the Power of the Divine Will, into One Fold and under One Shepherd" (216). The biblical metaphor has been altered, once again to mute what might be mistaken for Protestant overtones, but paradoxically even this alteration demonstrates Newman's commitment to Augustinian autobiography. The traditional Protestant form of closure concerns itself with the redemption of the individual soul; the Augustinian form recalls the communion of saints.

Despite the similarity of the prayers, however, Newman's closure is curiously different from its original, and the choice of *living* priests for the subjects of elegy signals the problem. In the *Confessions* Augustine appropriately gives life through words to the woman who gave him life through flesh. His elegy pays tribute to a woman now dead who, as he so clearly states, "brought me forth, both in the flesh, that I might be born to this temporal light, and in heart, that I might be born to Light eternal."[41]

Newman can write no such tribute to his mother—nor to father, brother, or sister. His mother had died before his conversion to Roman Catholicism, but that was not, of course, the obstacle. Had she lived, his conversion might very well have caused an irreconcilable breach, as it did with his sisters. More to the point, had his mother lived, Newman might never have converted. Issac Williams, his curate at St. Mary's and author of a memoir supplementary to the *Apologia*, suggests that Newman's mother corrected "that want of balance and repose in the soul, which [was] the malady of both brothers"; once she died, her sons lost this balance, Francis taking the direction of theological rationalism and John Henry, the direction of Roman Catholicism.[42]

If Williams is correct about the maternal influence, then the elegy that closes Newman's autobiography may be not only a conscious tribute, but also an unconscious series of substitutions. It substitutes first a memorial to his "dearest brothers of this House" for the elegy to his mother that he could not write. In this substitution, Newman consciously brings to fruition a notion introduced in the preface— that he, like Abraham, had "left 'my kindred and my father's house' for a Church from which I once turned away with dread" (12)—and reiterated throughout the *Apologia* in a complex of metaphors involving the loss of home, family, and friends.[43] He substitutes as well Ambrose St. John, "the link between my old life and my new," for the many links, both temporal and spiritual, that Augustine had to commemorate in book IX: his friend Alypius, his son Adeodatus, as well as his mother Monica, all of whom were "fellow-citizens in that eternal Jerusalem." Most significantly, Newman's elegy substitutes an apparent object of loss for the real object of loss. For it is not his brother priests (who are, after all, still alive) whom Newman mourns in this elegiac passage. Rather, it is the loss of his mother—absent from him now, perhaps absent eternally—that gives the elegiac closure of the *Apologia* its power.[44]

If the repetition of Augustinian figures allows Newman to bring the *Apologia* within a Catholic tradition, the repetition of a larger Augustinian form explains the final chapter, "Position of My Mind since 1845," and provides Newman with a means of reconciling a disjunction within the form of the English autobiography itself. In a seminal work on the genre, Wayne Shumaker has observed that the English autobiography, particularly in the Victorian period, is a "mixed mode": it combines exposition and narration—or, to describe it negatively, it represents something in between, a combination or an alternation of modes. Following Shumaker, most literary histori-

ans have viewed the development of the genre as a process of purifi-
cation: as the autobiography becomes self-conscious and self-assured,
it moves away from exposition and toward narration; it moves closer,
that is, to the novel.[45] These versions of literary history assume that
the most important characteristic of the genre is its factuality and the
most important development, its blurring of the boundary between
fact and fiction.

Newman, however, was a keener historian of the genre and a more
perceptive interpreter of the disjunction between narration and exposition. He understood the genre to be essentially hermeneutic, a
category that supersedes the label of fiction or non-fiction. He recognized, too, that the primary concern of autobiographers had traditionally been to find an adequate hermeneutic method. Thus, the
expository element was not dross to be refined, but the legitimate
articulation of principles that had governed the autobiographer's
interpretation of narrative all along.

This relation of narrative to exposition, of narrative to theology
and philosophy, is most clear in the arrangement of the *Confessions*,
and it is Augustine's clarity of generic intention and form that
Newman brings to the final chapter of the *Apologia*. Augustine's
narrative ends with book IX when, hearing the *tolle lege* of the young
child, he decides to abandon his professorship of rhetoric and seek
baptism at the hand of Ambrose. After the account of his conversion,
the mode of the *Confessions* shifts radically, from the narrative of books
I — IX to the exposition of X — XIII. John C. Cooper has explained this
shift in terms of the two meanings of the word *confessions*: Augustine
engages in *confessio peccati* in the narrative of his life from birth to
spiritual conversion; he shifts to *confessio fidei* in the personal reflections of book X and in the theological exposition of Genesis in books
XI — XIII.[46]

Although Cooper mentions only the common ecclesiastical distinction, he might also have cited evidence from the *Confessions* itself.
In book VII, Augustine anticipates the distinct forms that his work
will embody as he considers the value of past experience:

Upon these [false books] Thou therefore willedst that I should
fall, before I studied Thy Scriptures, that it might be imprinted

on my memory how I was affected by them; and that afterwards
when my spirits were tamed through Thy books, and my
wounds touched by Thy healing fingers, I might discern and
distinguish between *presumption* and *confession*; between those
who saw whither they were to go, yet saw not the way, and the
way that leadeth not to behold only but to dwell in the beatific
country.[47]

The key distinction, as my emphasis suggests, is between presumption and confession. It would be presumptuous for anyone to write an
exposition of doctrine, to make a *confessio fidei*, before undergoing
personal experiences that teach the truth of Christian doctrine.[48]
Such an exposition would be mere presumption or assumption, a
statement made before the fact or without the facts. For Augustine, in
other words, experiential confession comes first; doctrinal confession,
second. Hence the arrangement of the *Confessions*, with the narrative
books preceding the expository.

Newman observes this Augustinian arrangement in the *Apologia*
by detailing the process of his conversion in chapters I−IV and then
systematically setting forth his theological beliefs in the "Position of
My Mind since 1845." The first line of the final chapter announces
the cessation of narrative: "From the time I became a Catholic, of
course I have no further *history* of my religious opinions to *narrate*"
(184, italics mine). Like Pusey's translation of the *Confessions*, which
introduces books XI−XIII with the headnote, "Augustine breaks off
the history of the mode whereby God led him to holy Orders, in order
to 'confess' God's mercies," Newman's self-announcement signals a
breaking off. He concludes the historical narrative in order to begin a
confession of the "Creed of the Church" (185).

That Newman includes an explicit defense of Catholics who hold
the creed against Protestants who charge deceit and hypocrisy in no
way lessens the Augustinian impact. One obstacle to faith prior to
Augustine's conversion, an obstacle implanted and then nurtured by
the Manichees, was the Church's teaching on creation. Augustine's
exposition of Genesis I in books XI−XIII represents, in this context,
a confession of faith and a renunciation of former heresy, as well as a

direct defense of Catholic doctrine against its contemporary critics. If Newman's defense in chapter V addresses accusations of deceit and dishonesty, it is because they were, like the Manichean perversions of the fourth century, the pressing issues of his day. Just as the narrative of chapters I—IV answers charges of personal dishonesty, the exposition of the creed answers the more general Protestant charge that the Catholic church sanctions—and even encourages—deceit.

Newman's transition from narration to exposition at the end of the *Apologia* thus recognizes the formal mixture that had traditionally marked autobiography as a genre. More important, it represents an attempt to make the theological implications of narrative absolutely clear. At the conclusion of *Grace Abounding*, Bunyan had appended a list of "seven abominations in my heart" and seven good things that "the Wisdom of God doth order"—fourteen theological truths that his experience had taught him.[49] Thomas Scott, too, had added his "Observations," some of which, like the influence of prayer or the study of Scripture, made doctrinal assumptions. But neither Bunyan nor Scott was self-conscious as an autobiographer about the relation between the narrative he was presenting and the theology he espoused; indeed, Scott seems to assume that he has told his story "straight," uninfluenced by his theology.[50] With the *Apologia*, the autobiography becomes self-conscious as a genre: it realizes its hermeneutic intention. By formally distinguishing between the two modes of autobiography, Newman paradoxically re-integrates them and, in the re-integration, reflects upon the hermeneutic enterprise on which both narrative and theology depend.

5

Martineau's *Autobiography:*
The Feminine Debate
over Self-Interpretation

arly in 1877, the publishing house of Smith, Elder issued posthumously the *Autobiography* of Harriet Martineau. Except for the three-volume format, it was an unusual sort of Victorian work: Martineau had written her account in 1855 on what she thought was her deathbed, and the printed and bound volumes had lain dormant in her publisher's safe for over twenty years, awaiting her death.[1] The autobiographer, too, was not the usual sort: a deaf woman from the provincial town of Norwich, she had made her reputation as a writer of popular tales of political economy, illustrating with cheerful goodwill the doctrines of Bentham, Mill, and Malthus, and doing it so successfully that by the age of thirty she had become one of London's foremost literary lions. The most unusual thing about the *Autobiography*, however, was that Harriet Martineau had written it at all. For during the nineteenth century few women wrote and published their autobiographies, and virtually no women wrote within the main tradition of the spiritual autobiography or, like Martineau, attempted one of the secular variants so common for male writers.

William Matthews' standard bibliography of British autobiographies lists, for instance, twenty-seven examples of spiritual autobiography written during the nineteenth century: twenty-two by men, five by women.[2] The accounts by men are fairly conventional narratives of spiritual waywardness or malaise, conviction of sin, and eventual redemption—lesser or secular versions of autobiographical classics like Bunyan's *Grace Abounding*. None of the accounts written by a woman is, in fact, a true spiritual autobiography: one is a memorial for the minor poet Francis Ridley Havergal, assembled from biographical and autobiographical documents by her sister Maria; two others are diaries of spiritual meditation, written during periods of illness and doubt and later re-arranged by a friend; the fourth begins with an account of conversion, which an anonymous editor amplifies with a selection of personal letters but which soon becomes a daily record of "spiritual blessings" (including such benefits as a present of "dried buffins" from "dear brother S—" and "a plum pudding and sausage rolls" from "my dearest B—"); the fifth recounts a conversion to Catholicism, but it was written in 1926 and thus mistakenly included in the list of nineteenth-century autobiographies.[3]

Matthews' bibliography is not fully accurate or complete: his objective in compiling it, as he states in the preface, was "not completeness, but comprehensiveness."[4] Its representative evidence suggests, however, that women avoided the form of the spiritual autobiography—or perhaps, to use the passive in an appropriate context, that women were avoided by the form. Generally, they did not compose retrospective accounts of spiritual or psychological progress, they did not use principles or patterns derived from biblical hermeneutics to interpret their lives, and they did not attempt to substitute other systems of interpretation to create secular variants of the form. This absence of women from the ranks of spiritual autobiographers seems peculiar, given the abundance of self-writing they otherwise produced: the autobiographical novels of major writers like Charlotte Brontë and George Eliot, the memoirs of lesser known poets and storytellers like Elizabeth Missing Sewell, Mary Cholmondeley, and Mary Kirby, and the diaries of countless women who, like the mothers of the autobiographers Butler and Gosse, considered the practice of spiritual record-keeping a sacred duty. If women did not write the traditional form of autobiography, in other words, it was no lack of literary talent or introspective diligence that prevented them; these they possessed in full measure.

Most of the critical and historical discussions of autobiography ignore this absence of female participants during the nineteenth century, treating only the main (male) literary tradition and tacitly assuming the existence of a lesser literature written by women authors.[5] Several recent feminist studies attempt to redress the neglect, but add another error in literary history by suggesting that women, too, began to write spiritual autobiographies in the seventeenth century and continued to write them, uninterrupted, through the nineteenth and twentieth centuries. Assuming this approach, Estelle Jelinek's collection, *Women's Autobiography*, places essays on the emergence of women's autobiography in England and America before a study of Martineau's *Autobiography*, as if the spiritual accounts of the seventeenth and eighteenth centuries led naturally to works of the nineteenth, Martineau's autobiography being the representative, if also the finest example. The volume by implication suggests an unbroken literary tradition.[6]

Englishwomen of the seventeenth century did indeed compose retrospective accounts of their spiritual lives that resemble those of male contemporaries, but it is an inaccurate literary history that supposes women's participation in the subsequent autobiographical tradition from the seventeenth through nineteenth centuries. Of the spiritual autobiographies that William Matthews lists for the seventeenth century, nearly a third were composed by women, and unlike the nineteenth-century examples, all are genuine versions of the form. Four are narratives of spiritual struggle and conversion written by women as diverse as Elizabeth West, an Edinburgh servant girl; Jane Turner, a sea captain's wife; and Mary Rich, the fourth Countess of Warwick.[7] Two others relate the conversion and religious service of a Quaker and a Scottish Reformed minister. The Quaker account, Alice Hayes' *A Legacy, or Widow's Mite*, is, moreover, a classic of the genre—thoroughly retrospective in approach, every bit as hermeneutic in method as Bunyan's *Grace Abounding*, and far more engaging than George Fox's *Journal*.

When Hayes describes her conviction of sin, it is "the Day of Jacob's trouble" witnessed upon her. When she receives no assurance of salvation, she "roars" "like David" in Psalm 22: "*I was ready to say, my Bones were all out of Joynt; and in the Depth of Distress, the Enemy was very strong with his Temptations.*" She disputes with her husband and priest, who oppose her attendance at Quaker meetings, by quoting the Scriptures: "It is better to trust in the Lord, than to put confidence in Man." She defies opponents like her father-in-law, who threatens to chain her to a tree and starve her, by taking to heart the account of "what *Israel* of old passed through while in *Egypt's* Land, and by the Red Sea." Hayes is thoroughly intent upon interpreting her experience in terms of scriptural patterns, and she articulates the typological basis of her interpretation as forcefully as any male spiritual autobiographer. "We have all these great Benefits which do accrew to both Soul and Body," she writes, "in learning of Him who was the Pattern in every Age":

> *Moses* in the Mount, did his Work according to the Pattern, by the Wisdom of our God, and *David* His Servant, gave Orders unto his Son *Solomon* and the Elders, how to carry on, and build that great House which was in its Time. But now how much more Glorious is this Dispensation of Light and Grace, which shines from the *Son Himself, the express Image of the Father, into our Hearts*, whereby we may now see our Way, and follow the Pattern, and need not to stumble where Thousands have fallen.[8]

These biblical precedents are the same as those Bunyan cites, and like him, Hayes draws upon the same hermeneutic tradition of self-interpretation.

By the end of the eighteenth century, women like Alice Hayes had ceased to write spiritual autobiography, just when men like Cowper, Newton, Whitefield, and Scott were revitalizing the genre. The bibliographical evidence suggests, moreover, that nineteenth-century women did not attempt to create secular versions of the form to suit their particular needs; they did not write, for example, autobiographies of de-conversion like Edmund Gosse's *Father and Son* or accounts of conversions to "scientific" modes of analysis like John Beattie Crozier's *My Inner Life, Being a Chapter in Personal Evolution and Autobiography*. Instead, women turned to other forms of self-expression: inward to their private diaries or outward to the protection of family memoirs or the fictional guise of the novel.

In this context, then, Harriet Martineau's *Autobiography* is unusual—exceptional rather than representative of the forms of self-writing produced by Victorian women. Martineau produced this anomaly, I would argue, precisely because she understood the theological and generic traditions of the spiritual autobiography and chose to write within them rather than within what she recognized as a "feminine" mode of self-expression.[9] Her choice was by no means an uncontroversial one. With it she raised questions for women writers about gender and genre, about their relationship to dominant (male) literary traditions and the desirability of creating an autobiographical literature of their own.

Before discussing Harriet Martineau's *Autobiography* more fully, however, we might consider some versions of autobiographical writing that Victorian women did compose, in part to sketch an unknown segment of nineteenth-century literary history, in part to define the social and generic restrictions that woman writers faced when they chose the form of spiritual autobiography. Martineau wrote when the available forms of self-expression for women were three: (1) the private diary, (2) the family memoir—including that peculiarly Victorian form, the memoir of the clergyman's wife, and (3) the autobiographical novel. The most common of these, as Matthews' bibliography indicates, was the private diary, and it provided an inestimable number of Victorian women with a vehicle for both religious expression and emotional release.[10]

Such spiritual records were not intended for publication—at least not without the careful editing of a family member or friend. When published, an editor's note invariably preceded the text, disclaiming that publication was the author's motive. By mid-nineteenth century, this disclaimer had become a convention of the form, so that in compiling *The Earnest Christian*, the journals and letters of Harriet Maria Jukes, the editor simply begins:

> It seems almost unnecessary to say on the opening page of this little work, as is generally done when introducing a Memoir to the public, that the Letters and Journals which form the principal part of it, were never intended by the writer to meet the eye of any but near and dear friends. Unknown, and unheard of but to these *in life*, she would have been the last to think she should have been so remembered after her death.

The editor, a Mrs. H. A. Gilbert, is conventional, too, not only in her assumption that the Christian woman is a silent woman, untempted by thoughts of worldly acclaim, but that above all else she is a family woman. "The MS. was nearly all arranged for the sake of Mrs. Jukes' children," the preface explains, "knowing how precious such records would be to them when old enough to understand them."[11] It never occurs to Mrs. Gilbert that in the careful arrangement of personal manuscripts Mrs. Jukes might have had a public motive beyond the private one. Or if it occurs to her, she, like Mrs. Jukes, immediately represses it as unworthy of an earnest Christian woman.

The social prohibitions against publication were strong enough to prevent most women from attempting full-scale spiritual autobiographies. But these were not the only prohibitions, nor the generically significant ones.[12] In its essential form, the spiritual autobiography demands an introspective and retrospective view of personal experience and a consistent hermeneutic system with which to interpret that experience. The spiritual diaries and memoirs of Victorian women lack both. Typically, their accounts give discontinuous presentations of their lives, only occasionally retrospective and rarely coherent in self-analysis.

Francis Ridley Havergal, one of the few Victorian women who attempted writing a retrospective account, recognized the inadequacies of the feminine forms and tried to circumvent them. She wrote "a sort of little autobiography" for her sister Maria to read after her death, defending her choice this way: "I have always avoided keeping a diary, feeling certain that it never would or could be a strictly faithful picture of a passing soul-life; yet I think an account of the *past*, in a bird's-eye view, would be far easier to give in a true and uncoloured light than any memoranda of a *present*, which would be tinged with the prevailing hues of the moment, morning, noon, or twilight." Here a Victorian woman articulates the virtues of the traditional form of autobiography: its retrospective stance ("in a bird's-eye view"), its coherent self-interpretation ("a strictly faithful picture"), its consistency in judgment ("in a true and uncoloured light"). Yet her attempt to embody them in a spiritual account produced only a truncated narrative of her first twenty years. Even that was dismembered by her sister, who took a more conventional view of women's (auto)biography and "re-arranged" the original document. What remains in the *Memorials* is a more typically "feminine" form of self-expression, and it seems as discontinuous as the typical woman's diary of the period.

In the twentieth century, women writers have learned to exploit the diary's sense of the discontinuity of experience and its capacity for a multiplicity of interpretations. In so doing, they have created works of lasting literary merit, and critics are right to praise these "honest records of the moment, whitehot, which do not impose the order of the next day on the record of the previous day."[13] One might see the achievement of twentieth-century women writers, however, as a proverbial instance of making virtue of necessity, and inquire more fully into the frustration of nineteenth-century women for whom such achievements were impossible. Victorian women often turned to their private journals not because they desired to produce whitehot records of the moment, but because they were judged incapable of writing autobiography in its standard form.

This judgment came indirectly through religious, psychological, and biological observations on the capacity of the female mind. English Calvinists, Anglicans, and humanists had debated the issue of women's capacities for over two hundred years, disagreeing about whether women's inferiority was a matter of nature or simply of tradition.[14] Even late in the eighteenth century, Hannah More's

Strictures on the Modern System of Female Education (1799) reflects a view of women's mental capacities as fundamentally limited:

> In summing up the evidence...of the different capacities of the sexes, one may venture, perhaps, to assert, that women have equal *parts*, but are inferior in *wholeness* of mind, in the integral understanding: that though a superior woman may possess single faculties in equal perfection, yet there is commonly a juster proportion in the mind of a superior man: that if women have in equal degree the faculty of fancy which creates images and the faculty of memory which collects and stores ideas, they seem not to possess in equal measure the faculty of comparing, combining, analysing, and separating these ideas; that deep and patient thinking which goes to the bottom of a subject; nor that power of arrangement which knows how to link a thousand connected ideas in one dependant train, without losing sight of the original idea out of which the rest grow, and on which they all hang.[15]

More's comments appear in the context of advice to young women with literary aspirations and seem to derive, especially the final clause, from a popular application of David Hartley's associationist theory in *Observations on Man, His Frame, His Duty, and His Expectations* (1749).[16] But whether More meant her comments to be fully descriptive of the female mind or merely prescriptive of the kinds of literature that women ought to attempt, their implications for the composition of autobiography are devastating. The genre demands precisely the qualities that More believes the female mind to lack.

While More allows women a measure of fancy "which creates images," she denies them the power to arrange the images into a coherent, causal sequence; while she admits that women possess the faculty of memory "which collects and stores ideas," she denies them both the patience for "deep thinking" and the analytic capacity to compare or combine their ideas. One can scarcely imagine an autobiographer who could not arrange memories into a coherent sequence or who could not combine a series of experiences to delineate a pattern of growth or who could not compare ideas at two points in life to chart that growth. Such a writer—in the Victorian period at least—would be necessarily restricted to the diary form, which allows the recording of images and ideas of the moment but does not demand the synthesizing intellect that More thinks women lack.

If More is correct, in other words, women are generically unfit to write autobiography. Even if she was only *believed* to be correct, an absence of retrospective spiritual or psychological autobiographies by women could be a result. The latter seems to have been the case. More's *Strictures* were reprinted in thirteen editions of 19,000 copies, and they dominated attitudes toward female education well into the nineteenth century. Even as discerning a young woman as Harriet Martineau treated More as an authority in religious and educational matters, praising in an 1822 essay on female writers More's "perspicuity and accuracy" and signing herself "Discipulus."[17]

In an uncanny way, the second form of self-writing by Victorian women exhibits the qualities that Mrs. More describes as typically feminine, and thus seems to testify again to the incompatibility of the female mind and the traditional autobiography. William Matthews lists these works, most of them written by clergymen's wives or daughters, as a sub-category of spiritual autobiography, but they are in fact memoirs—vaguely religious, usually morally edifying. In subject, they range from Mrs. William Peter Griffith's *Reminiscences* of her work in Canada and New Zealand as the wife of a Methodist minister; to Mary Cholmondeley's *Under One Roof*, four character sketches of a family rectory in Shropshire; to Mary Kirby's *Leaflets from My Life* which, as its title suggests, tells a series of discrete tales of clerical life in the provinces, some involving the author, others merely recollecting the conversations of friends. In method, the accounts make no attempt to describe an individual struggle against sin or against the temptations of the world, flesh, and devil or against any more modern obstacles to spiritual well-being. Rather, they are deliberately communal accounts of experiences shared with a husband or, more frequently, a family.

The proliferation of these memoirs, peculiar to the mid- and late nineteenth century, demonstrates the need of Victorian women to find an alternative mode of self-remembrance and self-expression. What seems uncanny, however, is that even with an alternative to the direct presentation of the self, with the necessity of personal testimony to spiritual progress removed, the writers still seem incapable of composing anything more than fragmentary documents. They seem unable to discover or impose a coherent pattern in or upon their materials. They seem unable to engage in the act of interpretation.

Typical of this failure is Mary Kirby's *Leaflets*, which she calls a "narrative autobiography" but which is really a potpourri of anecdotes about her sister and their acquaintances. The table of contents reads like a list of the children's tales that she and her sister wrote for their livelihood—"Carnival of St. Valentine," "The 'Whipping Toms and the Vicar of St. Mary's,' " "The Fates are adverse to Elizabeth and her Lover"—and, titles aside, these do not represent a coherent sequence of episodes in her spiritual life or professional career.[18] Similarly, Mary Cholmondeley, a skilled writer with over a dozen novels to her credit, gives portraits of her father, mother, nurse "Ninny," and younger sister without attempting to describe their interrelations or suggest their influences upon one another. Cholmondeley initially states that she has chosen to draw these portraits precisely because she wants to present "in context" the writings of her sister, who died in late adolescence. But the reader must infer the context and relationships, for Cholmondeley describes only the individual family member whose portrait she is drawing.[19] And a third Mary—Mary Lisle, a silly woman who claims to write for moral edification and to "lose the sense of my own loneliness"—tacks together a series of reminiscences that become ludicrous in their unmeditated juxtapositions: she follows her memories of an aunt's gruesome death by fire with the delights of a pet squirrel, for example.[20] It is as if these autobiographers had read Hannah More—or some theorist of her ilk—and been convinced that they possessed no capacity for arrangement, no power to compare, combine or analyze, no ability to shape their own lives or their family histories into a coherent pattern.

Such women are, it is true, minor figures in the ranks of religious autobiographers and memoir writers, and the tendency to narrate anecdotes rather than interpret history is common among male memoirists, whether religious or secular. Even the best of the female Victorian memoir writers, Mrs. M. O. W. Oliphant, resists imposing a comprehensive self-interpretation on her experience, preferring to tell familial or literary anecdotes and only in the end suggesting a pattern for her literary career.[21] This difficulty with interpretation should have been less troublesome for writers of the religious memoir, which include the women quoted above. The familiar biblical patterns of interpretation, derived from typological hermeneutics, could as easily have been used in the memoir as in the spiritual autobiography (or in other forms that require an interpretation of religious experience: the spiritual diary, the funeral sermon, the religious biography). These patterns women knew but seemed not to use.

The difficulty lay not so much in the *act* of interpretation, I think, as in the *method* that the autobiographical tradition imposed upon them. If women wished to write autobiography, they had to use the language of the spiritual autobiographer. Male writers like Carlyle, Ruskin, Newman, and a host of others used this language with a confidence that only experience and authority can bring. In Newman's case, a formal theological education and extensive theological publication gave the experience; ordination gave the authority. In Carlyle's case, experience and authority came from an intense Calvinistic upbringing and a thorough reading in English and German theology, as well as from his vocation as philosopher.

Women possessed neither experience nor authority. They rarely had the formal education that would have allowed them to use a system of biblical hermeneutics with confidence (although some might, like Carlyle and Ruskin, have learned its principles through long church attendance and private study). More important, Victorian women did not have the authority to speak the language of biblical types. By Pauline injunction, they had been admonished to "learn in silence with all subjection." "I suffer not a woman to teach,"

St. Paul had written, "nor to usurp authority over the man" (I Tim. 2.11–12). By ecclesiastical decree, they were denied ordination in the Church of England during the whole of the nineteenth century, prohibited from interpreting the Scriptures to a congregation in most Dissenting sects, and banned from Methodist pulpits by the Convention of 1803.[22] John Wesley's comments to Sarah Crosby, a woman who felt the call to preach, are instructive: "Even in public you may properly enough intermix short *exhortations* with prayer; but keep as far from what is called preaching as you can; therefore never take a text; never speak in continued discourse without some break, about four or five minutes."[23] For Wesley the crucial issue is not public speaking but taking a biblical text—and, worse yet, expounding upon the text in "continued discourse." That sort of entry into hermeneutic territory was forbidden to women.

Wesley's comment is not as nasty as Samuel Johnson's, which compares "a woman's preaching" to "a dog's walking on its hind legs": "It is not well done; but you are surprised to find it done at all."[24] But ultimately it is Wesley's comment that is the more inhibiting for women who would engage in the kind of interpretation required for spiritual autobiography, for Wesley removes the source from which autobiographical interpretation proceeds. Moreover, Wesley represents the stance that became increasingly common during the eighteenth century as biblical hermeneutics came to be regarded as a privileged endeavor, one that required knowledge of the original biblical languages as well as a systematic use of interpretive principles and procedures.

No woman was denied, of course, the right to appropriate the lessons or models of the biblical text privately; indeed, from the pulpits that denied women the right to expound that text publically, they were encouraged to apply it to their personal lives. But such encouragement, delivered from the same mouths that repeated the Pauline injunction, implicitly told women they could handle the text only after a priest or a man (the Pauline text gave husbands a priestly authority over their wives) had interpreted it for them first. They were themselves unfit to deal critically with the text—that is, to expound or interpret it on their own.

That this judgment perplexed and provoked Victorian women is evident from the prose writing of the period, fictional as well as autobiographical. In her first novel George Eliot makes the Methodist decision to ban women from preaching the subject of familial controversy and the "resolution" to her heroine's career.[25] Charlotte Brontë makes the male authority to interpret biblical models for women a tacit concern in *Jane Eyre*, an explicit theme in *Shirley*. Harriet Martineau makes a male's refusal to explain a theological dilemma the crisis of her autobiography and the impetus for her search for a non-theological hermeneutics. For these women and others, the hermeneutic prohibition represented a historical fact which was, legitimately, a subject for prose writing. Their treatment of the fact, moreover, suggests that they understood its implications for the writing of autobiography—or, to put it more generally, for the shaping of their lives, whether in reality or in literature. For them, as for us, the two were intertwined.

Of Victorian women writers, Charlotte Brontë was perhaps the most sensitive to the barriers that prevented women from entering the domain of spiritual autobiography—just as Harriet Martineau was the most eager to surmount the barriers. Before turning to Martineau's response to the female autobiographer's dilemma, therefore, we might consider Brontë's exploration of the generic problem. It is no coincidence that Brontë chose to write autobiographical novels. They were, of course, the third alternative to traditional autobiography that women might take. As fiction, the novels provided Brontë with a means of interpreting the experiences of her past without exposing her private self or violating social and theological taboos. As novels that mimic the form of autobiography, moreover, they allowed her to explore self-consciously the conventions of a genre she found prohibitive and the implications of the hermeneutic prohibition for women who wanted to be autobiographers.

Jane Eyre is an experiment in the autobiographical mode: Brontë subtitled the novel "An Autobiography," presents it as a work edited by another (as women's accounts usually were), and makes her narrator's primary concern that of interpretation: interpretation for self-understanding and self-direction.[26] Critics of the novel have pointed out, moreover, that Brontë uses biblical types "to describe the moral and spiritual condition of [her] character[s]."[27] But Brontë does more than use types to delineate character. She discriminates nicely between when a woman may apply types and when she may not, between what aspects of a woman's life are accessible to typological interpretation and what aspects are beyond (or beneath) interpretation.

In the first third of the novel, Brontë allows her protagonist only to narrate her experience—without system, without interpretation. For these chapters, Jane's experience at the entrance to Lowood School becomes the emblem of her difficulty as autobiographer. She can see the name of the institution and read the biblical inscription below it: "Let your light so shine before men that they may see your good works, and glorify your Father which is in heaven." Jane cannot, however, make interpretive connections between what her eyes read and what the biblical text says: "I read these words over and over again: I felt that an explanation belonged to them, and was unable fully to penetrate their import. I was still pondering and signification of 'Institution,' and endeavouring to make out a connection between the first words and the verse of Scripture, when the sound of a cough close behind me, made me turn my head" (V, 42). The hermeneutic impulse is present (Jane feels the need for "explanation" and ponders "the signification"), but in this section of her autobiography, the biblical text provides no means of self-interpretation. Indeed, unlike the authorities at Lowood, she believes that it does not illumine her experience.

It is only when Jane falls in love with Rochester, discovers his mad wife in the attic, and flees Thornfield to avoid what she fears might become a moral bondage, that the biblical types begin to apply. Then the system of hermeneutics traditional in the spiritual autobiography gives meaning to her experience, and she attempts an interpretation of her narrative. On the morning she flees Thornfield, she reads in her experience a repetition of the tenth plague of Moses: "My hopes were all dead—struck with a subtle doom, such as in one night, fell on all the first-born in the land of Egypt. I looked on my cherished wishes, yesterday so blooming and glowing: they lay stark, chill, livid corpses that could never revive" (XXVI, 260). She recognizes this plague as a spiritual warning: she has made Rochester "an idol," "almost my hope of heaven," and has substituted an earthly Canaan for a spiritual one, in her dreams imagining beyond the "wild waters" of an "unquiet sea" "a shore, sweet as the hills of Beulah" (XV, 133). As she flees her Egypt and wanders (literally) in a wilderness, she continues the interpretation: "I could not turn, nor retrace one step. God must have led me on" (XXVII, 283). Moreover, as she views her life retrospectively some months later, she still recognizes a providential exodus: "Yes; I feel now that I was right when I adhered to principle and law, and scorned and crushed the insane promptings of a frenzied moment. God directed me to a correct choice: I thank his providence for the guidance" (XXXI, 316).

If Brontë allows a female autobiographer to interpret her experience with the traditional patterns of the spiritual autobiography, she at the same time makes us understand that Jane's interpretation is subversive: it violates hermeneutic rules. First of all, the male characters of the novel also use types to interpret Jane's character: Rochester calls her a vexatious Delilah over whom he "long[s] to exert a fraction of Samson's strength" (XXVII, 266), and St. John Rivers says he suspects in her "the vacillating fears of Lot's wife" which "incline [her] to look back" (XXXI, 318). As these men would have it, the types appropriate to delineate Jane's character are only those of Old Testament women—the lovers, wives, and mothers of the Bible who offer limited autobiographical models. Jane's attempt to apply the types universally (sexlessly), while in theory sound, becomes in practice subversive of cultural codes.

More important, when Jane tries to turn her interpretation into action, she meets with imperious resistance from St. John, who thinks he offers a more authoritative interpretation for her life. St. John, too, foresees an exodus—but the destiny he envisions is India, not Thornfield or Canaan. His text for Jane is the Revelation of St. John, "the vision of the new heaven and the new earth" (XXXV,

367), and when Jane refuses to apply his text to her life, he decrees that she has refused "the Christian's cross and the angel's crown" (XXXV, 370). Of St. John, Jane observes, "as a man, he would have wished to coerce me into obedience" (XXXIV, 360), and as a clergyman, St. John had the authority to expect obedience. Through Jane's comment Brontë recognizes the limits placed upon the woman who attempts to become an autobiographer, and at the same time she articulates her heroine's need to exercise hermeneutic freedom, to interpret her life for herself.

If a woman is to write autobiography, she must be allowed to use the language and conventions of the autobiographer, and Jane Eyre does finally shape her own account by using the traditional language and interpretive patterns. Bronte even allows her another sort of hermeneutic victory. At the end of the novel, when Jane returns to Thornfield, Rochester no longer thinks of her in gender-linked types. He has somehow learned the universal intention of the biblical models: instead of Delilah, she is now David to his Saul (XXXVII, 386). But in the world outside the novel, Brontë assumes no such enlightenment. Jane Eyre's autobiography makes its way into the world through the offices of a man, Currer Bell, who appears on the title page as the editor and who, according to Victorian convention, selects and arranges what a woman has to say about her life.

It is in this historical context, then, and with these generic precedents that Harriet Martineau published her *Autobiography* in 1877. According to her own testimony, the early part of her life seemed much in its misery like the childhood that Brontë depicts in the opening chapters of *Jane Eyre*. When Brontë's novel appeared, in fact, Martineau was "taxed with the authorship by more than one personal friend, and charged by others, and even by relatives, with knowing the author, and having supplied some of the facts of the first volume from [her] own childhood" (II, 324). But anyone who understood Martineau's temperament might have realized that *Jane Eyre*, however similar in biographical detail, was not for her a likely form of autobiographical expression. Martineau had little talent for Brontë's imaginative "making out"; indeed, after the age of eighteen, she claimed a total inability to invent fictions. More important, Martineau had no desire to circumvent a primary literary tradition simply because she was a woman or to write autobiographical fiction because it was a typical form of feminine self-expression. Throughout her career, she had consistently adopted male forms, and in writing an autobiography, that meant creating a thoroughly hermeneutic example of the genre.[28]

Martineau's response produced one of the few instances (perhaps the only instance) of a spiritual autobiography written and published by an Englishwoman during the nineteenth century, for the *Autobiography* is an account of genuine moral and intellectual growth. Written as a testimony to the regenerative power of philosophical positivism and as an illustration of that philosophy's law of human development, it is intended as a model for others, male and female, to follow in the interpretation of their lives. In order to make the genre of spiritual autobiography expressive of her own experience and philosophy, however, Martineau had to transform some of its most basic characteristics.

Of these, the most significant was the language of interpretation which, as Brontë so clearly recognized, depended upon a system of biblical hermeneutics that excluded women. Like her male contemporaries, Martineau understood this language and its patterns of interpretation thoroughly: as a young girl, she had been educated at the Reverend Issac Perry's grammar school in Norwich, a Dissenting academy for boys, and when her formal education ceased, she set herself a course of reading in theology and philosophy as rigorous as that of her college-bound brother.[29] As her autobiography recounts, she spontaneously thought and spoke in biblical patterns for over twenty years of her life. But biblical allusions and typological analogies are virtually absent from the *Autobiography*, at least as absent as one can imagine in a prose work written in English. Except for the discussion of American slavery, in which she repeats episodes of the Exodus as they were applied by slaves and abolitionists themselves, Martineau seems systematically to have expunged the old biblical language from her account of spiritual and intellectual development.

Without biblical typology to give coherence to experience, most autobiographers would have found themselves at a loss—without the traditional system yet without a comprehensive substitute. Women writers necessarily began with such a loss, and as Brontë's attempt at myth-making in *Shirley* suggests, substitutes were difficult to create. But in 1855 Martineau had a ready alternative. In 1851, four years before composing the *Autobiography*, she had begun an English condensation of Auguste Comte's six-volume *Cours de Philosophie Positive*, and in 1853 she published a two-volume translation of the work, *The Positive Philosophy of Auguste Comte*.[30] In the place of biblical types and language, she substitutes in her *Autobiography* the terminology of positivism and its "great fundamental law": that each race and humankind as a whole pass through three stages of development— "the theological, or fictitious; the metaphysical, or abstract; and the scientific, or positive."[31]

As in typological practice, these stages apply as readily to the individual human being as to the race, an application that Martineau explains in the first chapter of *The Positive Philosophy*:

> The progress of the individual mind is not only an illustration, but an indirect evidence of that of the general mind. The point of departure of the individual and of the race being the same, the phases of the mind of a man correspond to the epochs of the mind of the race. Now, each of us is aware, if he looks back upon his own history, that he was a theologian in his childhood, a metaphysician in his youth, and a natural philosopher in his manhood.

As the final sentence suggests, Martineau believed her own life to delineate the same stages, and thus she found in Comtian philosophy a formal and authoritative system of self-interpretation. She organizes her *Autobiography* according to the Comtian pattern, moving from an early religious period (1802–19) through what she calls a "metaphysical fog" (1819–39) to a final positivistic stage of thought (1839–55). Each stage encompasses roughly two books of the total six, with book V representing a transitional period between metaphysical confusion and her final positivisitic stance in 1855.

Explained this abstractly, Martineau's method sounds like a rather routine (and dull) substitution of one interpretive system for another, hardly an innovative solution to the dilemma of the woman autobiographer. But if the *Autobiography* is Comtian in form and method, it became so only despite obstacles as vexing as those Newman faced as a Catholic autobiographer and only because Martineau had wrestled with hermeneutic issues for thirty years. It came as the result of an intense struggle with the theological concept of predestination and an equally intense, if muted struggle with her brother Thomas over the right of young women to have such concepts explained.

At the center of the *Autobiography*, we find a crisis in hermeneutics. This crisis represents the classic dilemma of Eve and her daughters. According to Martineau, she had puzzled as a young girl over the old theological problem of foreknowledge and free will and had finally asked her older brother to explain it: "how, if God foreknew every thing, we could be blamed or rewarded for our conduct, which was thus absolutely settled for us beforehand" (I, 44). The young man had no answer for his shrewd little sister and so did what most young men would do: he told her she was too young to understand. Balked of a solution at age eleven, she spent much of the rest of her life formulating her own, a solution which she found first in Necessarianism and later in Comtian positivism. In the text of the *Autobiography*, the search for an adequate theological answer—indeed, for a hermeneutic system capable of explaining the intricacies of her experience—becomes the equivalent of Bunyan's search for the appropriate biblical type.

In essence what Martineau derived from Necessarianism was a principle: all action is determined by antecedent causes. That the principle might sound overly simple to those who did not embrace Necessarianism, she admitted in the *Autobiography*: "Some, no doubt, say of the doctrine that every body can prove it, but nobody believes it; an assertion so far from true as not to be worth contesting.... [I]t appears to me, now as then, that none but Necessarians at all understand the Necessarian doctrine. This is merely saying in other words that its truth is so irresistible that, when once understood, it is adopted as a matter of course" (I, 110). To the young girl, nonetheless, the revelation lay not so much in the principle itself, but in its

implications for moral action. What she had discovered independent-
ly of Tom and other male authority was that there is no "self-
determining power, independent of laws, in the human will" (I,
111).

Necessarians contended that every man or woman is the maker of
his or her own fortune. All action might be determined by antecedent
causes, but one's own actions and discriminations were necessary links
in the chain of cause and effect. As the Unitarian W. E. Channing
explained in a letter roughly contemporary with Martineau's discovery, "the apprehension that [men's] endeavours to promote their own
happiness will have a certain and necessary effect, and that no well-
judged effort of theirs will be lost, instead of disposing them to remit
their labour, will encourage them to exert themselves with redoubled
vigor; and the *desire of happiness* cannot but be allowed to have the same
influence upon all systems."[32] For daily life, Necessarianism gave
Martineau a "new method of interpretation" which she could apply to
her own behavior and to an infinite number of cases "with readiness
and ease" (I, 109). In her autobiography, the Necessarian method
assumes the function that typological principles and patterns hold in
the traditional spiritual autobiography. In effect, she creates a new set
of scriptures for the philosophical elect, defining that elect with the
same exclusivity that Bunyan describes in the Bedford Christians:
"[A]ll the best minds I know are among the Necessarians;—all indeed
which are qualified to discuss the subject at all" (I, 110).

In conjunction with the patterns derived from Comtian positivism, then, Martineau uses a Necessarian mode of analysis to
determine the influences upon the subsequent actions in her life. She
begins, logically, with the early religious phase. For the first third of
her life, Martineau had been an intensely pious Unitarian, a true
spiritual descendant of her Huguenot ancestors who had left France
after the revocation of the Edict of Nantes and settled in Protestant
East Anglia. Martineau explains her early religious phase just as one
would expect a Necessarian and Comtian to explain it: not as a period
of sinful error or unfortunate misdirection, but as the effect of specific
circumstances and influences and as the usual phase with which
intellectual development begins.

Explaining her early religiosity, for example, she notes that as an infant in delicate health she had been sent to convalesce in a farmhouse outside of Norwich, where her nurse was "a Methodist or melancholy Calvinist of some sort" (I, 12). This stay produced an immediate effect:

> I came home the absurdist little preacher of my years . . . that ever was. I used to nod my head emphatically, and say "Never ky for tyfles:" "Dooty fust, and pleasure afterwards," and so forth: and I sometimes got courage to edge up to strangers, and ask them to give me—"a maxim." Almost before I could join letters, I got some sheets of paper, and folded them into a little square book, and wrote, in double lines, two or three in a page, my beloved maxims. (I, 12)

It contributed to a lasting trait of personality as well: "It was probably what I picked up at Carleton that made me so intensely religious as I certainly was from a very early age" (I, 12).

So, too, did other religious experiences shape Martineau's personality permanently: from the childhood practice of writing sermon abstracts, she learned "the highest use in fixing [her] attention" (I, 33); from her obsession with tabulations of moral virtues and vices, she "made out that great step in the process of thought and knowledge, —that whereas Judaism was a preceptive religion, Christianity was mainly a religion of principles" (I, 36). She also learned to rival "any old puritan preacher in [her] free use of scripture," a lesson invaluable to a woman who later wanted not only to write spiritual autobiography but transform its interpretive mode.

Martineau neither attributes these incidents to providence, as the traditional autobiographer would, nor wastes time lamenting their deleterious effects, as an autobiographer like Ruskin or Gosse might. Her attitude is strictly Necessarian. The incidents occurred; they produced effects; the effects should be understood. To Henry Atkinson, her philosophical comrade and co-author, she explained in a letter reprinted in full in the *Autobiography*, that the old religious superstitions actually did her good as a child:

I have found the good of those old superstitions in my day. How it might have been with me (how much better) if I had had parents of your way of thinking, there is no saying. As it was, I was *very* religious (far beyond the knowledge and intentions of my parents) till I was quite grown up. I don't know what I should have done without my faith; for I was an unhealthy and most unhappy child, and had no other resource. (II, 288)

Moreover, as a Comtian, she accepts these early incidents of religiosity as predictable stages of a child's development:

Every child, and every childish tribe of people, transfers its own consciousness, by a supposition so necessary as to be an instinct, to all external objects, so as to conclude them all to be alive like itself; and passes through this stage of belief to a more reasonable view: and, in like manner, more advanced nations and individuals suppose a whole pantheon of Gods first,—and then a trinity,—and then a single deity;—all the divine beings being exaggerated men, regarding the universe from the human point of view, and under the influences of human notions and affections. (II, 280)

Absent from her analysis is a lingering sense of failure or shame, which she certainly felt at the time, but deems irrational to express now as a Comtian autobiographer.

The *Autobiography* continues to detail the metaphysical and positive phases of Martineau's life—with the same Necessarian detachment, the same dispassionate tone. Beginning with three prize essays for the Central Unitarian Association (1831), written to advocate the Unitarian faith "to the notice of Catholics, Jews, and Mohammedans" (I, 150), Martineau explains that she left the theological phase behind and entered into "those regions of metaphysical fog in which most deserters from Unitarianism abide for the rest of their time" (I, 156–57). The prize essays, which won her much acclaim among Unitarians and made her their "chosen expositor" (I, 158), she judges in retrospect to be "morbid, fantastical, and therefore unphilosophical and untrue" (I, 157), just as she identifies "the fundamental fault" of her later *Society in America* (1837) as "its metaphysical framework, and the abstract treatment of what must necessarily be a concrete subject" (II, 103) and criticizes the final work of her metaphysical phase, *Life in the Sickroom* (1843), for "the *débris* of the theological" it includes, debris compatible with only a metaphysical, not a positive order of society. "I gave forth," she explains, "the contemporary persuasions of the imagination, or narratives of old traditions, as if they had been durable convictions, ascertained by personal exertion of my faculties" (II, 173).

Actually, much of the detail that the *Autobiography* includes within the metaphysical phase has little to do with spiritual or intellectual development. Martineau recounts her inspiration for the immensely successful Practical Economy Series (1832−34), recollects anecdotes about famous London figures, and describes visits to slave plantations and abolitionist meetings in America.[33] Yet even amidst literary anecdotes and details of travel and disagreements with publishers, Martineau finds occasion to apply positivist principles. She uses the beginnings or endings of sections to reiterate these or the Necessarian basis of her autobiographical method. "Now the summer of my life was bursting forth without any interval of spring," she writes at the close of a period of great literary success.

> My life began with winter, burst suddenly into summer, and is now ending with autumn,—mild and sunny. I have had no spring; but that cannot be helped now. It was a moral disadvantage, as well as a great loss of happiness; but we all have our moral disadvantages to make the best of, and "happiness" is *not,* as the poet says, "our being's end and aim," but the result of one faculty among many, which must be occasionally overborne by others, if there is to be any effective exercise of the whole being. (I, 180−81)

The stance is philosophic to the core, accepting of the influences that could not be prevented, insistent upon the responsibility of adding to them one's own positive causes.

Once she has reviewed the factors contributing to her intellectual development between 1839 and 1844, the "five heavy years" that produced *Life in the Sickroom* and various controversial essays on mesmerism, Martineau has in effect brought her account of spiritual progress to its final stage. Not that she failed to grow morally and intellectually after 1844. That would have been contrary to the premise of her *Household Education*, which argues that education—the individual's improvement in intellectual skills and moral qualities—should be a lifelong occupation.[34] But although she had much more to recount of her studies and literary efforts, and although the encounter with Comte's *Cours de Philosophie Positive* occurred a decade later, her *Autobiography* had already delineated the three Comtian stages of progress, and there was little more to interpret.

As Martineau substitutes a Necessarian mode of interpretation and a Comtian pattern of development for the traditional principles and patterns of biblical typology, she inevitably revises several conventions of the spiritual autobiography: conventions of form (the dramatic conversion, the Pisgah vision) and of mode (the introspective stance). As evidence of the philosophical consistency that Martineau brings to her *Autobiography*, these revisions are significant in and of themselves. They are also significant for the possibilities they suggest for women's autobiography and, more broadly, for the shifts they anticipate in the entire genre, particularly in late nineteenth century attempts at "scientific" self-interpretation.

In both the conversion episode and the Pisgah vision, Martineau revises the conventions in order to deprive them of theological content and substitute her own philosophical principles. As she recounts her discovery of Necessarianism, for instance, she repeats the primary characteristics of religious conversion as they were understood in the nineteenth century. In *The Varieties of Religious Experience* (1901–02) William James lists them as (1) "the loss of all the worry, the sense that all is ultimately well," and "the willingness *to be*, even though the outer conditions should remain the same," (2) "the sense of perceiving truths not known before," and (3) "the objective change

which the world often appears to undergo."[35] Martineau describes
the same feelings: in her own words, a restoration of "peace" to her
"troubled mind," a new sense of life as "something fresh and wonder-
fully interesting," and an astonishment at "the vastness of the view
opened to me" and "the prodigious change requisite in my moral
views and self-management" (I, 109–10). Her language, too, echoes
the vocabulary of religious conversion: "I was like a new creature in
the strength of a sound conviction," she writes. Making metaphorical
St. Paul's blinding light, she recalls that "a new light spread through
my mind, and I began to experience a steady growth in self-command,
courage, and consequent integrity and disinterestedness" (I, 110).

Despite these resemblances to religious conversion, Martineau
takes care to label her experience a "revolution" rather than a conversion, and she avoids here as in the rest of the *Autobiography* any
explicitly biblical allusions. (The light, for example, is self-consciously offered as metaphor or, as James would call it, an internal
"photism.")[36] This combination of adherence to and deviation from
the conventional episode of conversion answers a need to control, as
autobiographer, the difference between past and present selves. As
her former self, Martineau had understood the discovery of Necessarianism to be a philosophical version of the experience that Dissenting
theology called conversion; at the time it occurred, she had interpreted it (perhaps recorded it in a private diary) in conventional
terms—that is, in the old theological language. As her present self,
she prefers to explain the experience as "revolution," a word she uses
throughout the *Autobiography* to mean a necessary and total change,
the inevitable result of antecedent causes (II, 447). Thus, the theological language is omitted, superseded by the philosophical.

The juxtaposition of past consciousness and present understanding
creates what Jean Starobinski describes as stylistic "redundancy," a
feature of autobiographical writing that "may disturb the message
itself." Style in autobiography has the function of establishing a
relation between the author and her past. "The past," Starobinski
explains, "can never be evoked except with respect to the present: the
'reality' of by-gone days is only such to the consciousness which,

today, gathering up their present image, cannot avoid imposing upon them its own form, its style."[37]

Martineau uses style in the conversion episode to establish a relationship between author and past reality (and between author and reader) that she wishes: the reality of the past self is indeed disturbed, but deliberately so in favor of the message of the present. One effect of the episode is to vitiate the confidence of Christians who offer internal phenomena as evidence of salvation. Martineau's own "revolution" undermines the validity of internal evidence per se, for it makes clear that anyone, even a Necessarian and philosophical atheist, can experience the phenomena of conversion. Internal phenomena cannot thus prove divine election or the validity of a theological position. A corollary is one that William James was later to adopt as the premise of his work: that conversion is not exclusively a Christian experience.

Yet might we not also say of Martineau's style, to reverse Starobinski's formula, that the language of by-gone days imposes itself, too, on the reality of the present? Does not her reliance upon Pauline metaphors of conversion, however effaced in the *Autobiography*, disturb the message of the present that she intends to convey? Throughout her life Martineau worried about precisely this problem. In describing spiritual phenomena particularly, she feared that her use of the traditional language of theology might delude readers into believing that she meant something orthodox when in fact she intended to be quite unorthodox. To Henry Atkinson, she proposed inventing a new vocabulary for their joint *Letters on the Laws of Man's Nature* (1851), but when Atkinson argued that philosophers must use familiar language in order to communicate to their readers, she abandoned the notion.

Whether or not his argument is valid, Martineau compromises in the *Autobiography* between it and her original plan by resorting to some traditional language while superimposing Comtian terminology upon it. This compromise, never fully satisfactory, nonetheless becomes her working out of Comtian principles in a specifically literary context. Comtian doctrine would suggest that, just as women and men who have reached the "positive" stage can correctly review the earlier phases of their lives, so she, as autobiographer, can review the earlier phases of the spiritual autobiography and transform or re-define the generic conventions according to a more enlightened philosophy. As Comtian philosopher, then, Martineau can maintain what she considers the valid features of the literary form, while stripping it of false theological debris. This process creates the layering of styles that Starbonski calls "redundancy."

Martineau's revision of the conversion episode achieves a subtlety of style in its balance between past and present selves, between repetition of and deviation from conventions of form. In contrast, her version of the Pisgah vision seems rhetorically heavy-handed. In the final episode of the *Autobiography*, titled "Prospects of the Human Race" in announcement of its generic intention, there is only the autobiographer's present self to deliver the message. That self is intent upon divesting its language of the theological and radically transforming the convention of autobiographical closure. Whereas Bunyan, for instance, uses the Pisgah vision to promise his readers the blessing of Canaan or Cowper assures himself of an earthly repose in God's mercy, Martineau uses the prospect vision to point out the delusiveness of the Christian doctrines of immortality and bodily resurrection and then to castigate the Church for the "moral injury and suffering" perpetrated "by the superstititions of the Christian religion" (II, 436, 444).

What she means in the first instance is that, scientifically speaking, bodily resurrection represents an impossible reversal of natural processes: the evidence for such a doctrine or the immortality of the soul simply does not exist. What she means in the second is more original. Martineau came to believe that the Christian obsession with death and final judgment was morally injurious: it focuses attention on the self rather than on others to whom one has social and moral responsibilities (II, 436).

Martineau revises the Pisgah episode to show—both in action and in philosophy—how one ought to face death. She begins with her own deathbed scene, a convention of the spiritual memoir, and describes her repose in the prospect of death and the calm assurance of the

"cheerful,—even merry—little party we are at home here" (II, 440).
In ironic contrast, she quotes the responses of Christian strangers and
acquaintances who are "kind enough to interest themselves in my
affairs": the one who sends a New Testament ("as if I had never seen
one before"), intimating modestly that, although she may feel happy,
she "ought not to be"; the one who insists "that Christian consola-
tions are administered to [her] by God without [her] knowing it"; and
the others who send her religious books and tracts "too bad in matter
and spirit to be safe reading for my servants; so instead of the
waste-basket, they go into the fire" (II, 441, 443). With these
personal anecdotes, Martineau demonstrates the superiority of her
philosophical views for the conduct of the individual man or woman.
She is also concerned, however, to show their superiority on a universal plane.

This intention she initiates (strangely) by transcribing a letter
written in 1849 in which she virtually predicts the Crimean War. In
the letter Martineau divides Europe into two opposing forces ("Asiatic despotism" versus the enlightened nations of western Europe) and
prophesies "a long and bloody warfare" for "the first principles of
social liberty." "It is my belief," she writes, "that the war has actually
begun, and that, though there may be occasional lulls, no man now
living will see the end of it" (II, 451, 454). Apart from its obvious
interest to a mid-Victorian audience, caught up in the Crimean War,
quoting such a letter makes no sense at this point in the *Autobiography*.
Indeed, it seems to be a lapse in an otherwise careful revision of the
Pisgah convention. Why should a letter predicting war be Martineau's choice to demonstrate the superiority of Necessarianism and
Comtian philosophy? And why should she prefer an old letter to a
direct statement of her current views?

What Martineau seems to have intended is an illustration on the
historical level of Necessarian and Comtian principles in their prophetic function and, by illustration, of their superiority to Christian
prophecy. Typically, at the close of a spiritual autobiography the
author looks ahead with his readers to the joys of Canaan—by which
he means an immortal life in heavenly bliss. To Martineau this sort of
prophecy, with its claim to know by divine revelation the unknow-

able, is spurious. A "prophecy" that uses antecedent causes to foresee
future events, however, is possible. A Necessarian, through astute
analysis of the European political situation, might follow the causes to
their necessary result and hence predict a conflict of Asiatic despotism
against western enlightenment or, more specifically, of Russia and
her allies against England and hers.

Written before the outbreak of the Crimean War, the letter
additionally serves as a formal validation of Martineau's authority as
prophet, and it confers more generally the right to prophesy about the
future of the human race. This prophecy closes the *Autobiography* as a
restatement of the Comtian philosophy that has informed the entire
work; in its pure exposition, it repeats the formal closure that we have
seen before in Bunyan's "Conclusion," Carlyle's Book Third, and
Newman's "Religious Opinions since 1845." Martineau notes "the
successive mythologies" that have arisen and then declined. She
declares that the last, Christianity, "is now not only sinking to the
horizon, but paling in the dawn of a brighter time. The dawn is
unmistakable; and the sun will not be long in coming up. The last of
the mythologies is about to vanish before the flood of a brighter light"
(II, 461). That flood is, of course, the light of scientific fact and
positivist philosophy. In that light "the immoralities which have
attended all mythologies" will disappear, humankind will arise "to a
capacity for higher work than saving themselves," and the race will be
"trained in the morality which belongs to ascertained truth" (II,
461).

If Martineau writes here with a heavy hand, she does so consciously
to make her intentions obvious. No reader can miss the intensity with
which she attacks Christian morality and denigrates the spiritual
autobiography, with its emphasis on individual conversion, for its
fundamental selfishness. The obviousness results from a singleness of
voice, from Martineau's fear of verbal ambiguity, and from the
expositional mode itself. We should also note, however, some less
than explicit intentions. The closing prophecy allows, I think, an
otherwise muted expression in the *Autobiography* of Martineau's deep
frustration as a woman and woman writer. In its strident tone and
assertive prophecy, the passage is unusual. It fails to view universal

history with the same absence of blame or censure that Martineau
maintains in her personal history, and it singles out Christian theology specifically for the devastating moral and psychological effects it
has had upon human lives, including her own and those of other
women.

We should remember that the initial hermeneutic crisis of Martineau's *Autobiography* focuses on the theological question of foreknowledge and free will: "how, if God foreknew every thing, we
could be blamed or rewarded for our conduct, which was thus
absolutely settled for us beforehand" (I, 44). As a young girl, Martineau had felt the impact of Christian theology assigning blame and
reward for her actions, yet she had found this theology unable to
explain its authority for doing so. We should remember, too, that she
identifies Christian theology (in the guise of an older brother) with
male authority, which is insistent upon its rights but ungrounded in
its assertions. Martineau's anger at this alignment of power and
ignorance does not express itself directly here or elsewhere in the
Autobiography because of other decisions she has made about autobiographical conventions. Rather, the "Prospects of the Human Race"
section becomes her response to patriarchal Christian authority. It
envisions a better world, free of gender restrictions; through its
Necessarianism, it answers the questions of predestination and free
will; and, most important, its answer is formulated by a woman.

In such revisions of autobiographical conventions of form, Martineau embodies an implicit argument about the approach women
should take to convention and authority generally—whether social,
religious, or literary. Rather than confront conventions angrily or
reject a dominant literary tradition out of hand, Martineau's example
suggests first an understanding of the forms and then a revision
according to an enlightened philosophy. Her position may seem, in
Elaine Showalter's terms, more like a "feminine" than a "female"
response, involving an "imitation of the prevailing modes of the
dominant tradition." But in no sense does Martineau represent an
"internalization" of the dominant tradition's "standards of art" or "its
views on social roles."[38] Her example suggests, in fact, that the best
way to avoid such internalization is through self-conscious literary

revision. And her *Autobiography* demonstrates the possibility of creating, through revision, a thoroughly original work.

Martineau's originality as a woman writer displays itself throughout the *Autobiography* in its confrontation of a dominant male tradition and its insistence upon gender-free patterns of human development. In the history of autobiography as a genre, Martineau is original in another respect: in 1855, she may well have been the first English autobiographer to substitute a scientific model of self-interpretation for the traditional patterns of biblical hermeneutics. Moreover, her revision of a major autobiographical convention of mode—the introspective stance—marks a third innovation within the genre which had significant effect upon subsequent autobiographers' treatment of the "self."

As a Comtian, Martineau had committed herself to a form of autobiography that depicts "the growth of a human mind" (I, 52), but not to one that focuses obsessively on the self. Indeed, she rejects traditional notions of the self, which she considers merely metaphysical substitutes for the theological concept of the soul. Metaphysicians find it necessary, she explains in her redaction of Comte, to preserve "the unity of what they [call] the I, that it might correspond with the unity of the *soul*, in obedience to the requisitions of the theological philosophy, of which metaphysics is...the final transformation."[39] Instead of detailing the minute fluctuations of an inner being in which she does not believe, or despairing as later writers would about the impossibility of inscribing the self in the text, Martineau chooses to trace in the *Autobiography* the forces that contribute to the growth of a mind—and these forces, while including the internal, consist in greater proportion of the observable and external.

Tracing external influences is not in itself an innovative act for the writing of spiritual autobiography. Bunyan discusses the influence of the Ranters upon his spiritual belief, to cite only one instance from *Grace Abounding*, and Newman makes "the circumstances in which I had been placed" one of two primary influences in his conversion to

Roman Catholicism.[40] But Newman also acknowledges opinions that were "the birth of my own mind" as the second primary influence— assuming, as he does, that the Spirit of God participated in such births. Martineau will have nothing to do with Newman's second source of knowledge. In her estimate it produces a faulty interpretation of life, the sort a "captive" might make "from the gleams and shadows and faint colours reflected on his dungeon walls." When she discovered Necessarianism and positivism, she explains, she "got out of the prison of my own self, wherein I had formerly sat trying to interpret life and the world" (II, 333). "To form any true notion whatever of any of the affairs of the universe," she insists, "we must take our stand in the external world,—regarding man as one of the products and subjects of the everlasting laws of the universe, and not as the favourite of his Maker" (II, 333−34).

In the *Autobiography*, Martineau takes her stand in the external world by regarding herself as the product of universal laws. This shift in perspective anticipates a general shift within the genre that becomes noticeable later in the century with Darwin's *Autobiography*, Butler's *The Way of All Flesh*, Spencer's *Autobiography*, the American *Education of Henry Adams*, and numerous lesser autobiographies that approach the individual man or woman as scientific specimen. In these accounts, as in Martineau's, it is the principle of antecedent causes that determines what materials the autobiographers select from the past and what interpretations they make of their lives.

We might describe this new stance in traditional narrative terms as the assumption of a new point of view, but Martineau would approve the terminology only so long as it is "point of view" and not simply "view." To her, "views" are for those "still within the dogmatic circle or the metaphysical wilderness." "Point of view" represents "the grand difference" between "the dogmatists, the metaphysical speculators, and the positive philosophers": "The first take their stand on tradition, and the second on their own consciousness. . . . We, seeing the total failure in the pursuit of truth consequent on [the latter] choice of a standpoint, try to get out of the charmed circle of illusion, and to plant our foot in the centre of the universe, as nearly as we can manage it, and, at all events, outside of ourselves" (III,

324–25). Although she does not articulate the difference, this assumption of a new "objective" stance places the autobiographer in a position once occupied by God. In Augustine's *Confessions*, it is only God who can stand outside the self and view man objectively; man is bound to the "narrow mansion of the soul."[41] Martineau might have accepted the metaphor (substituting "prison" for the euphemism "narrow mansion"), but disagreed with Augustine that God could "enter in" and "enlarge it"—or, for that matter, that enlarging the soul could improve man's perspective on himself.

In the *Autobiography* the assumption of an objective point of view follows logically from the scientific method Martineau chooses. It follows also from a personal rejection of the self-laceration that conventionally accompanies the introspective stance and from a deep understanding of the means by which women could gain authority as writers. As a Unitarian, Martineau had never shown much tolerance for the evangelical plea of utter worthlessness: as R. K. Webb neatly sums up her attitude, "to her Cowper was a mere slave to God."[42] As a Necessarian, she considered it requisite to deny any "morbid appetite for pathological contemplation,—physical or moral" (II, 148). Castigating oneself for physical and moral deficiencies or treating them, in the Christian sense, either as trials or temptations about which to feel shame was a waste of time. Necessarians simply accepted their condition as the natural result of antecedent factors and did their best in future actions to add beneficial factors to those over which they had no control.

In the writing of autobiography, Martineau's attitude encouraged a shift away from episodes of failure toward experiences of moral and intellectual growth; it encouraged, too, an elimination of blame, either of oneself or others. Her autobiography achieves, as a result, an evenness of tone and almost scientific detachment—and the authority that both of these bring. It is a rare autobiographer who can look back on a childhood and youth, as emotionally stunted as that described in *Jane Eyre*, and observe calmly that her life "began in winter" and "had no spring," but still be "satisfied in a higher sense than that in which the Necessarian is always satisfied" (I, 180–81).

It is a rare woman autobiographer, too, who understands the

importance of such a statement. The satisfaction of the Necessarian, of which Martineau speaks, is not that of emotional expression or personal justification, but that of analyzing the separate pieces of a life, of seeing how they fit, of interpreting their relationships and thus life itself, in a "positive" spirit—that is, according to "what can be rigorously demonstrated from and sustained by facts" (III, 308). The testimony to such satisfaction by a woman writer is the best evidence against the claim, made fifty years earlier in More's *Strictures on Female Education*, that women have not the capacity "of comparing, combining, analysing, and separating ideas," nor that "deep and patient thinking which goes to the bottom of a subject." Martineau's *Autobiography* testifies not only to women's capacity, but to their power to use it.

If Martineau's *Autobiography* represents a solution to the dilemma of the woman autobiographer, it was not the only solution nor one that all Victorian women writers considered satisfactory. In fact, during the nineteenth century women writers introduced a debate, implicitly if not explicitly, over the forms and modes of self-interpretation they should attempt. Martineau's position in this debate seems clear: women should engage the main tradition of autobiographical writing, and they should adopt universal patterns of interpretation, systems that apply to all humankind. Charlotte Brontë's position seems less certain. In *Shirley*, the novel after *Jane Eyre*, Brontë again explores through autobiographical fiction two methods of self-interpretretation: the culturally accepted method of Caroline Helstone, the more imaginative attempt of Shirley Keeldar.

Caroline Helstone takes upon herself the role of the benevolent spinster, adhering closely to biblical models of women but hoping all the time that someone will say she need no longer follow them. Caroline wants the biblical text itself to change. When Joe Scott reminds her of the Pauline injunction to silence, for example, she responds with an ill-founded hope that the words don't mean what they say: "I dare say, if I could read the original Greek, I should find that many of the words have been wrongly translated, perhaps misapprehended altogether. It would be possible, I doubt not, with a little ingenuity, to give the passage quite a contrary turn; to make it say, 'Let the woman speak out whenever she sees fit to make an objection.' "[43] While Caroline engages in wishful thinking, lacking the hermeneutic skills to effect her desire, Shirley chooses to ignore the traditional biblical types and instead creates her own self-interpreting myth. Outside in the evening air, away from the parish church, she envisions the first woman, whom she calls alternatively "Eve," "Eva," and "a woman-Titan," and whom she imagines "bore Prometheus," from whose breast was "yielded the daring which could contend with Omnipotence: the strength which could bear a thousand years of bondage,—the unexhausted life and uncorrupted excellence, sisters to immortality, which, after millenniums of crimes, struggles, and woes, could conceive and bring forth a Messiah" (360). The syntax of her vision re-constructs biblical and mythical history: while the parallel phrases logically seem to describe the hero Prometheus and hence masculine achievements, they culminate in feminine acts of conception and birth and thus in effect describe "Eva," the woman who is the focal point of history and the mother who nourishes these two young would-be autobiographers.

Shirley never completes the myth within the novel, but one can sense the possibility for women's self-writing that Brontë imagines. Instead of attempting autobiography in the primary tradition with universal models, as Harriet Martineau did, women writers might create their own patterns of interpretation—and a separate autobiographical tradition.

As far as literary history goes, Charlotte Brontë and Harriet Martineau never discussed the problem of women's autobiography face to face. They did, however, have a rather serious falling out over Brontë's final novel, *Villette*, and the point of disagreement connects directly to their different approaches to women's autobiography. Responding to Brontë's request for criticism on *Villette* but without realizing that the work was autobiographical, Martineau complained that in the novel "all the female characters, in all their thoughts and lives, are full of one thing, or are regarded by the reader in the light of that one thought,—love. It begins with the child of six years old, at the opening . . . and it closes with the last page." According to Martineau, this view was not only obsessive but false: "It is not thus in real life. There are substantial, heartfelt interests for women of all ages, and under ordinary circumstances, quite apart from love."[44] Martineau refers to "real life," but as she understood quite well, the real lives of women were in large measure created by the autobiographical lives that women writers chose—or had the power—to tell. To create an autobiography in which the interests and hence the shape of a woman's life were presented as fundamentally different from those of mankind was to approve a separate autobiographical tradition for women and thus finally to acquiesce in the exclusion of women from a primary literary tradition. Unlike Brontë's autobiographical novels, Martineau's *Autobiography* allows no such distinctions.

Both writers agreed, then, that women needed to abandon the hermeneutic system of the traditional spiritual autobiography. But they disagreed about what should replace it. The difference their works represent is the legacy that nineteenth-century women left for their successors to resolve.

6

Gosse's *Father and Son*:
The Evolution of
Scientific Autobiography

Harriet Martineau's *Autobiography* may have been the first English attempt at a "scientific" autobiography, but in the history of the genre, it represents as much a midpoint in 150 years of autobiographical writing by scientists as it does an origin for scientific modes of self-interpretation. The first autobiographies by writers legitimately called scientists—James Ferguson's *Short Account* (1773), Joseph Priestley's *Memoirs* (1806), and Richard Watson's *Anecdotes of the Life* (1817)—were published considerably earlier, although they were not scientific in any formal sense.[1] Ferguson, a self-taught astronomer famous for his orreries and eclipsareons, wrote an account of his life in preface to his *Select Mechanical Exercises*, but, formally, the *Short Account* resembles other memoirs of self-education and public achievement, "a testimony of the vigour of native intellect under circumstances of the greatest depression," as one edition describes it.[2] Priestley's *Memoirs* and Watson's *Anecdotes*, too, are unoriginal in form and method. Both accounts reveal men more theological than scientific in temperament, despite their early contributions to chemistry, and both adopt the models of contemporary autobiographical literature, Watson assembling a form of life and letters and Priestley writing an account of spiritual progress (or regress) that resembles, in its intertextuality, Thomas Scott's *The*

Force of Truth.[3] None of these writers felt a need to modify traditional forms of self-presentation or self-interpretation as a result of their scientific pursuits.

There was, in fact, no need for early scientists to avoid the conventions of autobiographical writing. Most of their accounts are versions of the *res gestae* memoir—either simple chronologies of experiment and invention, like James Ferguson's, or more elaborate books, like Robert Munro's *Autobiographical Sketch*, detailing matters of education, research, and public honor—and the conventions of the memoir changed little, even after the spread of Darwinian models to the social sciences.[4] Those works that were genuine autobiographies, like Priestley's, retained the conventional patterns of spiritual and intellectual development and exhibited little tension between convention and content. Priestley describes his experiments with electricity and air in the same terms that he describes his publications in theology, and if his narrative details a movement from orthodoxy to Arianism, it is a movement initiated by his study of theology, not science. In his view, all of his activities contributed to his conviction that "a wise Providence was disposing every thing for the best."[5]

The reasons for such compatibility between the old forms and the new science begin with the kinds of research that eighteenth-century Englishmen conducted. For all their novelty, neither Ferguson's discoveries in astronomy nor Priestley's experiments with air gave a direct challenge to biblical models of understanding the self and the world. Moreover, the motives that compelled these scientists to write were traditional ones. Even in the nineteenth century, most scientific autobiographies are either private memoirs, like Darwin's sketch for "my children or their children," or substitutions for official biographies, like Huxley's attempt to avoid "the more or less fulsome inaccuracies" of a biography that "some importunate person proposes to write."[6] Most, too, are sequential records of major discoveries, focusing on colleagues or circumstances that served as catalysts and including anecdotal material wherever it seems interesting or amusing. If there are hidden motives in these accounts, they are motives of fame and public honor, not of generic reform. As Bertram Hopkinson, son of the inventor of the dynamo and himself a scientist, explained: "[O]ne whose labours have lain in pure science or in the construction of engineering works cannot hope for immortality." The scientist

> adds, perhaps, a few stones to the vast and ever-increasing edifice of human knowledge and at first, no doubt, those stones are identified with him and bear his individual marks. But as time goes on those marks are inevitably obliterated. The lines which divide his work from that of his contemporaries become less definite and the stones that he laid become merged into the general whole.[7]

For those scientists who wished to prevent, as Hopkinson did, the early obliteration of such individual marks, the appropriate autobiographical form was the memoir. *Res gestae* memoirs called for the enumeration of public achievements, rather than the interpretation of more private aspects of life; they did not require the comprehensive hermeneutics of the traditional autobiography.

Although the early accounts by scientists tended to assume the form of memoirs, and although the incompatibility of traditional autobiography and scientific models became evident later in the nineteenth century, there were some indications at mid-century of the direction that a new autobiography might take. These indications, in the personal accounts of Darwin, Huxley, and their lesser contemporaries, suggest the possibility of replacing biblical hermeneutics with scientific methods of interpretation and of otherwise expanding or revising the autobiographical form. They foreshadow the serious attempts at scientific autobiography that we find later in Herbert Spencer and Samuel Butler and the crisis in the autobiographical genre that we find in Edmund Gosse.

Among the most prominent of these indications in Darwin's *Autobiography* (1876) is the attempt at a scientific methodology, particularly in the initial segments of self-presentation. Darwin considered himself, first and foremost, a practitioner of the Baconian method. Throughout his life, as Nora Barlow has documented, he insisted upon the primacy of the observation and collection of data, and he firmly dismissed "speculation" and "a strong tendency to generalise" as "an entire evil."[8] In the *Autobiography* Darwin notes with evident pride that, from the beginning of his scientific study in 1837, he "worked on true Baconian principles, and without any theory collected facts on a wholesale scale."[9] This insistence upon collection rather than theoretical speculation appears in his approach to autobiographical composition, which in microcosm imitates his life's work.

In the first pages of the *Autobiography*, Darwin simply gathers the facts. He tells of his love of angling and hunting, confesses his theft of peaches and invention of deliberate lies, describes his early piety, his mediocrity at school, his fleetness as a runner, his passion for natural history, "and more especially for collecting"—all without reference to a comprehensive pattern or theory of life, without apparent concern for literary coherence.[10] In this undirected gathering of facts, the opening of Darwin's *Autobiography* is markedly different from, say, Newman's *Apologia*, which self-consciously begins with a record of supernatural premonitions that came to the young boy. Darwin does not anticipate the course of his future as Newman does. Only after the facts have been collected does he offer a generalization about the "qualities which at this time promised well for the future," and then he does not attempt to incorporate all the facts or offer a comprehensive theory.[11] Some facts remain random data.

Few scientific autobiographers after Darwin exhibit his rigor in the patient collection of facts. Indeed, one amusing result of the publication of Darwin's *Autobiography* is the slavishness with which his scientific successors imitate the master and in effect make his account conventional, right down to admissions of mediocrity at school and episodes of angling, bird-nesting, and hunting.[12] Nonetheless, Darwin's influence can be felt in what James Olney has called the "objective" stance of the *Autobiography*, a more general indication of the direction that scientific autobiography would later take.

As Olney suggests, Darwin intends to be "as objective and as detached" in his "private-experiential" book as he had been in his "public-scientific" work: "As if he were a coral reef in the South Seas, Darwin deliberately looks at himself from without, studying a creature, presently not living, to whom a series of things happened in the past and over whom a series of changes came in sixty-seven years of life."[13] The objective stance begins in the prefatory paragraph of the *Autobiography*, where Darwin explains, "I have attempted to write the following account of myself, as if I were a dead man in another world looking back at my own life."[14] It continues in the account of his early life where Darwin mixes tales of both piety and moral laxity, of his achievements and his faults. And, for the reader of the *Autobiography*, the sense of objectivity is intensified by the editorial emendations of his son, Francis, who deleted private remarks to wife and family, as well as negative comments about friends and a deeply personal discussion of religion as Darwin saw it eroded away by his discoveries in science.[15]

Olney considers this attempt at scientific objectivity to have been detrimental for the *Autobiography* and, indeed, for autobiographical writing generally. In his view, it is not simply that Darwin's concern with "an abstractable process divorced from the living organism" runs counter to the genre's commitment to the individual self; it is also that Darwin's scientific objectivity wreaked a terrible vengeance on the autobiographer himself. Darwin "tried to deny a half and more of the psychic organism, and that whole and outraged organism," Olney believes, "took its revenge on this attempt of Darwin's at self-effacement or self-destruction . . . in the form of all the various, plainly psychosomatic illnesses."[16] Yet even if Darwin suffered from psychosomatic ailments, and even if the ailments were causally connected to his scientific stance of objectivity, we might question whether autobiography must foreground psychic concerns, either as evidence or explanation.[17] Certainly, in light of Victorian attempts at scientific self-explanation, we might question whether autobiography must focus on the individual self and whether, in fact, it is possible to take another view of Darwin's "objectivity."

Before Darwin, Harriet Martineau had argued that scientific—or, in her terms, positivistic—autobiography must forego the language of the self. In order "to form any true notion whatever of any of the affairs of the universe," she insisted, "we must take our stand in the external world,—regarding man as one of the products and subjects of the everlasting laws of the universe."[18] With the adoption of this

"stand in the external world" (and with it the demise of theological
and metaphysical modes of understanding), Martineau envisioned a
release from "the prison of the self." Her "external" stand is the
"objective" stance of Darwin's account, and if her vocabulary is more
Comtian than Darwin's, the position she argues is nonetheless his
own. Martineau identifies this position, we should note, with intellectual and emotional "release," not with the "self-destruction" that
Olney describes.

Late in the nineteenth century, scientific autobiographers would
try to take literally Martineau's "stand in the external world" and look
at themselves as "objects." They would call their accounts "natural
histories" and treat themselves as specimens; they would begin their
lives not with themselves, but with their progenitors. Darwin's
cousin Francis Galton, for instance, makes the first chapter of
Memories of My Life an analysis of the "six nearest progenitors, namely
the two parents and four grandparents," who "bequeathed very
different combination of [traits] to their descendants."[19] Galton
includes in the bequeathal both physical traits (which lead him into a
discussion of the bronchitis and asthma he inherited from his great-
grandfather, Samuel Galton) and what he terms "an hereditary bent of
mind" (which leads to a discussion of the evolutionary receptivity he
and his cousin Charles inherited from their grandfather, Erasmus
Darwin). Such "objectivity" was a logical conclusion of the scientific
stance. And even if Galton's theories of human heredity and eugenics
do not seem to us scientific, his approach had significant possibilities
for the form of the autobiography.

It is in Herbert Spencer's *Autobiography* (1904), however, that the
implications of Darwin's work become fully evident. In his preface,
Spencer introduces his account as "a natural history of myself," and,
like Galton, begins not with his birth but with his "extraction."[20]
For seventy pages, Spencer details his family antecedents, noting the
"nonconformist tendency" of the maternal Bretells, the "prudence" of
the paternal Spencers, the regard for "remote" rather than "immediate results" of both, and so on. Not only does Spencer analyze the
dominant characteristics of parents and grandparents, he also cites
those of his father's siblings, for "family-traits," he argues, may be

"displayed in other lines of descent."[21] At the conclusion of "Family Antecedents," as he calls the first part of his autobiography, Spencer sums up the traits common to members of his family and evident in himself: "independence, self-asserting judgment, the tendency to nonconformity, and the unrestrained display of their sentiments and opinions; more especially in respect of political, social, religious, and ethical matters."[22]

These traits establish the interpretive strains of the work, which then repeats and develops examples of Spencer's own independent spirit and forthright intellectual manner. Although much of his autobiography after part I reverts to the conventional *res gestae* form, Spencer never forgets to remind his readers of the effects of his inherited characteristics. He notes the predictable "disregard of authority" during boyhood: "The mere authoritative statement that so-and-so is so-and-so, made without evidence or intelligible reason, seems to have been from the outset constitutionally repugnant to me."[23] He notes, too, the "independence of judgment" intensified through contact with his father, the rebellion against an arbitrary educational regime during his youth, and the tendency throughout life to "castle-building," which he relates to the "regard for remote results" of his nonconformist ancestors and to the "constructive imagination" inherited through the paternal line.[24] What is remarkable about the *Autobiography* is not simply this unity of narrative and theme, but the explicit articulation of the scientific hermeneutics which informs both. For Spencer, as for Newman, autobiographical narrative and hermeneutic system cohere.

Such coherence testifies to the evolution of the scientific autobiography as a literary form. In Darwin's *Autobiography*, there had been an incipient version of a Baconian method and a stance of objectivity, but no self-conscious discussion of interpretive principles.[25] Moreover, because Darwin's account was in form more closely related to the memoir than to the developmental autobiography, it did not attempt a comprehensive interpretation of his life. Nevertheless, when Darwin did generalize, he chose his language from a fund of scientific metaphors— and here the potential for scientific autobiography is significant. At various points Darwin calls his passion for collecting "innate," he questions whether the quality of "humanity" is "natural or innate," and he sees in the gradual development of mental rather than physical pursuits "the primitive instincts of the barbarian slowly yield[ing] to the acquired tastes of the civilized man."[26] Such interpretations are local or partial, but they appear without reference to theological categories of good and evil and with the same avoidance of moral questions that characterizes the *Origin of Species*. Implicitly, they replace old generic conventions with new scientific metaphors.

The occasional scientific metaphors in Darwin's *Autobiography* become more pervasive attempts at scientific self-interpretation in the accounts of his successors. Whereas Darwin hesitates to apply evolutionary theory full-scale to an individual life, autobiographers after him are less cautious. In a short personal memoir, for instance, Thomas Huxley comments that the boys in his public school "were left to the operation of the struggle for existence among [them]-selves."[27] Galton interprets his quick understanding of the concept of natural selection as an inherited trait: "I felt little difficulty in connection with the *Origin of Species*," he notes in *Memories of My Life*, "but devoured its contents and assimilated them as fast as they were devoured, a fact which perhaps may be ascribed to an hereditary bent of mind that both its illustrious author and myself have inherited from our common grandfather, Dr. Erasmus Darwin."[28] And Robert Munro, who testifies that the effect of Darwin's *Origin* "was virtually to change the whole tenor and prospects of my future life," shapes his *Autobiographical Sketch* into "a description of the successive steps by which a country lad[,] without possessing any exceptional ability either inherited or inspired by the social environment," may attain "to a position of some distinction in the scientific world" and "be an inspiring object-lesson to others who harbour the laudable ambition to emerge from the proletarian rut."[29] These autobiographers show a fervent commitment to extending Darwin's evolutionary metaphors and to "facing the world" resolutely, as Huxley put it, "when the garment of make-believe by which pious hands have hidden its uglier features is stripped off."[30]

Spencer's *Autobiography* represents the realization of this new "facing of the world" without the hermeneutics of the pious. The "creed of Christendom" had been from his youth, as Spencer explains, "evidently alien to my nature, both emotional and intellectual,"[31] and thus his account shows no inclination to religious modes of thought. His *Autobiography* is not, however, a facing of the world without hermeneutics. Four years after he completed the work, in an appendix entitled "Reflections," Spencer articulated the scientific theories that inform his interpretation of his life. Like Newman's final chapter of the *Apologia*, the theories present in expository form the hermeneutic principles latent in the autobiographical narrative.

Spencer begins with reflections on supernatural doctrines of metempsychosis which, in his view, deny "a relation between character and bodily structure" and which work against scientific theories of the human organism. He then argues a "connexion between mind and brain," one that exists "in both amounts and kinds": "Mind is not as deep as the brain only," he posits, "but is, in a sense, as deep as the viscera."[32] With this hypothesis in view, Spencer re-interprets his past—here proceeding not chronologically, but systematically. He discusses "psycho-physical connexions," including the alimentary and cardiovascular structures that he inherited from his parents and that both influenced and inhibited his intellectual, emotional, and ethical activities throughout life.[33] Building upon "these psycho-physical interpretations of character," he moves to more purely "psychical" considerations, analyzing the structure and working capacity of his brain. These considerations lead him finally to an analysis of his intellectual traits—the capacity for intuition, the synthetic tendency, the analytic tendency, and the ability to discern inconspicuous analogies—all of which he considers rooted in the physical and, in part, transmitted through heredity.

Within these scientific categories, the episodes of his life become not narrative pieces, but evidence for a hermeneutic system. That Spencer understands the connection between narrative and hermeneutics is clear from the "Reflections," which describe his books as the "products of experience" that "have been organized into a coherent whole" and his autobiography as the addition of personal evidence to a coherent theory of life. In the "Reflections," too, he identifies the motivating force of his life as "the conception of Evolution in its comprehensive form": "the desire to elaborate and set it forth was so strong that to have passed life in doing something else would, I think, have been almost intolerable."[34] That comprehensive form of evolution was the hermeneutic possibility Spencer bequeathed to posterity. It was possible, as he had shown, to avoid the traditional categories of theological hermeneutics. One might root an understanding of the self in a psycho-physical theory of life and apply a pattern of evolution autobiographically to the individual organism.

It is one of the ironies of literary history that Spencer's *Autobiography*, begun in 1866, should not have been published until 1904, the year after Samuel Butler's literary executor released *The Way of All Flesh*. Spencer's work provided the basis for a new form of autobiographical writing, one with a coherent scientific theory to replace the old biblical hermeneutics and with a new method for examining the antecedents and experiences of the individual human being. But Butler's work, begun a decade after Spencer's, was published first in 1903.[35] Because it was sensational in its satiric content as well as innovative in form, it became the more memorable attempt at "scientific" autobiography.[36]

Like Spencer, Butler introduces a scientific method for interpreting the self, one that treats the protagonist of his (pseudo)autobiography as a scientific specimen. *Ernest Pontifex, or The Way of All Flesh* was the original title of the work, but Butler deliberately ignores Ernest for the first sixteen chapters, concentrating instead on family antecedents. Chapter 1 treats old George Pontifex, the unpretentious carpenter who lived in harmony with nature and bequeathed to some of his descendants his musical ability, manual dexterity, and generally complaisant temperament. Chapter 2 introduces his son, George Jr., the successful Victorian businessman who inherited his mother's obstinacy and father's intelligence, without his father's sense of humor or tastes for music and drawing. Chapter 3 presents Theobald Pontifex, the miserable scion of George Jr., worn-out from the remarkable achievements of the previous generation and no more able, as an offspring of the Pontifex race, to "repeat its most successful performances suddenly and without its ebbings and flowings of success than the individual can do" (19). Chapters 4 through 16 continue to analyze, through the consciousness of Edward Overton, Butler's adult alter ego, the history of the Pontifexes prior to Ernest's birth and thus his genetic inheritance. As in Spencer's *Autobiography*, the emphasis throughout the early chapters of *The Way of All Flesh* falls upon what Spencer termed the psycho-physical and psychical traits of its subject's recent ancestors.

With this analysis of family antecedents, Butler offers a scientific theory of heredity and human development. In the original preface to the novel, R. A. Streatfeild suggested that Ernest Pontifex's tale may be read "as a practical illustration of the theory of heredity" embodied in *Life and Habit* (1878), and various critics since have discussed the influence of Butler's theory of "purposive" evolution, an original blend of concepts from Lamarck and Erasmus Darwin which stresses the "oneness of personality between parents and offspring" and the offspring's "unconscious" memory of "certain actions which it did when in the person of its forefathers."[37] Had Butler written his autobiographical novel a few years later, he might instead have turned to psychological theories of the self and to Freud's concept of parricide as "the principle and primal crime of humanity as well as of the individual."[38] Butler's concern in self-interpretation focused, after all, on the conflict between parents and offspring, of which his own unhappy familial situation was a prime example.[39] His representation of that situation in *The Way of All Flesh*, moreover, anticipates Freud in its understanding of the oedipal nature of the father-mother-son triangle: it is his father, not his mother, whom Ernest considers his enemy, and the source of the rivalry between father and son is Christina, from whom both Ernest and his father desire unequivocal love and attention.[40] Freud's work might have provided a vocabulary with which to discuss this Victorian father-son relationship, with its rivalry for sexual and financial power.

Writing before the advent of Freudianism, however, Butler turned to evolutionary theory, the most sophisticated science of his day, and interpreted his past in biological rather than psychological terms. In his view, all forms of life, the human included, demonstrate a conflict between the older forms (the parent generation) and newer, modified forms (the offspring). In his notebooks he commented that the common antipathy between human parents and children was "part of the same story with the antipathy that prevails throughout nature between an incipient species and the unmodified individuals of the race from which it is arising": "The first thing which a new form does is to exterminate its predecessor; the old form knows this and will therefore do its best to prevent the new from arising. Every generation is a new species up to a certain point—and hence every older generation regards it with suspicion."[41]

The novel offers a similar explanation for our common desire to do away with our parents and for the consequent parental struggle to preserve life and authority. Overton laments that human beings must endure an unpleasant situation that other animals are spared: "Why should the generations overlap one another at all? Why cannot we be buried as eggs in neat little cells with ten or twenty thousand pounds each wrapped round us in Bank of England notes, and wake up, as the sphex wasp does, to find that its papa and mamma have not only left ample provision at its elbow but have been eaten by sparrows some weeks before we began to live consciously on our own accounts" (71). Ernest articulates an equally cynical view: "Certainly there is no inherent love for the family system on the part of nature herself. . . The ants and the bees . . . sting their fathers to death as a matter of course" (91).

Such conflicting responses in the novel fit within Butler's larger theory of personality, described in *Life and Habit* as "many component parts which war not a little among themselves."[42] What is noteworthy about *The Way of All Flesh* as (pseudo)autobiography, however, is not simply that Butler offers a "scientific" theory to explain a generational conflict, nor even that he places this conflict within a larger theory of heredity and "unconscious memory," eventually allowing Ernest to recover the almost forgotten traits of his great-grandfather George, but that, as an experiment in autobiographical form, Butler self-consciously substitutes a scientific theory for a religious system of interpreting his protagonist's experience. At the same time that

Overton is offering a scientific analysis of Ernest's behavior, the narrative structure of the novel is undermining the conventional episodes of the spiritual autobiography.

We can trace this narrative movement by examining the "key" events of Ernest's life: his baptism, confirmation, ordination, and marriage. Each of these conventional episodes presents itself as a moment of significance, as a starting point or turning point in Ernest's life. At birth he is specially baptized with water from the River Jordan; at confirmation he feels that he has "arrived at one of the great turning points of his life, and that the Ernest of the future could resemble only very faintly the Ernest of the past" (166); at ordination he experiences a spiritual awakening and feels again "that the turning point of his life had come" (196); and at marriage he thinks "of the wonderful goodness of God towards him" (273). These turning points represent the "conversions" of Ernest's spiritual autobiography, and Butler satirizes each for the disaster it brings and for the false significance it claims. Ernest's baptismal waters have been dirtied and then sopped up "as though they had been a common slop" (67); the true meaning of his confirmation asserts itself in the burning of his father's effigy; his ordination soon leaves him "appalled at the irrevocable nature of the step" that "he had taken much too hurriedly" (200); and his marriage turns out to be a union with an alcoholic and polygamist. These key episodes demonstrate the nugacity of traditional religious hermeneutics.

If Butler's treatment of narrative structure insists that religious systems cannot provide direction for Ernest's life, his narrator also suggests that more reliable sources of human understanding may be found in science or natural history. When Ernest finally collapses from the weight of religious convention, the remedy that Overton pursues is one of "crossing," a new "scientific" treatment of fresh exposure, assimilation, and change that Butler had formulated in *Life and Habit*. Such "crossing" brings Ernest in contact first with the larger mammals of the Regent's Park Zoo but eventually with Darwin's theories of evolution and the descent of man. "Of course," Overton remarks, "he read Mr. Darwin's books as fast as they came out and adopted evolution as an article of faith" (317).

Overton describes Darwinian theory as a new creed, an "article of faith," and, indeed, in *The Way of All Flesh* Butler's own version of Darwinianism replaces the conventional articles of biblical hermeneutics. Yet we might ask if, ultimately, Butler considered it a sufficient replacement. In the first two volumes of the novel, contemporaneous with his work in *Life and Habit*, he seems to have embraced evolutionary theory as a superior system for understanding human development, individual and corporate both. By the time he composed the third volume, however, Butler had misgivings. The semi-satirical example of "crossing," a concept he had presented seriously in *Life and Habit*, suggests as much. Moreover, in the penultimate chapter of *The Way of All Flesh*, Butler parodies his own religious and scientific publications in his descriptions of Ernest's writings—which, as Overton remarks, "rang with the courage alike of conviction and of an entire absence of conviction" (343). Even in *Life and Habit*, Butler formulates a coherent theory of heredity, but warns his readers against accepting it unskeptically: "Above all else," he comments, "let no unwary reader do me the injustice of believing in *me*. In that I write at all I am among the damned."[43]

The skepticism about scientific systems that Butler only hints at becomes a primary focus in Gosse's *Father and Son*, a work that both embodies an attempt at scientific autobiography and self-consciously critiques it. In writing his *Autobiography*, Spencer had introduced an evolutionary model, fully confident of its superiority to biblical (or any other) hermeneutics. Similarly, Butler had replaced religious patterns of self-interpretation with more modern scientific models, if finally expressing some doubt about their validity. It was Gosse, however, who raised the crucial question of scientific autobiography and hermeneutic authority.

Like Butler's (pseudo)autobiography, Edmund Gosse's *Father and Son* delineates a generational conflict between a father committed to religion and a son requisitive of new ideas. Given the description of the conflict in the first chapter, between a man "born to fly backward"

and a son destined to be "carried forward," the reader anticipates Edmund's substitution of a new autobiographical hermeneutic for the old biblical typology that was the mainstay of his father, Philip Henry Gosse.[44] Certainly, the preface to the autobiography intimates a generic conflict within the text to come. Its language falls into patterns of opposition—between solemnity and merriment, tragedy and comedy, the record of spiritual struggle and a genuine slice of life. It seems conscious, too, of a violation of traditional generic boundaries. "It is not usual," Gosse explains, "that the narrative of a spiritual struggle should mingle merriment and humour with a discussion of the most solemn subjects . . . But life is not constituted thus, and this book is nothing if it is not a genuine slice of life" (4). A defense of generic violation such as Gosse makes here—on the grounds of empirical evidence and in the terms of "scientific," slice-of-life realism—suggests a conflict between older and newer forms of autobiographical writing and a revision, if not a replacement, of the older form.[45]

Despite the dialectical formula of "backward" and "forward," however, there are no clear generic oppositions in *Father and Son* to parallel the generational struggle. Unlike Butler's *Way of All Flesh*, in which a scientific theory clearly replaces conventional religious forms of self-analysis, or Ruskin's *Praeterita*, in which an extroverted form of memoir vies with an introspective form of spiritual analysis, Gosse's autobiography tangles the generic elements. The thematic conflict between science and religion produces no generic equivalent. At times, Gosse offers scientific metaphors as a means of interpreting the self, but if they contest the spiritual form of his father's religion, they do not finally supersede it. Instead, Gosse hints of many generic possibilities and sends contradictory signals—not only of tragedy and comedy, but of biography and autobiography, of document and diagnosis, of spiritual narrative and genuine slice of life.[46]

What we are witnessing is the breakdown of a coherent generic form. In place of the traditional autobiography, with its comprehensive narrative pattern and hermeneutic system, we find the substitution, locally, of other patterns and modes of self-interpretation. Science offers one of these modes, and for Gosse its metaphors serve a crucial function. Science cannot interpret the self authoritatively, however—at least not in *Father and Son*.

But this is to anticipate the conclusion of an argument rather than to offer its basis. For, in spite of local substitutions, the primary literary genre that gives shape to *Father and Son* is the spiritual autobiography, even when Gosse works against it. Gosse imbibed the typological hermeneutics characteristic of the form as he grew up, the spiritual milk and meat of the Bible and other devotional literature being served up regularly with family meals. He knew literary examples of the form through his religious tradition, the Plymouth Brethren being among the few nineteenth-century sects that continued to write intensely hermeneutic, almost Bunyanesque versions of the spiritual biography and autobiography.[47] And he also knew the form of spiritual autobiography directly through family tradition. As James Hepburn has described, Gosse's grandfather underwent and recorded a religious conversion to Wesleyan Methodism: "He was walking in Fleet Street and suddenly saw 'Christ risen and received into heaven as my accepted Righteousness.'" His father, too, left a religious memoir that narrated the events leading to a decision "to live a new, a holy life; to please and serve God."[48]

It was not these autobiographical texts, however, but the spiritual diary of his mother that most directly influenced the writing of *Father and Son*. Gosse quotes from his mother's diary extensively, almost obsessively—eight times in contrast to the two instances he cites his father's. All eight quotations focus on his mother's decision to "dedicate" her son to God, or they describe the effects of her religious beliefs upon the shape of his life. Moreover, the only other texts that Gosse quotes to any significant extent are spiritual memoirs written *about* his mother—one by his father, another by a family friend, Anna Shipton—and, again, in quoting these memoirs, Gosse focuses on his mother's illness, especially the deathbed scene of dedication. Perhaps his mother's diary and the biographical memoirs account for some of the anxiety about generic violation that the preface to *Father and Son* betrays.

Gosse's first citations from his mother's diary concern his dedication, virtually from birth, to the service of God. Opening "a locked volume," which he claims has been "seen until now, nearly sixty years later, by no eye save her own," Gosse turns an actual key and supplies the metaphorical key to his life:

> We have given him to the Lord; and we trust that He will really manifest him to be His own, if he grow up; and if the Lord take him early, we will not doubt that he is taken to Himself. . . . Whether his life be prolonged or not, it has already been a blessing to us, and to the saints, in leading us to much prayer, and bringing us into varied need and some trial. (9)

This dedication—a typological repetition, we later learn, of Hannah's dedication of her son, the prophet Samuel—determines the pattern by which Edmund's life will be developed. Because Emily Gosse believes that her son, like Samuel, will serve God in some major role, she contemplates in her diary (and discusses with husband, servants, and saints) the possible destinies he might face, from becoming the Charles Wesley of his age to serving in the tropics in "the field of missionary labour" (19). Because she believes that inventing stories is a sin, a conviction she records in her diary, she forbids Edmund to read fictitious narratives of any kind, whether religious or secular in content (16 – 17). And because she believes in a "covenant God" (38), she secures the original dedication on her deathbed, binding her husband and son to it. The scene of binding is narrated in both biographical memoirs and repeated in *Father and Son* in some of the same language, but with greater dramatic power: "When the very end approached, and her mind was growing clouded, she gathered her strength together to say to my Father, 'I shall walk with Him in white. Won't you take your lamb and walk with me?'" The dedication was "sealed with the most solemn, the most poignant and irresistible insistence, at the death-bed of the holiest and purest of women" (41 – 42).[49]

The fact that Gosse discloses the contents of the locked diary "now, nearly sixty years later," suggests that he finds in it a key to his life and, in a special sense, to its written form in *Father and Son*. The pre-interpretation that the diary contains must be countered by Gosse, the adult autobiographer. If he reveals what before only his mother's eyes had seen, it is to re-interpret it from his own perspective. In this sense, *Father and Son* is virtually an answer to his mother's diary. It rejects of the interpretation of his life that she sought to impose, and thus attempts to avoid the influence of the traditional form of spiritual autobiography, whether in diary or hermeneutic narrative.

In a generic sense, however, Gosse's autobiography does not avoid the form of spiritual autobiography—either by rejecting it, as Ruskin does in *Praeterita*, or by substituting another, as Martineau does in her *Autobiography*. Rather, *Father and Son* embraces the traditional form by means of parody. Gosse's parody is not the usual sort, an "exaggerated imitation of a work of art,"[50] but a sophisticated version that involves the repetition of formal generic patterns with a displacement of meaning.

In common usage, *parody* suggests the extreme or abnormal, the ludicrous or malicious, but in Gosse's vocabulary, the term designates a formal rather than an intentional relationship. Gosse distinguishes between *imitation*, which involves a duplication of the structure, style, and content of some original work, and *parody*, which involves a repetition of the structure or style of the original work, but with a new or different content. In *Father and Son*, the literary work that illustrates this distinction between imitation and parody is his own first "book." Indeed, it is this "book" that necessitates the distinction.

At the age of ten, Gosse suggests, he had unwittingly created just such a parody of the scientific treatise, his father's literary form, by preparing a series of "little monographs on seaside creatures." These he assembled into a book, "arranged, tabulated and divided as exactly as possible on the pattern of those which my Father was composing for his 'Actinologia Britannica.'" The description of his method is significant:

> I wrote these out upon sheets of paper of the same size as his
> printed page, and I adorned them with water-colour plates,
> meant to emulate his precise and exquisite illustrations. . . . I

invented new species, with sapphire spots and crimson tentacles and amber bands, which were close enough to his real species to be disconcerting. . . . The subject did not lend itself to any flow of language, and I was obliged incessantly to borrow sentences, word for word, from my Father's published books. (95–96)

As he interprets this activity, Gosse insists that the juvenile work cannot be called *imitation* because he did not simply copy his father's studies of sea anemones. The term he insists upon is *parody*. In parody, a formal continuity is maintained, but content is altered; that is, his juvenile work replicates the size of his father's book, uses the same paper, and contains the same formal combination of plates and words, while it invents a different content. The content may be fictitious, as occurs when Gosse invents what he should have copied scrupulously from nature, or it may be displaced, as results when he borrows his father's words to refer to creatures that do not exist in the reality that scientific treatises seek to explore. Satiric intention, ridicule and mockery, however, have nothing to do with parody—at least not essentially or consciously, as Gosse defines it. He claims that his intention was "innocent and solemn" (95).

This example allows Gosse to suggest that parody as a form need not, in and of itself, signal destructive or ironical intention. Whether such a distinction between formal and intentional matters can be maintained is questionable, and Gosse's insistence on the possibility of being "innocent and solemn" is perhaps motivated more by his own present guilt than by a faultless logic. Innocence aside, however, it is worth considering Gosse's attempt at the distinction as it relates to his autobiography, for in it lies a clue to the generic revision of *Father and Son*.

The parodic book that young Gosse creates resembles a mode of repetition that Hillis Miller has described in his study of Victorian and modern novels, *Fiction and Repetition*. Following Gilles Deleuze, Miller posits two forms of repetition: (1) a Platonic repetition which, "grounded in a solid archetypal model," establishes the world as icon and "embodies basic metaphysical beliefs in origin, end, and an underlying ground that makes similarities identities," and (2) a

Nietzschean repetition which, against the Platonic, "posits a world based on difference," and thus suggests that similarities are merely simulacra, "ungrounded doublings which arise from differential interrelations among elements which are all on the same plane."[51] In Miller's terminology, we might say that Philip Henry Gosse wrote his book assuming the first mode of repetition, believing in the world as icon; he justified his scientific investigation "by regarding it as a glorification of God's created works," as "one more tribute humbly offered to the glory of the Triune God."[52] His son Edmund uncannily assembles his book according to the second mode of repetition, creating a world of multiple simulacra. The sea creatures he draws and describes resemble those contained in his father's book, but the resemblance is a false one. His words and images, the usual means of verbal and visual representation, feign reference to real things. His style may be the hard realism of the scientist, a realism he associates with Pre-Raphaelite painting, but his imaginary sea creatures resemble nothing, and his words and images refer to nothing. The effect was "disconcerting," Gosse remembers—they literally disturb, as the adjective suggests, the harmonious union of word and world that his father's book conceives.

The form of parody that Gosse describes in his juvenilia is a prefiguration of the form that his mature autobiography assumes. But whereas the childish book represents an "innocent and solemn" parody, *Father and Son* is a more deliberate version of the second form of repetition, a version which calls into question the theological underpinings of the spiritual autobiography and the possibility of certain meaning which that form traditionally embodies. Generically, Gosse maintains formal continuity with the main English tradition of spiritual autobiography, including the lesser examples in his own familial tradition. While maintaining formal continuity, however, he alters or displaces the traditional content. Words, phrases, and sentences create episodes that are simulacra; they use the language of genuine spiritual experience to expose a feigned or hollow experience that the language tends to (or tries to) disguise.

Whether Gosse would go the whole way with Nietzsche and posit a world of similarity/simulacra against his father's world of similarity/identify seems unlikely. It is true that *Father and Son* begins with a dialectic, presented as a struggle between a father "born to fly backward" and a son who "could not help being carried forward," and that Gosse describes the result of this struggle in terms of different languages: "There came a time when neither spoke the same language as the other, or encompassed the same hopes, or was fortified by the same desires" (5). But it is also true that Gosse was in many ways conservative. Even in his rejection of his father's spiritual system, he maintained a belief in God, Christ, and the Christian "scheme of the world's history,"[53] and he had little tolerance for contemporary thinkers like Samuel Butler who did go the way with Nietzsche and embrace a world of contradictory and mutually self-exclusive meanings. Butler might have been willing to see "the texture of the world" as "a warp and woof of contradiction in terms; of continuity in discontinuity, and discontinuity in continuity"; of subject and countersubject.[54] Gosse nonetheless considered the holder of such a view an "inspired 'crank,'" rejecting the extremity of such intellectual and spiritual rebellion.[55]

Whatever his philosophical position, the definition of parody that Gosse constructs in chapter viii becomes the formal basis of his self-presentation throughout *Father and Son*. It illumines his method of composition in the two central episodes of the book: his public baptism (viii) and his de-conversion (xii). It suggests as well his parodic revision of the system of biblical hermeneutics standard in the spiritual autobiography. And it anticipates his fundamentally skeptical use of scientific metaphors in the later chapters of his book.

In writing of his public baptism, Gosse calls the experience the "central event" of his "whole childhood": "Everything, since the earliest dawn of consciousness, seemed to have been leading up to it. Everything, afterwards, seemed to be leading down and away from it" (103). This statement sounds as if it belongs in a traditional spiritual autobiography. Gosse also describes his baptism, however, as an illusion, an instance of perhaps "temporary sincerity"; it was, like other instances he witnessed at his father's chapel, a "simulacrum of a true change of heart" (108). Both versions of his response must figure into the account of baptism. In the episode, then, as the subject, is the paradoxical convergence of an apex and an illusion, of a central event that poses as substance but is really simulacrum. In it also, as the formal difficulty, is the presentation of this convergence in a way that maintains the centrality of the event while simultaneously revealing its illusory nature.

Gosse's solution is parody. Conceptually, Gosse makes his baptism central by presenting it as the fulfilment of his "dedication": just as his parents, modern-day Elkanahs and Hannahs, had given their child to the service of the Lord, so in this episode the saints debate whether he in fact is "another infant Samuel" (100), thus meriting admission to their communion at the tender age of ten years. Structurally, too, Gosse gives the baptism centrality by making it the dramatic climax of the autobiography, placing it in the position conventionally assumed by conversion. In the evangelical doctrine of the Plymouth Brethren, baptism was inseparable from conversion, the public act bearing witness to an inner, personal experience, and not, as among what Gosse calls "pedobaptists," the public act anticipating or promising a future experience. As Philip Gosse understood the doctrine and taught his son:

> There must be a new birth and being, a fresh creation in God . . . There might have been prolonged practical piety, deep and true contrition for sin, but these, although the natural and suitable prologue to conversion, were not conversion itself. . . . The very root of human nature had to be changed, and, in a majority of cases, this change was sudden, patent, palpable. (98—99)

This understanding of conversion provides the basis for parody, by means of a transference of what occurs in the religious ritual to what is recorded in the literary account.

The direct relationship of a formal, public act to an inner "birth and being" is what the written spiritual autobiography, like the sacrament of baptism, claims to represent. In Hillis Miller's terms, spiritual autobiography claims the world as icon, embodying "basic metaphysical beliefs" in "an underlying ground that makes similarities identities." In Gosse's terms, both baptism and the writing of autobiography are acts of imitation. They reproduce publically—visibly, patently, palpably—a personal, if invisible reality. They attempt a coherence of form and content. They embody a belief in the possibility of the sign converging with its meaning.

In retrospect, Gosse suggests that his public baptism began as an act of imitation: "[A]s I look back, I see that I was extremely imitative, [that] the imitative faculty got the upper hand" (98). But what began as imitation soon became parody: form became emptied of—or displaced from—content. While the formal procedures of baptism were maintained, the coherence of form and meaning was lost, and young Edmund proceeded into baptism without the requisite "deep and true contrition for sin" or the act of grace that conversion embodies.

What makes this parody in Gosse's terms (rather than satire, as it would be in Butler's work) is the loss of coherence coupled with the young boy's attitude, which was initially innocent and sincere. Critics like James Woolf tend to blame the loss of coherence upon the father, upon his "pathetic" desire "to secure" his son "finally, exhaustively, before the age of puberty could dawn, before [his] soul was fettered with the love of carnal things" (98). But Gosse's account deliberately refrains from assigning culpability. It never suggests that, previously or potentially, a coherence of form and meaning existed for the young boy. That question is left indeterminate.

Whatever the case, in the climax of the episode, Gosse offers not the burning coal of Isaiah sanctifying a young boy's lips (100) but the tongue of a ten-year-old put out in mockery of other children, "to remind them that I now broke bread as one of the Saints and that they did not" (106). With baptism Gosse's childhood seems to end, as does his innocence and sincerity. His moral majority begins on 12 October, "almost exactly three weeks after [his] tenth birthday" (103), when he is physically immersed and a "sonorous voice" seems "to enter [his] brain and empty it, 'I baptize thee, my Brother, in the name of the Father and of the Son and of the Holy Ghost'" (106). At this point in the autobiography, too, a generic emptying begins. All events *after* the baptism acknowledge its significance, but they attempt to undo it.

The undoing occurs throughout the second half of *Father and Son*, but becomes most urgent in the final stage of the process, a second parodic episode which attempts a more complex form of parody. Whereas the baptismal episode works by placing a (self)deceptive experience at the center of the autobiography and then by defining explicitly what a true conversion would entail, the final episode of *Father and Son* relies similarly upon structural position, but creates parody through a revision of autobiographical conventions. Conventionally, the final episode of the spiritual autobiography takes the form of a Pisgah vision. In the *Confessions* Augustine closes the narrative books with a prayer for his parents, "my fellow-citizens in that eternal Jerusalem which Thy pilgrim people sigheth after from their Exodus, even unto their return thither." In *Grace Abounding* Bunyan meditates on a text from Hebrews that sums up the movement of biblical history toward the Second Coming, "Ye are come unto mount Sion and unto the city of the living God, the heavenly Jerusalem." In Cowper, the promise of a new life with the Unwins becomes an entry into an earthly Canaan, a type of the heavenly paradise, and in Carlyle, Teufelsdröckh's wanderings end as a prospect from a "skyey Tent, musing and meditating, on the high table-land, in front of the Mountains."[56] For Gosse, the Pisgah vision occurs on a late summer afternoon, as he gazes down from one of the windows of his father's Devonshire villa onto "a labyrinth of garden sloping to the sea, which twinkled faintly beyond the towers of the town":

There was an absolute silence below and around me, a magic of suspense seemed to keep every topmost twig from waving. Over my soul there swept an immense wave of emotion. Now, surely, now the great final change must be approaching. I gazed up into the faintly-coloured sky, and I broke irresistibly into speech. "Come now, Lord Jesus," I cried, "come now and take me to be forever with Thee in Thy Paradise." (164–65)

The experience has its origin in Moses' vision on Mount Nebo, when the prophet overlooks the promised land from the plain of Gilead even "unto the utmost sea" (Deut. 34:1–4) and escapes death, being translated directly into God's presence. Its language is complicated by St. John's apocalyptic vision of the new Canaan, Gosse's "Come now, Lord Jesus" echoing the final words of the Revelation: "He which testifieth these things saith, Surely I come quickly: Amen. Even so, come, Lord Jesus" (Rev. 22:20). And the episode is enriched by the tradition of spiritual and secular autobiography from Augustine to Wordsworth, the garden setting finding its *locus classicus* in the *Confessions* and the saturation of natural scenery showing the influence of Romantic epiphanies in such works as *The Prelude*.

These biblical and literary traditions also provide the means of parody. When Wordsworth returns from a country dance and, at dawn, views a similarly rapturous scene:

> The sea lay laughing at a distance; near
> The solid mountains shone, bright as the clouds,
> Grain-tinctured, drenched in empyrean light
> And in the meadows and the lower grounds
> Was all the sweetness of a common dawn—

he feels assured that he is a "dedicated Spirit" and walks on "in thankful blessedness." When Augustine similarly "leans out from a window overlooking a garden and contemplates a vision of God's world," his vision, as Roger Porter has pointed out, unites him with Christ and connects his soul's rebirth "with the resurrection of the whole Christian community."[57] Augustine hears a voice from a neighboring house, "as of a boy or girl, I know not, chanting, and oft repeating, 'Tolle lege'"; he interprets it as a command from God to open the book, and in obeying, he experiences "a light as it were of serenity infused into my heart, all the darkness of doubt vanished away."[58] Gosse's experience repeats Augustine's, but parodically. Gosse leans out the window, but what he hears is the "chatter of the boys returning home" and then a tea-bell, "the last word of prose to shatter my mystical poetry." The light of serenity that in Augustine dispels spiritual darkness becomes, in Gosse, a natural light, whose "colour deepened, the evening came on" (165).

It seems strange to Gosse, even in retrospect, that this religious experience should have ended in parody. He writes that, before the episode, he had experienced no "doubt or hostility to the faith," but on the contrary, "a considerable quickening of fervour" (163). He calls the experience "the highest moment of my religious life, the apex of my striving after holiness" (165)—and the emphasis on the first-person pronoun suggests that, in this instance, the spiritual impetus came from within rather than from external pressure. Yet, once again, the episode represents form without substance, form devoid of meaning. Does it then, like the baptism, represent another parodic reduction of conventional motifs? And is it a reduction that implies a rejection of (even derision for) evangelical religion and the form of spiritual autobiography through which that religion has traditionally found expression?

It is possible to blame the failure of religious ecstacy upon Gosse himself, upon an inner absence that manifests itself in what he calls a "theatrical attitude" (165). "Theatrical" suggests a kind of play-acting, a stance of artificiality or superficiality, and thus a fundamental disjunction of form and meaning. Yet the "theatrical attitude" is recognized and labeled such only in retrospect: "I waited awhile, watching; and *then* I felt a faint shame at the theatrical attitude I had adopted" (165, italics mine). In fact, this theatrical attitude is another instance of the imitation that Gosse earlier defined in non-pejorative terms: an expression of a genuine desire to repeat a form in order to experience or validate its content. It does not, at least not initially, represent parody.

Nevertheless, the final episode follows the same pattern that marks earlier attempts at imitation. Just as Edmund had replicated the form of his father's scientific treatises or imitated the ritual of public baptism, so he here repeats the formulae of visionary experience. As in other instances, an action that begins as spiritual imitation becomes parody. The experience is emptied of its traditional or pre-ordained meaning; its content is lost or displaced.

This pattern of parodic repetition that Gosse inscribes in *Father and Son* testifies to his own lack of spiritual experience—and to something more. The loss of a certain correlation between form and meaning, action and substance, undercuts the authority of traditional religious formulae and the validity of the form of spiritual autobiography. It acknowledges that repetition of formulae or literary forms, even in sincerity, cannot assure meaning nor guarantee a continuity between one's personal experience and that of others who have expressed themselves in similar forms. Similarities may turn out to be simulacra.

This was no small discovery in the history of spiritual autobiography, and its effect upon the typological basis of the genre was significant. Typological hermeneutics depended upon a continuity of meaning; it implied a version of repetition in which form and meaning had genuine correspondence. When the possibility of such continuity was disturbed, the typological basis of self-interpretation could no longer be engaged in the usual way. As Gosse empties the key episodes of spiritual autobiography of their meaning, then, he also empties the hermeneutic system upon which those episodes depend of its authority. That authority is not re-invested in a single, alternative system, as it is in Martineau's or Spencer's autobiographies or in Butler's *The Way of All Flesh*. Instead, it is dispersed to a variety of interpretive strategies, which are applied locally rather than comprehensively.

Such patterns of emptying and dispersal become the mode of the second half of Gosse's account, and we might consider in detail one culminating pattern in chapter xii, where Gosse recollects the hermeneutic practice of his parents in its full power. This episode involves the abandonment of their hermeneutics, but includes also the introduction of other metaphors—scientific and literary—in its place.

In chapter xii Gosse again recollects his dedication to the "manifest and uninterrupted and uncompromised 'service of the Lord,' " and his parents' understanding of that event. The act of dedication, extreme even by the standards of the Plymouth Brethren, involves a direct appropriation of a biblical type:

> In their ecstasy, my parents had taken me, as Elkanah and Hannah had long ago taken Samuel, from their mountain-home of Ramathaim-Zophim down to sacrifice to the Lord of Hosts in Shiloh. They had girt me about with a linen ephod, and had hoped to leave me there; "as long as he liveth," they had said, "he shall be lent unto the Lord." (147)

The role of an "infant Samuel" is not unusual in spiritual auto-biography. (Ruskin's mother, for example, had similar plans for her son.) But his parents' complete immersion in the language of Scripture is—at least in the nineteenth century. Their thinking illustrates a typological system which treats experience as a repetition of patterns pre-ordained by the Word of God. And the syntax of the passage itself suggests the power of their language system. What begins as a simile—as Elkanah and Hannah did X, so my parents did Y— collapses from comparison to identification, with no differentiation between the actions of a righteous couple in age of Israelite judges and Christian parents in the nineteenth century. According to the syntax, it is Philip and Emily Gosse who descended from the mountains, sacrificed at Shiloh, and clothed their son in a linen ephod. What appears to be an interpretation here is nothing less than a total assimilation of the parents' action into the originating type.

Or perhaps this is the ultimate form of typological interpretation. For what typology aims at—at least in autobiographical writing—is an understanding of personal experience completely and exclusively within the framework of biblical patterns and principles. It seeks to *merge* the contemporary into the biblical in the legal sense of that verb: to "lose character or identity by absorption into something else" (OED). Thus, the Pauline ideal of beholding Christ in the mirror and being transformed into his image (2 Cor. 3:18) describes visually what typology attempts verbally: a loss of self-identity through absorption into the types—which are, finally, patterns of Christ.

The absorption is total for Gosse's parents. They have no consciousness of a separation between their lives and the Scriptures, and
they employ typology with what must be called hermeneutic naiveté.
Gosse the autobiographer, however, is fully conscious of their system
qua system. He understands that it operates so powerfully for them
precisely because they do not think of it in such terms. This is why he
calls it, in retrospect, the "Great Scheme," admitting that he cannot
resist the "mortuary honour of capital letters" (147). The mortuary
label becomes a means of negating the scheme, of deadening its effect.
Yet verbal mortuarization proves not to be an effective means of
negation, and Gosse's technique of parody, so effective in the baptism
and conversion episodes, does not operate here.

Instead of parody, Gosse tries a dispersal of interpretive authority.
Immediately after this passage, he counters his parents' interpretation
of his life with a biblical alternative: Gehazi, the servant of Elisha.
Like Gehazi, he suggests, he was more interested in material profit
than in spiritual service, and when his step-uncle offered him a
position in banking, only to have the offer refused by his father, he
was sharply disappointed: "I felt very much like Gehazi, and I would
fain have followed after the banker if I had dared do so, into the night.
I would have excused to him the ardour of my Elisha, and I would
have reminded him of the sons of the prophets—'Give me, I pray
thee,' I would have said, 'a talent of silver and two changes of
garments' " (148−49). The writing serves as counterexample, the
truth of Gosse's experience testifying against his father's interpretation. In the extremity of its choice—Gehazi was a type of the
"avaricious and ungodly man" and his punishment with leprosy, "the
proper emblem of the polluted stage of his soul"—it has the potential
to become parody.[59] But Gosse suppresses this potentiality, allowing
neither an exaggeration of the form of interpretation nor a displacement of its traditional meaning. Instead, the counterexample attempts to limit the power of the Great Scheme. It prevents the
autobiographical self from being assimilated into the biblical model
and keeps the two elements of the analogy distinct through the
manipulation of possessive pronouns and conditional verbs. It stays

conscious of the fact, unlike the example it counters, that this is an act of interpretation.

Despite its hermeneutic distinctions, the counterexample does not significantly disrupt the system of interpretation within which Gosse's parents operate and his own autobiography struggles. Gosse seems unable to parody here, perhaps because the Great Scheme is too powerful in its reading, too inclusive in its understanding of human motivations. Although elsewhere he does attempt to parody the form of typological interpretation, in this culminating example what he substitutes for the traditional system of biblical typology is not a system at all but an unsystematic series of local interpretations, each one adopted to read a particular passage of his life.

Identifying these local interpretations has been the effort of other literary critics, and their discoveries need not be repeated here, even to argue against the inclination to impose upon *Father and Son* a single generic category.[60] Two of these local interpretations, however, are suggestive of Gosse's stance toward hermeneutic systems in autobiographical writing and representative as well of the end of the tradition of Victorian autobiography. These interpretations—one scientific, the other literary—follow the Samuel and Gehazi example and counterexample in chapter xii, although one could as easily examine other scientific or literary analogies in *Father and Son* to demonstrate the unsystematic nature of Gosse's approach.

The first example uses the speckled soldier-crab, a sea creature from his father's aquarium, and like the Gehazi correlation, it follows close upon the account of his parents' dedication of their son to the Lord. As if in response to their typological vision of his joyful departure from his "mountain-home of Ramathaim-Zophim" to serve and "sacrifice to the Lord of Hosts in Shiloh," Gosse records his actual feelings upon leaving Devonshire to work in London:

> I compared my lot with that of one of the speckled soldier-crabs that roamed about in my Father's aquarium, dragging after them great whorl-shells. They, if by chance they were turned out of their whelk-habitations, trailed about a pale soft body in

search of another house, visibly broken-hearted and the victims
of every ignominious accident. (161)

The tone of the comparison is elegiac rather than celebratory; its
mode, biological rather than biblical. It allows the adolescent Gosse
to explain to himself and in his own terms the reluctance he feels upon
leaving home, his fear of danger and of exile. More important, it
provides Gosse the autobiographer with an interpretation that cannot
be incorporated into the Great Scheme.

The effect of this biological mode of interpretation can be gauged
by comparing it to a similar example in *Grace Abounding*. In its
explicit anthropomorphism and visual keenness, it resembles Bunyan's comparison of himself to "a Bird that is shot from the top of a
Tree": so "down I fell . . . into great guilt and fearful despair."[61] In
Bunyan, however, the local metaphor is immediately subsumed into a
more comprehensive hermeneutical act. By the next sentence, Bunyan is analyzing his sin as a type of Esau's betrayal: "And withal, that
Scripture did seize upon my Soul, *Or profane person, as Esau, who for one*
morsel of meat sold his Birthright." In Gosse, the comparison remains a
local one, neither superseded by a biblical model nor incorporated
into a scientific system of interpretation. Beyond its visual keenness,
it has limited authority. Biological metaphor is not elevated to the
status of system. It never becomes fully "scientific."

Nonetheless, it does have a personal effect. Like Gosse's earlier
comparisons of his soul to a flower in a crannied nook (12) or his state
to that of "a small and solitary bird, caught and hung out hopelessly
and endlessly in a great glittering cage" (111), it provides a means of
resisting his father's powerful language system. "The clearness of the
personal image affected me as all the texts and prayers and predictions
had failed to do," he notes, commenting on the caged-bird image. "I
saw myself imprisoned for ever in the religious system which had
caught me and would whirl my helpless spirit as in . . . concentric
wheels" (111). Visual keenness silently counters a hegemony of
language.

A verbal resistance follows the visual, originating in the discovery of forbidden literature and manifesting itself in an ability to create metaphors and make literary allusions. Throughout Gosse's childhood, most literature (but specifically fiction) had been prohibited as sinful lie-telling and antagonistic to his religious dedication. That this should necessarily have been so Gosse denies, arguing that the prohibition only served to remove "supernatural fancy" from his psyche and make him "positive and skeptical" (17). Gosse's argument has authority, in part because it derives from an autobiographical tradition—including Wordsworth's *Prelude*, book V, and Mill's *Autobiography*, chapter III—that gives priority to imaginative literature in the growth of the human mind. But the autobiographical tradition may here blind Gosse to the truth of his own autobiographical insight. The use of literary example and language in *Father and Son* is more ambivalent than Gosse explicitly acknowledges. The creative acts of the young boy, which the autobiography preserves and extends, challenge the biblical hermeneutics of his father even more effectively than do the biological metaphors.

Most of the literary examples seem innocent enough, like the use of *Aurora Leigh* to describe his haphazard education (91) or the quotation from Coleridge to evoke his first encounter with poetry, "a breeze mid blossoms playing" (93). A few are nasty but apt, like the lines from *Paradise Lost* ("so huge a rout / Encumbered him with ruin") used to suggest his father's fall from popularity with the publication of *Omphalos* and, by association, his father's Satanic pride (62). But innocence and aptness do not account for their collective power. These literary analogies and allusions, five times as frequent as the scientific, are substitutions for biblical patterns of interpretation. In most instances, they do not complement a biblical scheme; they contradict it.

The text of *Father and Son*, like its texture, reveals what Gosse cannot admit. Its narrative belies his argument that literature enfolds its reader in "supernatural fancy," and the texture of its literary examples not only belies, but reenacts the means by which "supernatural fancy" is exposed for what it is. When Gosse cites Prospero's speech to Caliban from *The Tempest*, for example:

> I pitied thee,
> Took pains to make thee speak, taught thee each hour
> One thing or other, when thou didst not, savage,
> Know thine own meaning, but wouldst gabble, like
> A thing most brutish; I endowed thy purposes
> With words that made them know.

—his interpretation concentrates on the power that books give to articulate "the image and the idea" out of "darkness into strong light" (153−54). The interpretation assumes a creative, constructive power, one that Gosse identifies with poetry or, more broadly, with literary writing. He makes this interpretation, however, only by suppressing the counterspeech of Caliban:

> You taught me language, and my profit on't
> Is, I know how to curse.

The negating, destructive impulse of language is felt in the texture of the literary example, whether or not Gosse foregrounds it in his interpretation. It is as much a part of what the reader understands about a literary substitution for a biblical hermeneutic as Gosse's direct statement of constructive power is—perhaps more so because it replicates the process and effect of the substitution.

In a compelling reading of *Father and Son*, Vivien and Robert Folkenflik have suggested that the primary movement traced in the autobiography is that from the Word of God to a personal word: "The informing principle of this portrait of the artist as a young man is the opposition of the child's attempt to find the authentic word to his father's belief in 'The Word,' the fundamentalism of the Plymouth Brethren." They suggest, too, that Gosse finds a personal language in "the language of fiction," which "both reaffirms his inner self and permits him to escape the sterility of feeling himself as other."[62] This reading accurately stresses Gosse's opposition, both as protagonist and autobiographer, to the Word of God and his turn to the language of fiction as a substitute of word for Word. We might question, however, whether the language of fiction can ever reaffirm (or confirm) an "inner self"; an understanding of the former may, as Paul de

Man has suggested, preclude an affirmation of the latter.[63] Gosse himself was never deceived about the possibility of fiction providing an "authentic" word. For him, authenticity—in its fundamental sense of originality, priority, and authority (a word which derives from the same Latin root)—was an impossibility. Hence his piecemeal substitutions in *Father and Son* of discrete scientific and literary interpretations for a comprehensive biblical system.

We can sense the absence of an authentic, authoritative word throughout *Father and Son*. It is noticeable in passages like the climactic one of chapter xii, which deals explicitly with Gosse's abandonment of biblical hermeneutics and recreates narratively his movement from one interpretive system to another. It is noticeable in many less dramatic passages, which demand that Gosse by some means interpret his reality.

The hermeneutic predicament that the absence of authority creates for Gosse—and, indeed, for all late and post-Victorian autobiographers—can be illustrated with one such undramatic passage, a seemingly simple moment that involves an act of retrospection with little apparent self-interpretation. It appears in chapter vi (77–78), where Gosse attempts to recreate through figuration the Devonshire coast as it existed during his childhood and where that figuration brings into play competing literary, biblical, and scientific systems. The passage, which I read as an example of a late Victorian mode of self-interpretation and as an emblem of generic demise, begins this way:

> Half a century ago, in many parts of the coast of Devonshire and Cornwall, where the limestone at the water's edge is wrought into crevices and hollows, the tide-line was, like Keats' Grecian vase, "a still unravished bride of quietness."

One expects the Keatsian simile to control the subsequent memory, to evoke a desire for permanence and create a sense of loss, perhaps even to testify to the truth of beauty rather than the truth of religion or science. The simile does, in a sense, accomplish these things. As

the reader moves through the passage, its latent promise of loss
becomes a manifest threat:

> These rock-basins, fringed by corallines, filled with still water
> almost as pellucid as the upper air itself, thronged with beauti-
> ful sensitive forms of life,—they exist no longer, they are all
> profaned, and emptied, and vulgarised.

If, however, this language interprets the memory of the unspoiled
Devonshire coast by means of literary simile, its mortal "rock basins"
of "still water" fulfilling Keats' immortal and "still unravished" urn
even (paradoxically) in their emptying and profanation, the passage in
no sense offers a comprehensive interpretation of Gosse's experience.
Within it, other means of interpretation contribute to—and compete
with—the literary.

There is the biblical, for instance. The rockpools at the water's
edge, Gosse continues, lay "undisturbed since the creation of the
world": "if the Garden of Eden had been situate in Devonshire, Adam
and Eve, stepping lightly down to bathe in the rainbow-coloured
spray, would have seen the identical sights that we saw now." The
sense of rockpools "undisturbed" since the creation of the world
augments the initial suggestion of an "unravished" urn, and the
imagined Adam and Eve, like the figures in Keats' ode, contribute to
a sense of a "paradise" that might be and has been "violated." These
two systems of understanding experience—and ultimately the interpretations they produce—are competitive. One soon realizes this fact
if one tries to find a single adjective for the world Gosse describes: Is it
prelapsarian? eternal? (im)mortal? (im)mutable? Such labels suggest
different schemes of time and different stances vis-à-vis experience.

No longer can a biblical hermeneutic provide, as in a pre-critical
era, a comprehensive understanding of experience. In Gosse we
witness "the eclipse of biblical narrative," the inability of the biblical
text to encompass the experience of the modern age or its inhabitants.[64] But neither can another single system replace the biblical.
For if Gosse uses a biblical figure to supplement the Keatsian, he then
adds a scientific to supplement them both: "The exquisite product of
centuries of natural selection has been crushed under the rough paw of

well-meaning, idle-minded curiosity." How does this biological metaphor, with its allusion to the scientific system of the *Origin of Species*, fit with the others? What adjective now can describe the world Gosse recollects: Darwinian? evolutionary? material?

In reading narrative, whether fictional or autobiographical, we tend to grant authority to final moments as to first instances, to ends as to origins. In this passage, however, because the scientific reading occurs last, it does not thereby gain authority. For Gosse there would be too much irony in granting an evolutionary metaphor such authority, and there are too many literary and biblical figures that appear subsequently in *Father and Son* to draw that conclusion anyway. All three systems—literary, biblical, scientific—allow possible and alternative recollections of the past, and all three occur throughout Gosse's autobiography as modes of self-interpretation. The reader may choose among them and, like the autobiographer, view experience according to his wont.

A multiplicity of interpretive systems allows the autobiographer great freedom in self-writing, and in *Father and Son* Gosse used this multiplicity to create one of the finest autobiographies in the English tradition. Post-Victorian autobiographers knew even greater freedom. Whereas the goal of early Victorian autobiographers, like Carlyle, had been to revitalize biblical hermeneutics or, like Newman, to adapt its conventions to particular religious concerns, late Victorian autobiographers maintained little interest in any system of biblical hermeneutics. Scientific autobiographers had not only suggested new modes of examining the self, thus making it possible to revise or recreate the conventions of the genre. In their effective displacement of biblical hermeneutics, they had also made possible the introduction of many other metaphors of the self, scientific and non-scientific. Gosse's easy alternation of the biological and literary illustrates this possibility and suggests the future for autobiographical writing.

Greater freedom brings its own disadvantages, however. As modern theories of poetic development have suggested, strong poets are created in and by their struggles with strong poetic precursors: in Harold Bloom's words, "Weaker talents idealize; figures of capable imagination appropriate for themselves."[1] Not only weaker talents, but weaker precedents are at issue here. Strong autobiographers, we might also say, are created in and by their struggles with strong generic precedents. The Victorian writers of this study—Carlyle, Newman, Martineau, Ruskin, and Gosse—represent both corporately and individually the strongest autobiographers of the English tradition. These autobiographers had known what their generic materials were. They had worked within (and against) a strong autobiographical tradition, and thus, paradoxically, they had known the real possibility of creating sophisticated literary works.

That possibility was more real for them than for their successors who faced a weakened generic tradition. The great Victorian autobiographies had depended on a hegemony of biblical hermeneutics and a common fund of autobiographical conventions. With the end of that hegemony and a diffusion of the conventions, the creation of what I have called hermeneutic autobiography became more difficult. After the publication of the last Victorian autobiographies by Spencer, Butler, and Gosse, the form that had developed from Bunyan's *Grace Abounding*, continued in the spiritual accounts of the eighteenth century, and then flourished in the Victorian era, met its demise. The autobiographical impulse still found expression in other literary genres, but bereft of the hermeneutic imperative that had made the Victorian autobiography a self-conscious literary tradition.

❧ NOTES ❧

CHAPTER 1

1   *The Works of John Ruskin*, ed. E. T. Cook and Alexander Wedderburn (London: George Allen, 1903–12), IV, 348–49, n. 4.

2   *Praeterita*, in *Works*, XXXV, 11.

3   The other paradox is, of course, that such conventions allow freedom. Although he avoids the concept of convention, Michael G. Cooke notes that "the ultimate paradox of autobiography" is that "the more it is beset with limits, the more it enables its subject to survive and define (i.e., limn and delimit) himself. No other literary form . . . has such limits or such tight-rope precariousness *as form;* no other form has such personal freedom." See his "'Do You Remember Laura?' or, The Limits of Autobiography," in the *Iowa Review*, 9 (1978), ii, 72.

4   Avrom Fleishman's recent *The Figures of Autobiography: The Language of Self-Writing in Victorian and Modern England* (Berkeley and Los Angeles: Univ. of California Press, 1983) treats Augustine's *Confessions* as the originating book and traces examples of Augustinian figures in a variety of well-known English autobiographies. While recognizing the importance of Augustine's work in the western tradition, my own account of English literary history differs from Fleishman's in two significant ways: (1) I take the practice of biblical typology to be the source of many of the figures that Fleishman identifies as specifically Augustinian, a practice that was more widespread in England in the seventeenth through nineteenth centuries than familiarity with the *Confessions*; (2) I take the spiritual autobiographies of the late seventeenth and eighteenth centuries, rather than the *Confessions*, to be influential in the development of English forms of the genre, in large part because they were well known, and Augustine's work was less so until Newman and Pusey re-introduced it to Victorian readers in the 1830s (see chapter 4).

5   John N. Morris, *Versions of the Self: Studies in English Autobiography from John Bunyan to John Stuart Mill* (New York: Basic Books, 1966), pp. 3–6. The distinction between introspective autobiography (also called "subjective" or "developmental" autobiography) and the more public, *res gestae* form is extensively treated by Wayne Shumaker in *English Autobiography: Its Emergence, Materials, and Form* (Berkeley and Los Angeles: Univ. of California Press, 1954), pp. 56–97. I follow the common practice of designating the latter form "memoir"

195

to distinguish it from the introspective "autobiography," while recognizing that during the nineteenth century this distinction in terminology was not consistently maintained.

6 "Eigentlich gehört nur das zur Hermeneutik was Ernesti Prol. 4 subtilitas intelligendi nennt. Denn die [subtilitas] explicandi sobald sie mehr ist als die äussere Seite des Verstehens ist wiederum ein Object der Hermeneutik und gehört zur Kunst des Darstellens." Discussed by Richard E. Palmer in *Hermeneutics: Interpretation Theory in Schleiermacher, Dilthey, Heidegger, and Gadamer* (Evanston: Northwestern Univ. Press, 1969), pp. 85−86, and by Hans W. Frei in *The Eclipse of Biblical Narrative: A Study in Eighteenth and Nineteenth Century Hermeneutics* (New Haven: Yale Univ. Press, 1974), pp. 341−42.

7 Palmer, pp. 85−86. Hayden White's distinction between explanation by "emplotment" and explanations by "formal argument" or "ideological implication" provides another way of explaining the act of writing autobiography. As White points out, writers of history provide "meaning" by the kinds of plots they choose to shape the historical data; but they also provide "meaning" (or "interpretation") by "formal, explicit, or discursive argument" and by their statements about "the nature of historical knowledge and the implications that can be drawn from the study of past events for the understanding of present ones" (see his *The Historical Imagination in Nineteenth-Century Europe* [Baltimore: Johns Hopkins Univ. Press, 1973], pp. 7−29). Using White's distinctions, one might say that autobiographers (who are, after all, personal historians) give their lives meanings with explanations by "emplotment," but they give priority to explanations by "formal argument" or "ideological implication."

8 Shumaker, esp. chaps. 5−8; Roy Pascal, *Design and Truth in Autobiography* (London: Routledge and Kegan Paul, 1960); and William C. Spengemann, *The Forms of Autobiography: Episodes in the History of a Literary Genre* (New Haven: Yale Univ. Press, 1980), esp. pp. xiii−xvii. Spengemann's approach has been particularly useful in recent critical discussions because it raises the question of historical development, a matter too often excluded in theoretical studies of the genre.

9 Throughout most of this book, I shall use the masculine pronouns, "he" and "his," when referring to the autobiographer and his work. My reasons are historical: as I explain in chapter 5, Victorian women seldom wrote this genre.

10 Medieval exegetes might have called some versions of this application *tropological* rather than *typological,* but Protestants, who adhorred allegory and the notion of interpretive "levels," used the term *typology* to designate all interpretation that accepted the original biblical character or event as a real, historical fact. See George P. Landow's important discussion of typological practice in England in *Victorian Types, Victorian Shadows: Biblical Typology in Victorian Literature, Art, and Thought* (Boston: Routledge and Kegan Paul, 1980), as well as Erich Auerbach's seminal "Figura," in *Scenes from the Drama of European*

Literature (New York: Meriden Books, 1959). The standard Victorian discussion of typological hermeneutics is Patrick Fairbairn's two-volume *The Typology of Scripture* (1900; rpt. Grand Rapids: Baker Books, 1975), which was originally published in 1847.

11 John Bunyan, *Grace Abounding to the Chief of Sinners,* ed. Roger Sharrock (Oxford: Clarendon Press, 1962), p. 2.

12 Many other episodes in *Grace Abounding* follow this pattern, which continues to shape the autobiographical episode well into the Victorian period, as Shumaker intuited when he noticed the preference for "summary" over "scene" and treated Victorian autobiography as a "mixed mode." See esp. his comparison of Anthony Trollope's *Autobiography* and the parallel scene from *The Three Clerks,* pp. 158—84.

13 Bunyan, sec. 132—33. Henceforth, section numbers will be cited in the text.

14 *Works,* IV, 348—49, n. 4.

15 G. A. Starr, *Defoe and Spiritual Autobiography* (Princeton: Princeton Univ. Press, 1965), p. 27, and Morris, p. 102.

16 William Cowper, *Memoir of the Early Life of William Cowper, Esq., Written by Himself, And never before published.* (London: R. Edwards, 1816), p. 11.

17 Ibid., p. 12.

18 See the publisher's preface, ibid., pp. vi—vii and xvi.

19 Ibid., p. 83.

20 Elizabeth West, *Memoirs, or Spiritual Exercises of Elizabeth West: Written by her Own Hand* (Glasgow: John Bryce, 1766), pp. 35, 90.

21 Alexander Cruden, *The Adventures of Alexander the Corrector* (London: n.p., 1754). In real life, Cruden was the author of a much-respected concordance to the Bible; in his autobiography, he is a post-figuration of Joseph and a host of other men—including, as his title suggests, Alexander the Great.

22 Thomas Scott, *The Force of Truth: An Authentic Narrative, of the Religious Experience and Wonderful Conversion of the late Rev. Thomas Scott, D.D.* (New Haven: Nathan Whiting, [1820]), pp. 124, 127. To his contemporaries Scott was known as "the theologian of the Evangelicals," primarily because of the massive biblical commentary he published between 1788 and 1792. Although considerably different in temperament, he became a close friend of John Newton and, through him, of William Cowper.

23 Ibid., p. 20

24 Ibid., p. 84.

25 Ibid., p. 27.

26 Starr, p. 48. Starr refers not to Scott, whom he does not discuss, but to similar eighteenth-century accounts.

27 The high proportion of natural incidents in Cowper's autobiography marks it as a pre-Romantic work, a precursor of autobiographies like Ruskin's *Praeterita.* Although roughly contemporary with Cowper (and, indeed, after his conversion, a friend of both Cowper and Newton), Scott is a rationalist in tempera-

ment, much like the young John Stuart Mill before his crisis.

28 I borrow the term *graphocentricity* from Denis Donohogue's *Ferocious Alphabets* (Boston: Little, Brown, 1981).

29 See, e.g., Harold Bloom, *The Anxiety of Influence: A Theory of Poetics* (New York: Oxford Univ. Press, 1973).

30 For a discussion of this ideal of progress, see. R.S. Crane, "Anglican Apologetics and the Idea of Progress, 1699−1745," *Modern Philology*, 31 (1934), 273−301 and 349−82.

31 Cf. Bunyan's response to the "Scripture language" of the Bedford Christians (sec. 37−38). Initially he feels excluded from this community of believers because he cannot understand their discourse: "they spake with such pleasantness of Scripture language, and with such appearance of grace in all they said, that they were to me as if they had found a new world, as if they were people that dwelt alone." By later writing an autobiography in such language, he demonstrates his membership with the community and in effect exhibits "the true tokens of a truly godly man" (sec. 40).

32 William Wordsworth, "From *The Recluse,*" *Selected Poems and Prefaces,* ed. Jack Stillinger (Boston: Houghton Mifflin, 1965), p. 45.

33 William York Tindall, *John Bunyan, Mechanick Preacher* (New York: Columbia Univ. Press, 1934), pp. 22−41.

34 Francesco Spira, *A Relation of the Fearful Estate of Francis Spira, After he turned Apostate from the Protestant Church to Popery* (Hartford: John Babcock, 1798).

35 Earl Miner, ed., *Literary Uses of Typology from the Late Middle Ages to the Present* (Princeton: Princeton Univ. Press, 1977).

36 See Hans Frei's discussion in *The Eclipse of Biblical Narrative*, pp. 251−55. As Frei points out, the application of the text has always been important to the devout—hence its emphasis among Pietists in Germany and later among evangelicals in England, even to the neglect of *subtilitas intelligendi* and *subtilitas explicandi*.

37 Richard Baxter, *A Paraphrase on the New Testament, with Notes, Doctrinal and Practical, Fitted to the Use of Religious Families, in their Daily Readings of the Scriptures* (London: Richard Edwards, 1811), p. iii. Baxter published the first edition in 1685.

38 All cited in U. Milo Kaufmann, *The Pilgrim's Progress and Traditions in Puritan Meditation* (New Haven: Yale University Press, 1966), pp. 81−92.

39 P[hilip] Doddridge, *The Family Expositor, Or, A Paraphrase and Version of the New Testament with Critical Notes, and a Practical Improvement of Each Section,* 7th ed. (London: T. Longman, 1792), p. xi.

40 Hannah More, *The Works of Hannah More* (New York: Harper and Brothers, 1854), II, 216. More's *Strictures on the Modern System of Female Education* make it clear that she believes these deficiencies to result from sexual rather than personal traits: [I]f women have in an equal degree the faculty of fancy which

creates images, and the faculty of memory which collects and stores ideas, they seem not to possess in equal measure the faculty of comparing, combining, analysing, and separating these ideas; that deep and patient thinking which goes to the bottom of the subject; nor that power of arrangement which knows how to link a thousand connected ideas in one dependant [sic] train, without losing sight of the original idea out of which the rest grow, and on which they all hang" (*Works*, I, 367).

41   See, e.g., his sermon, "The Scapegoat," in Henry Melvill, *The Golden Lectures* (London: James Paul, n.d.), which uses typology to argue the evangelical view of a vicarious atonement.

42   See, e.g., "Honey from the Rock," in Henry Melvill, *Lectures on Practical Subjects, Delivered at St. Margaret's, Lothbury* (New York: Stanford and Swords, 1853).

43   Ibid., pp. 30—31. In *Victorian Types, Victorian Shadows* Landow quotes Melvill's defense of this practical application of biblical history: "We are not to regard the Scriptural histories as mere registers of facts, such as are commonly the histories of eminent men: they are rather selection of facts, suitableness for purposes of instruction having regulated the choice" (p. 38).

44   Scott may have continued to repeat the practical lessons of the biblical text, but his understanding of the interpretive act was radically different from Baxter's, as his formal separation of critical and practical notes suggests.

45   David Couzens Hoy, *The Critical Circle: Literature, History, and Philosophical Hermeneutics* (Berkeley and Los Angeles: Univ. of California Press, 1978).

CHAPTER 2

1   Wayne Shumaker defines autobiography thus in *English Autobiography*, p. 106. The distinction between modal and generic terms derives from Alastair Fowler, who in *Kinds of Literature: An Introduction to the Theory of Genres and Modes* (Cambridge: Harvard Univ. Press, 1982) points out that "terms for kinds" can "always be put in noun form ('epigram'; 'epic'), whereas modal terms tend to be adjectival." See pp. 106—18 and 130—48 for Fowler's instructive discussion of kind (genre), mode, and subgenre.

2   Thomas Carlyle, *Sartor Resartus*, ed. C. F. Harrold (New York: Odyssey Press, 1937), p. xxx. Citations throughout the chapter will be to this edition.

3   Johann Wolfgang von Goethe, *The Autobiography of Johann Wolfgang von Goethe*, trans. John Oxenford (1848; New York: Horizon Press, 1969), p. 3. The account begins: "On the 28th of August, 1749, at midday, as the clock struck twelve, I came into the world, at Frankfurt-on-the-Main. My horoscope was propitious: the sun stood in the sign of the Virgin, and had culminated for the day; Jupiter and Venus looked on him with a friendly eye, and Mercury not adversely; while Saturn and Mars kept themselves indifferent; the moon alone,

just full, exerted the power of her reflection all the more, as she had then reached her planetary hour. She opposed herself, therefore, to my birth, which could not be accomplished until this hour was passed."

4　Roy Pascal, *Design and Truth in Autobiography* (Cambridge: Harvard Univ. Press, 1960). Pascal's title alludes, of course, to Goethe's title *Dichtung und Wahrheit*.

5　Fleishman, pp. 1—39.

6　George Levine, *The Boundaries of Fiction: Carlyle, Macaulay, Newman* (Princeton: Princeton Univ. Press, 1968), pp. 22—24. Levine is adapting Northrup Frye's terminology in the *Anatomy of Criticism* (Princeton: Princeton Univ. Press, 1957), pp. 303—14.

7　Besides Bunyan's *Grace Abounding*, another seminal example in the English tradition is George Fox's *Journal*, which Carlyle's allusions in "An Incident in Modern History" suggest he knew as well. Because Fox's account uses the Quaker form of autobiography, first narrating his conversion and then recording in diary style the journeys from meeting to meeting, it was somewhat less influential in the English literary tradition. It represents, however, the standard Quaker form of autobiographical narrative.

8　John Bunyan, *Grace Abounding to the Chief of Sinners*, ed. Roger Sharrock (Oxford: Clarendon Press, 1962), p. 2. Further citations will be to this edition of the text, but will be given by section number to make reference to other editions easier.

9　In "The Myth of the Fall: A Description of Autobiography," *Genre*, 12 (1979), 45—67, Martha Ronk Lifson argues the widespread use of the Fall pattern throughout Western autobiography, and supplementing her evidence, Avrom Fleishman treats the Fall as the central figure of the nineteenth century in *Figures of Autobiography*, pp. 116—20. It is probably futile to argue the dominance of the Fall versus the Exodus, since patterns of fall, exile, and return occur in most spiritual accounts. For the theological as well as apologetic reasons I discuss later, I treat the Exodus as the basic pattern of the English autobiography.

10　In J. Hillis Miller's terms, Bunyan consciously allows only a Platonic form of repetition, which "establishes the world as icon," to influence the narrative and hermeneutic form of *Grace Abounding*. This passage suggests, however, that a Nietzschean form of repetition, which "defines the world of simulacra," enters unconsciously. See J. Hillis Miller, *Fiction and Repetition: Seven English Novels* (Cambridge: Harvard Univ. Press, 1982), pp. 1—21.

11　In *The Secular Pilgrims of Victorian Fiction: The Novel as Book of Life* (Cambridge: Cambridge Univ. Press, 1982), Barry V. Qualls similarly points out that the English Editor gives Teufelsdröckh's "bagged materials their *familiar* shape": "The Editor gives a Bunyanesque structure to a Romantic's quest; he sorts Diogenes' scribblings into the shape of Christian's progress" (p. 20).

12　Carlyle's conjunction of Genesis and Exodus here helps clarify Avrom

Fleishman's point that a central figure for nineteenth-century autobiography is "the myth of the Fall" (see *Figures of Autobiography*, pp. 116−20). It is important to note, however, that virtually all Victorian autobiographers invoke the Exodus, while only some include a Fall. Those who, like Carlyle, include the Fall do so self-consciously, quite aware that they are grafting a Romantic figure onto an older generic tradition.

13   Elizabeth W. Bruss, *Autobiographical Acts: The Changing Situation of a Literary Genre* (Baltimore: Johns Hopkins Univ. Press, 1976), p. 11.

14   It is significant that at this point in Book Second the choice can be designated as neither Editor's nor subject's exclusively, but as the examples in this paragraph suggest, one that belongs to both. Protagonist and autobiographer have moved nearer each other in time and perspective, a movement represented in the breakdown in distinctions between Teufelsdröckh and his Editor.

15   See G. B. Tennyson, *"Sartor" Called "Resartus": The Genesis, Structure, and Style of Carlyle's First Major Work* (Princeton: Princeton Univ. Press, 1965), pp. 201−15.

16   Johann Wolfgang von Goethe, *The Sufferings of Young Werther*, trans. Bayard Quincy Morgan (New York: Frederick Ungar, 1957), p. 98.

17   Joseph Sigman, "Adam-Kadmon, Nifl, Muspel, and the Biblical Symbolism of *Sartor Resartus*," *ELH*, 41 (1974), 240−43.

18   John Stuart Mill, *Autobiography*, ed. Jack Stillinger (Boston: Houghton Mifflin, 1969), p. 81.

19   Walter L. Reed, "The Pattern of Conversion in *Sartor Resartus*," *ELH*, 38 (1971), 413−14.

20   C. F. Harrold, *Carlyle and German Thought* (New Haven: Yale Univ. Press, 1934), p. 5; see also his introduction to the Odyssey Press edition, p. xxxiv.

21   Tennyson suggests an Augustinian as well as a Calvinistic influence, quoting Augustine's "Descend, so that ye may ascend" to explain "The Everlasting No" and using the Augustinian "trial of the center" to discuss "The Centre of Indifference." See *"Sartor" Called "Resartus*," pp. 296, 310.

22   This failure is apparent in Harrold's formulation itself: "a brilliant metaphorical adaptation of German idealism, in its *terms* and *concepts*, to the surviving intellectual *design* bequeathed by Calvinism." "Terms" and "concepts" mingle with "design," but at no point does Harrold clarify what he means by the relationship of concept to design, of idea to form. Nor is it even clear that by "design" he means narrative form (although many of the footnotes in his critical edition suggest that he does). Forty years later Reed repeats the confusion, even as he disagrees with Harrold's statement. Quoting Basil Willey that "the Christian reader" will notice in *Sartor Resartus* "a lack of conformity with the established pattern of conversion: there is no contrition, no reliance upon grace or redeeming love, but on the contrary, much proud and passionate self-assertion," Reed argues that "Christian tradition and doctrine" fail to provide "a

model" for Teufelsdröckh's pattern of conversion (p. 413). Reed is correct that Teufelsdröckh fails to meet doctrinal standards, but wrong to equate doctrine with narrative pattern. He is also wrong to quote Willey in his support. For while Willey discusses Carlyle's deviations from the traditional conversion experience, he also takes note of Carlyle's literary predecessors. Carlyle's "description of this ordeal," he writes of the incident on the Rue St. Thomas de L'Enfer, "reminds one of Bunyan's in *Grace Abounding*." See Basil Willey's *Nineteenth Century Studies: Coleridge to Matthew Arnold* (New York: Columbia Univ. Press, 1949), p. 114—15.

23   David J. DeLaura's recent discussions of Goethe's influence upon Carlyle and Arnold, especially through *Werther, Wilhelm Meisters Lehrjahre*, and *Dichtung und Wahrheit*, remind us that we should not separate these influences either. Goethe himself revised the traditional Christian model of suffering and purgation into a pattern for the secular *Bildungsroman* and into what DeLaura identifies in Arnold as the "suffering-'one'-wise man-throne" causal sequence. See "Arnold and Goethe: The One on the Intellectual Throne," in *Victorian Literature and Society: Essays Presented to Richard D. Altick*, ed. James R. Kincaid and Albert J. Kuhn (Columbus: Ohio State Univ. Press, 1984), pp. 197—224, and "Heroic Egotism: Goethe and the Fortunes of *Bildung* in Victorian England," in *Johann Wolfgang von Goethe: One Hundred and Fifty Years of Continuing Vitality*, ed. Ulrich Goebel and Wolodymyr T. Zyla (Lubbock: Texas Tech Press, 1984), pp. 41—59.

24   Fairbairn, I, 16. The two volumes of Fairbairn's work were originally published in the 1840s.

25   Thomas Scott, *The Holy Bible, Containing the Old and New Testaments, with Original Notes, Practical Observations, and Copious References*, 6 vols. (New York: Williams and Whiting, 1810), s.v. Matt. 2.9—12. The first edition was published in England between 1788 and 1792 and soon became the most widely read commentary on the Bible.

26   David Friedrich Strauss, *The Life of Jesus Critically Examined*, trans. George Eliot (1846; Philadelphia: Fortress Press, 1972), p. 163.

27   Ibid., pp. 174.

28   E. S. Shaffer, *'Kubla Khan' and The Fall of Jerusalem: The Mythological School in Biblical Criticism and Secular Literature, 1770—1880* (Cambridge: Cambridge Univ. Press, 1972), p. 22 ff. In "Sterling, Carlyle, and German Higher Criticism: A Reassessment" (*Victorian Studies,* 26 [1983], 269—85), Anthony J. Harding also discusses the English knowledge of German biblical scholarship in the 1820s.

29   As Carlyle emphasizes the multiple authors and texts, his phrases also suggest an idea of an interpretive community, anticipatory of that described by Stanley Fish in *Is There a Text in This Class?* (Cambridge: Harvard Univ. Press, 1980), esp. pp. 303—71.

30 David Friedrich Strauss, *The Christ of Faith and the Jesus of History: A Critique of Schleiermacher's The Life of Jesus*, trans. Leander E. Keck (Philadelphia: Fortress Press, 1977).

31 Pascal, p. 16.

32 Quoted by Harrold, p. 166, n. 3.

33 In this context, the philosophical segments of Book Third represent the conventional exposition of the hermeneutic assumptions on which the narrative depends. For Newman's very different reworking of this autobiographical convention, see chap. 4.

CHAPTER 3

1 John D. Rosenberg discusses Ruskin's reverence for Carlyle in *The Darkening Glass: A Portrait of Ruskin's Genius* (New York: Columbia Univ. Press, 1961), p. 141, n. 6.

2 *The Works of John Ruskin*, ed. E. T. Cook and Alexander Wedderburn, Library Edition (London: George Allen, 1903-12), V, 427. The title of the appendix is "Plagiarism." All citations of Ruskin's works will be to this edition.

3 According to Rosenberg, p. 141, "Carlyle created in *Past and Present* the idiom Ruskin was to perfect in *Unto This Last*." Both employed "the ethics of the Gospels and the rhetoric of the Prophets" in a "moving indictment of England's Mammonism."

4 *Praeterita* (III.i.23), in *Works*, XXXV, 496. Hereafter, citations to Ruskin's autobiography will give volume, chapter, and section numbers of *Praeterita* rather than page numbers in the *Works*.

5 *Works*, IV, 349, n. 4.

6 The subtitle in the original edition is "Outlines of Scenes and Thoughts perhaps Worthy of Memory in my Past Life."

7 See the proof sheets of the first edition, Osborn Collection, Beinecke Rare Book and Manuscript Library, Yale University.

8 *Works*, XXXV, 72.

9 See George P. Landow, *The Aesthetic and Critical Theories of John Ruskin* (Princeton: Princeton Univ. Press, 1971), esp. ch. 5.

10 It may be that Ruskin uses a metaphorical formulation to obscure the relationship of the language he uses and the reality he wishes (or does not wish) to represent. It may be that he hopes through metaphor to fool his parents (or the spirit of his parents as readers). Given their religious predilections and interpretive habits, they would interpret his metaphor in a spiritual sense. Or perhaps, on the anniversary of his father's birth, he needs to fool himself.

11 Pierre Fontenay, "Ruskin and Paradise Regained," *Victorian Studies*, 12 (1969), 347—56; George P. Landow, "Introduction," *Approaches to Victorian Autobiogra-*

phy, ed. George P. Landow (Athens: Ohio University Press, 1979), p. xxxv; Elizabeth Helsinger, "The Structure of Ruskin's *Praeterita*," in *Approaches to Victorian Autobiography,* pp. 87−108; Heather Henderson, "'That there should be time no longer': Revelation and Recurrence in *Praeterita,*" Conference on Victorian Autobiography and Autobiographical Fiction, 5−6 August 1983, Santa Cruz, California; and Fleishman, p. 174−88.

12   Fleishman, p. 175. In most of these readings, the initial assumption (or final critical argument) has been that *Praeterita* belongs within the tradition of spiritual autobiography and that Ruskin has employed the conventions of the genre (whether called archetypal patterns, biblical types, or common topoi) in a traditional way to interpret his life and give coherence to his autobiography. Occasionally, critics of *Praeterita* have admitted to a generic confusion within the work, but usually it is to prove its ultimate unity. Even Helsinger, who tellingly suggests that "Ruskin seems to have tried to follow two conflicting models for autobiography," comes finally to this point.

13   Claudette Kemper Columbus, "Ruskin's *Praeterita* as Thanatography," in Landow, ed., *Approaches to Victorian Autobiography,* pp. 109−27.

14   Throughout *Praeterita* Ruskin's strategies of resistance develop from a tactic implicit in the "Christ Church Choir" passage quoted above. The periodic reminders of Old Testament types, of *The Pilgrim's Progress* and other works of typological interpretation, serve the same purpose in *Praeterita* as Bunyan's frequent allusions to the Exodus do in *Grace Abounding*—but with reverse effect. Whereas Bunyan uses types to interpret an episode of his experience or to sum up a period of his life, Ruskin refers to them to deny their hermeneutic validity. His critique of Old Testament typology and spiritual allegory expresses a conviction that Abraham's experience and Christian's pilgrimage were not— and still are not—translatable into a real, historical situation. Further, it suggests that typology and allegory claim to make a connection between two realities that cannot be made and can only trouble the man who puts faith in such connections.

15   Frei, pp. 3−8.

16   Ibid., pp. 4−5.

17   The Fountainbleau section was the last that Ruskin composed in his initial draft of the autobiography. If we consider it as the conclusion to a sequence of episodes focusing on the problem of interpretation, we can see that Ruskin has shifted from witty criticisms of typology in the opening chapters, to substitutions of other interpretive modes, to a discovery of the problematic nature of interpretation itself. Since these episodes represent a chronological account of Ruskin's intellectual development, and since Ruskin consulted his yearly diaries as he composed them, the sequence probably charts Ruskin's increasing uneasiness about typological hermeneutics during the 1830s, '40s, and '50s.

18   See the 1885 diary entries in the Osborn Collection for 22−23 February; 16, 22, 29 March; and 20−21 April, as well as the remnants in *Praeterita,*

I.viii.167–76, and in the appendix, "Prize Poems," in *Works*, XXXV, 614. Some of Ruskin's early attempts were quite successful; as "Prize Poems" explains, he won the prestigious Newdigate prize at Oxford.

19   "Preface," *Works*, XXXV, 12. The preface was written on the anniversary of his father's birthday, 10 May 1885. Ruskin wrote in what was "once my nursery in his old house."

20   See the diary entry for 21 April 1885.

21   Taken from the fourth ode of Horace, the title of chapter viii retains something of Ruskin's original intention to record that segment of his life spent under the protection of the Muses. The ode begins, however, with a question that had long plagued Ruskin: "auditis, an me ludit amabilis insania?" "Are you listening? Or does a pleasant feeling of inspiration delude me?"

22   This last quality, "invention," was precisely what Ruskin believed he lacked as a poet. In the diary entry for 22 March 1885, he noted, "I had not the slightest power of invention. My brain in this is as powerless as an animal's." His deprecatory self-analysis, so striking in this passage of the draft of *Praeterita*, contains many of the "essential qualities" he attributes to Byron, but used as a measure of his own failure.

23   George Gordon, Lord Byron, *Childe Harold*, I.23, in *The Works of Lord Byron* (Boston: Phillips, Sampson, 1853).

24   Jerome G. McGann, *Fiery Dust: Byron's Poetic Development* (Chicago: Univ. of Chicago Press, 1968), p. 38.

25   Michael Cooke, *The Blind Man Traces the Circle: On the Patterns and Philosophy of Byron's Poetry* (Princeton: Princeton Univ. Press, 1969), pp. 96–97.

26   Rosenberg, p. 223.

27   3 March 1887, *The Diaries of John Ruskin*, ed. Joan Evans and John Howard Whitehouse (Oxford: Clarendon Press, 1956–59), III, 1141.

28   Mss. of *Praeterita*, Osborn Collection, Beinecke Rare Book and Manuscript Library, Yale University.

29   *Diaries*, III, 1144 (3 January 1888). See also III, 1142 (26 April 1887).

30   Frequently, he managed their demands by ignoring their letters. See, e.g., his entry for 4 January 1846 in *Diaries*, I, 321–22: "I received in passing through Lausanne . . . a short letter from my Father, full of most unkind expressions of impatience at my stay in Venice. I had been much vexed by his apparent want of sympathy throughout the journey, and on receiving this letter my first impulse was to write a complaining and perhaps a bitter one in return. But as I drove down the hill from Lausanne there was something in the sweet sunshine between the tree trunks that made me think better of it. I considered that I should give my father dreadful pain if I did so, and that all this impatience was not unkindly meant, but only the ungoverned expression of extreme though selfish affection. At last I resolved, though with a little effort, to throw the letter into the fire." In a sense, Ruskin's transcription of the letters at the end of volume II represents a substitution for actions such as this one. In the substitution, both parents and

child appear better than, in fact, they were: the parents write appreciative letters, and the son respectfully preserves them in his autobiography.

31   *Works*, IV, 349, n. 4.

32   John T. McNeill, ed., *Calvin: Institutes of the Christian Religion*, trans. Ford Lewis Battles (Philadelphia: Westminster Press, 1975), p. 35. For Ruskin the issue was also a social one. He describes Bunyan as a "fat, vacant, vulgar" and Herbert as "high-bred, keen, severe, thoughtful." Always somewhat ashamed of his family's middle-class origins, he had no desire to associate himself with the less than refined aspects of his family's religion.

33   *Diaries*, I, 322 (4 January 1846). The revelation at Nyon is not the only conversion-like experience that Ruskin's diaries record. On 2 July 1854 at Lucerne, for instance, he writes: "I hope to keep this day a festival for ever, having received my third call from God, in answer to much distressful prayer" (II, 497–98). In the autobiography, however, Ruskin gives only the episode at Mont Blanc the weight of a religious and poetic epiphany.

34   See *Works*, II, 233–35, for the original version of the poem.

35   One might assume that Ruskin suppressed these lines in 1887 because they seemed arrogant. He had, in fact, noticed that flaw in 1845 when he had sent the verses home to his parents, commenting "I am really getting more pious than I was," and "perhaps a shade too modest into the bargain, as you will perceive, by my comparing myself to Moses and Elijah in the same couplet." I would argue, rather, that Ruskin suppressed the stanza because he could not admit, in an autobiography intended as "a dutiful offering," he had failed to live up to the vocational expectations that his parents had for him.

36   See, e.g., Columbus, "Ruskin's *Praeterita* as Thanatography," in Landow, ed., *Approaches to Victorian Autobiography*, pp. 112–15.

37   With this understanding of the subjectivity of biblical hermeneutics, Ruskin states his decision not to convert to Roman Catholicism but to remain (at least nominally) in the faith in which he had been raised. Despite the fact that he found evangelical Protestantism intellectually untenable and Roman Catholicism aesthetically appealing, he was not apt material for a conversion like Newman's. "From John Bunyan and Issac Ambrose," he explains, "I had received the religion by which I still myself lived, as far as I had spiritual life at all; and I had again and again proof enough of its truth, within limits, to have served me for all my own need, either in this world or the next" (III.i. 17). The point is clear: Ruskin no longer expects to find hermeneutic certainty or "true religion"; personal need has become for him the basis of religious practice.

CHAPTER 4

1   John Henry Cardinal Newman, *Apologia pro vita sua*, ed. David J. DeLaura (New York: W. W. Norton, 1968), p. 11. Citations will be to this text, which

is based upon the 1886 edition that includes all of Newman's emendations. In preparing this chapter, I have also consulted Martin J. Svaglic's definitive edition (Oxford: Clarendon Press, 1967) and benefited frequently from the help his and DeLaura's notes have provided.

2   The original title, *Apologia pro vita sua*, was restored in 1873, along with a subtitle adapted from the 1865 edition, *Being a History of his Religious Opinions*.

3   See Colby's "The Poetical Structure of Newman's *Apologia pro vita sua,"Journal of Religion*, 33 (1953), 47, and Svaglic's "The Structure of Newman's *Apologia,"* *PMLA*, 66 (1951), 138.

4   On epic allusions and Aristotle's *Poetics*, see Colby, pp. 47—57; on biblical motifs and the influence of dramatic structure, see Svaglic, pp. 138—48; on fictional techniques, see William R. Siebenschuh, "Art and Evidence in Newman's *Apologia,"* *Biography*, 3 (1980), 314—30; and on logical structure and the relation to the *Grammar of Assent*, see Jonathan Robinson, "The *Apologia* and the *Grammar of Assent,"* in *Newman's Apologia: A Classic Reconsidered*, ed. Vincent Ferrer Blehl and Francis X. Connolly (New York: Harcourt, Brace, and World, 1964), pp. 145—64, and Robert A. Colby, "The Structure of Newman's *Apologia Pro Vita Sua* in Relation to His Theory of Assent," *Dublin Review*, 460 (Summer 1953), 140—56. The evidence for these non-autobiographical approaches depends upon what the work includes or what Newman's other works suggest—e.g., allusions to classical epics, biblical motifs of spiritual warfare, a love of the theater, a knowledge of Aristotle's *Poetics*, or symbolic details characteristic of fiction. While providing illuminating commentary on the *Apologia*, such approaches imply that work is better treated in generic categories other than that of autobiography. Avrom Fleishman's recent *Figures of Autobiography* has begun to correct this generic misconception by reminding us of the classic autobiographical topoi that the *Apologia* invokes, but it does not examine systematically either the English or Augustinian traditions that inform the work.

5   "Autobiographical Memoir," in *Autobiographical Writings*, ed. Henry Tristram (New York: Sheed and Ward, 1957), p. 79. Newman wrote this memoir in the third person for his colleagues, particularly Ambrose St. John, to use after his death: "not so much for publication, as in order to show them what, in my own judgment, should in a Memoir be said about me, and how, viz., in respect to matter, manner, and length" (p. 24).

6   Ibid., p. 80.

7   Doddridge's chapter titles outline the same process of conversion that Newman describes: "The careless sinner awakened" (II), "The awakened sinner . . . cautioned against delay" (III), "The sinner arraigned and convicted" (IV), "The sinner stripped of his vain pleas" (V), "The sinner sentenced" (VI), "The helpless state of the sinner under condemnation" (VII), "New of salvation by Christ" (VIII), "The doubting soul . . . assisted" (XIII), "The assistance of the Spirit of God" (XV), "The Christian urged to . . . an express act of Self-dedication" (XVII), and so on.

8   Tristram, p. 80.

9   Philip Doddridge, *The Miscellaneous Works of Philip Doddridge, D.D.* (London: William Ball, 1839), p. vi.

10 Scott, *The Force of Truth*, p. 127. The autobiography was published originally in England in 1779.

11 Ibid., p. 87.

12 Ibid., pp. 45—48.

13 Ibid., pp. 51—52.

14 For a discussion of Scott's commentary, see chap. 2, n. 25.

15 Bunyan, sec. 15; John Newton, *An Authentic Narrative*, in *Works of the Rev. John Newton* (New York: Robert Carter, 1847), I, 87—89.

16 Scott, *The Force of Truth*, pp. 93, 108.

17 Ibid., p. 110.

18 Ibid., p. 110—11, 114. As Scott tells it, he acquired his evangelical doctrines by reading the Anglican divines, but complemented his theological reading with an intense study of the Scriptures, in which he had "ransacked the Bible" (the unfortunate verb is his) "to bring as much Scripture evidence for my direction as possible."

19 In *The Art of Autobiography in 19th and 20th Century England* (New Haven: Yale Univ. Press, 1984), p. 178, A. O. J. Cockshut suggests that the primary difference between Catholic and Protestant autobiographies lies in their presentation of conversion: "The Catholic view is that conversion is the beginning of a journey; or, perhaps better, a decisive change of direction. . . . The Protestant view tends to telescope several stages of Catholic experience into a unique, momentary action." While this distinction holds generally, it is also the case that many Protestant autobiographers, like Scott, view their conversions as a sequence of gradual changes and that the metaphor of the journey is as common among Protestant autobiographers as among Catholic. More important for the English autobiographer, I think, is the choice of a hermeneutic mode.

20 Sacvan Bercovitch, *The Puritan Origins of the Self* (New Haven: Yale Univ. Press, 1975), p. 15.

21 Alice Hayes, *A Legacy, or Widow's Mite, Left by Alice Hayes, to Her Children and Others* (London: T. Sowle, 1723), p. 31.

22 Newton, I, 79.

23 Ibid., 95—98.

24 Cruden, p. 39.

25 See Landow, *Victorian Types, Victorian Shadows*, pp. 23—28.

26 Tristram, p. 53.

27 As Margery S. Durham observes, Newman frequently uses the motif of return to the Mother Church to express his sense of exile, and on one occasion, he associates this motif with Abraham's archetypal journey ("The Spiritual Family in Newman's *Apologia*," *Thought*, 56 [1981], 422—23). But this association is a limited and local one, subsumed into a maternal pattern which is alien to the English spiritual autobiography.

28 Henry Chadwick, *The Early Church* (Harmondsworth, England: Penguin Books, 1967), p. 211. As Chadwick explains, the controversy had both political and doctrinal causes, and in the matter of politics, the Roman See was far more powerful than the African. In the end, Rome achieved a significant victory— but one, sadly, that separated congregations within the African church and created an antagonism against Rome that exists to the present day among Armenian, Coptic, and Ethiopian Christians.

29 This section of the *Apologia* does narrate, as Newman insists; but the sequence of events that it narrates concerns his discovery, during the Long Vacation of 1839, of the method of interpretation that led to his conversion in 1845. That discovery now determines the form of his autobiography.

30 On these occasions, Newman says that he determined to be guided "not by imagination, but by my reason": any "new conception of things should only so far influence me, as it had a logical claim to do so" (100). Here is another parallel with Thomas Scott, who gave priority to reason and denied the influence of "impulses, impressions, visions, dreams, or revelations."

31 Martin J. Svaglic, "Why Newman Wrote the *Apologia*," in *Apologia pro vita sua*, ed. DeLaura, p. 385.

32 I use here DeLaura's translation of Augustine's "Quapropter securus iudicat orbis terrarum, bonos non esse qui se dividunt ab orbe terrarum, in quacumque parte orbis terrarum" (see his edition of the *Apologia*, p. 98, n. 5).

33 According to Wiseman, the question is "essentially one of fact rather than of right; that is to say, the very circumstances of one particular Church being out of the aggregation of other Churches, constituted these judges over the other, and left no room for questioning the justice of the condemnation. St. Augustine has a golden sentence on this subject, which should be an axiom in theology." See Nicholas Wiseman, "Tracts for the Times: Anglican Claims of Apostolical Succession," *Dublin Review*, 7 (1839), 154.

34 Weintraub's argument appears throughout *The Value of the Individual: Self and Circumstance in Autobiography* (Chicago: Univ. of Chicago Press, 1978), but see esp. pp. 49, 91–92. See also the limited number of English translations of the *Confessions* listed in the *British Museum General Catalogue of Printed Books* for the years prior to 1838, as well as the evidence of Howard Helsinger ("Credence and Credibility: The Concern for Honesty in Victorian Autobiography") and Phyllis Grosskurth ("Where Was Rousseau?") on the negligible influence of Augustine's *Confessions*, both published in Landow, ed., *Approaches to Victorian Autobiography*, pp. 26–63.

  William C. Spengemann (pp. 1–33) and Avrom Fleishman (pp. 53–69) treat Augustine's *Confessions* as the seminal work in the English and American traditions, but neither gives convincing historical evidence for the claim. The forms of autobiography that Spengemann describes as intrinsic to the *Confessions* do not influence the autobiographers he discusses in any direct sense; indeed, these forms function primarily as a means of organizing his own discussion, and one can find "historical," "philosophical," and "poetic" elements in many of the autobiographies that he identifies as representing only one form.

Fleishman's book is more trustworthy as literary history, but it should be noted that the "figures" Fleishman associates with Augustine are, with two interesting exceptions, common types readily available to autobiographers from the Bible itself and in particular from St. Paul's account of conversion. The two exceptions, which Fleishman describes initially but does not mention in his chapter on Newman, are uniquely Augustinian: the admonition by a children's game and the terminology of a medical crisis. Significantly, both appear in Newman's account of his conversion, the first in an allusion to the Dick Whittington legend (98–99), the second in the crisis state (121–22) I describe below.

35 Edward Bouverie Pusey translated the *Confessions* in 1838 for *The Library of the Fathers of the Holy Catholic Church*.

36 *The Confessions of Saint Augustine*, trans. Edward B. Pusey (1838; New York: Collier Books, 1961), p. 79.

37 Ibid., pp. 79–80.

38 Ibid., p. 82.

39 On the rhetorical effects created by Newman's use of nostalgia here, see David J. DeLaura's essays, "The Allegory of Life: The Autobiographical Impulse in Victorian Prose," in Landow, ed., *Approaches to Victorian Autobiography*, pp. 342–44, and "Some Victorian Experiments in Closure," *Studies in the Literary Imagination*, 8 (1975), 19–35. What DeLaura identifies in the latter essay as the "almost maternal or conjugal emotions" associated with St. John (23), I read (below) as a submerged elegy to Newman's mother.

40 *Confessions of Saint Augustine*, pp. 151–52.

41 Ibid., pp. 141–42.

42 Issac Williams, *The Autobiography of Issac Williams . . . As Throwing Further Light on the History of the Oxford Movement* (London: Longmans, Green, 1892), p. 61.

43 For a catalogue of these metaphors, see Sydney Mendel, "Metaphor and Rhetoric in Newman's *Apologia*," *Essays in Criticism*, 23 (1973), 357–71.

44 Newman's contemporary, Alfred Tennyson once said, in writing the "elegiacs" that would become *In Memoriam*, that the saddest words he knew were those of Catullus, "Frater Ave atque Vale," because they were so final. Newman's stance, of course, is thoroughly Christian, lacking the pagan sense of absolute finality. But in his substitution of the elegiac object, Newman expresses both Christian reconciliation and an unspeakable loss.

45 So at least Shumaker suggests when he writes of the gradual evolution during the nineteenth century from exposition to a "fully novelized form" and Spengemann also implies when he describes a formal modulation from the "historical" to the "philosophical" to the "poetical," the last category represented primarily by autobiographical novels, *David Copperfield, The Scarlet Letter*, and (the one exception) *Sartor Resartus*. See Shumaker's *English Autobiography*, esp. chs. 6–8,

and Spengemann's *The Forms of Autobiography*, esp. pp. xv—xvii. Cf. also Roy Pascal's preference in *Design and Truth in Autobiography* (Cambridge: Harvard Univ. Press, 1960) for Victorian autobiographies that are already novelistic in form, such as Charlotte Bronte's *Villette* and Charles Dickens' *David Copperfield*.

46 John C. Cooper, "Why Did Augustine Write Books XI—XIII of the Confessions?" *Augustinian Studies*, 2 (1971), 42.

47 *Confessions of Saint Augustine*, p. 112.

48 This passage and others like it call into question Spengemann's reading of books I—IX, which argues that the *Confessions* treats experience only as an illustration of doctrinal pronouncements or a topic of exegesis, "never as something of interest or value in itself" (p. 11). It also calls into question his more general theory that the three parts of the *Confessions* (I—IX, X—XII, and XIII) are discontinuous, "the narrative mode and theological ideas of each succeeding part invalidat[ing], or at least qualify[ing], the assumptions behind the structure and doctrine of each preceding part" (p. 2).

49 Bunyan, pp. 102—03.

50 Scott, *The Force of Truth*, pp. 92—136.

CHAPTER 5

1 *Harriet Martineau's Autobiography, with Memorials by Maria Weston Chapman*, 3 vols. (London: Smith, Elder, 1877). All citations are to this edition, the first two volumes of which have been re-issued recently in facsimile (London: Virago Press, 1983).

Both R. K. Webb's *Harriet Martineau: A Radical Victorian* (London: Heinemann, 1960) and Mitzi Myer's "*Harriet Martineau's Autobiography*: The Making of a Female Philosopher," in *Women's Autobiography: Essays in Criticism*, ed. Estelle C. Jelinek (Bloomington: Indiana Univ. Press, 1980), pp. 53—70, give accounts of the composition of Martineau's autobiography, treating particularly its philosophical contexts. My approach diverges significantly from Myer's— and, indeed, from the approach in Jelinek's volume—in viewing Martineau's account as an aberration from, rather than as a representative example in, a tradition of women's autobiography.

2 See the index to William Matthews, *British Autobiography: An Annotated Bibliography of British Autobiographies Published or Written Before 1951* (Berkeley and Los Angeles: Univ. of California Press, 1955).

3 *Memorials of Francis Ridley Havergal*, ed. M[aria] V. G. H[avergal] (London: James Nisbet, [1880]); *Memoir of Mary Ann Gilpin of Bristol, Consisting Chiefly of Extracts from Her Diary and Letters*, 2d ed. (London: Edmund Fry, 1841); Eliza Edward, *Diary of a Quiet Life* (n.p.: n.p., 1887); *Memoir of Sarah Elizabeth Stacy* (Norwich: Josiah Fletcher, 1849); anonymous, *Experiences* (London: J. M. Watkins, 1926).

4   Matthews, p. x.

5   My own early essay on the autobiography of Mrs. M. O. W. Oliphant ("Audience and the Autobiographer's Art," in Landow, ed., *Approaches to Victorian Autobiography*, pp. 158—74) succumbs to this error by beginning with a conventional definition of autobiography and then attempting to make her work fit the definition. A more fruitful approach would recognize first that Oliphant's work is not conventional autobiography, but a memoir or a series of recollections, which she only half-successfully gave coherence to after the death of her intended editor, her eldest son Cecco.

6   Jelinek, ed., *Women's Autobiography,* esp. pp. 21—70. Later in the volume, however, in "Anais Nin's Diary in Context," p. 207, Lynn Z. Bloom and Orlee Holder attempt an important distinction between the autobiographical writings of men and women: "the typical [man's] autobiography [is] a summing up, a review of the whole life or an important segment of it. . . . It is structured, orderly. . . . [W]omen's autobiographies tend to be much less clearly organized, much less synthetic. Therefore, they are more like diaries, honest records of the moment." This distinction provides an important clue to the absence of retrospective spiritual autobiographies by nineteenth-century women.

7   *Memoirs, or Spiritual Exercises of Elizabeth West: Written by Her Own Hand* (Glasgow: John Bryce, 1766); Jane Turner, *Choice Experiences of the Kind Dealings of God, before, in, and after Conversion* (London: H. Hils, 1653); and *Autobiography of Mary Rich, Countess of Warwick,* ed. T. C. Croker (London: Percy Society, 1842). I have been unable to locate the fourth autobiography under the title that Matthews lists, *An Account of Anne Jackson.*

8   *A Legacy, or Widow's Mite, Left By Alice Hayes, To Her Children and others* (London: J. Sowle, 1723), pp. 15, 28, 30, 47, 68—69.

9   According to Elaine Showalter's distinction, the adjective "feminine" would apply to Martineau's own work in that it represents an "imitation of the prevailing modes of the dominant tradition" and perhaps an "internalization of its standards of art" (see *A Literature of Their Own: British Women Novelists from Bronte to Lessing* [Princeton: Princeton Univ. Press, 1977], p. 13). I discuss this issue of imitation later in pp. 153—55, but here I would distinguish Martineau's *Autobiography* from the "feminine"literature of her contemporaries by pointing to its significant revision of the dominant tradition and by suggesting that, while Martineau may accept some of the prevailing standards of art, she does not internalize "its view on social roles."

10   The keeping of a private diary probably grew out of the practice, common in dissenting sects of the seventeenth and eighteenth centuries, of writing a brief autobiographical account at the time of conversion or confirmation and then reviewing the account periodically (but especially before taking communion) to check on spiritual progress. For an interesting description of this practice in eighteenth-century Scotland, see the *Memoirs, or Spiritual Exercises of Elizabeth West.*

11   *The Earnest Christian: Memoirs, Letter, and Journals of Harriet Maria, Wife of the late Rev. Mark R. Jukes,* comp. and ed. Mrs. H. A. Gilbert (London: Seeley, Jackson, and Halliday, 1858), pp. iii—iv.

12   Socially, women had never been encouraged to make their spiritual lives a matter of public interest, even in the seventeenth and early eighteenth centuries when some were required to write (or at least recount) them before taking communion. In the Puritan Church of Visible Saints, for instance, men who sought admission presented their testimonies of conversion publically to the congregation; women presented their accounts privately to the minister. See Carol Edkins, "Quest for Community: Spiritual Autobiographies of Eighteenth-Century Quaker and Puritan Women in America," in Jelinek, ed., *Women's Autobiography,* pp. 39—52.

Some of the more remarkable early spiritual accounts by women nonetheless found a publisher and thus a wider audience. By the late eighteenth century, however, there is a significant decline in the publication of such women's autobiographies, despite the increased publication of similar accounts by men. This decline may be related to a process of religious and literary "gentrification": as members of dissenting sects rose in social status and as the genre simultaneously became more respectable for middle and upper class men, it paradoxically became less possible for women to write and publish their own spiritual accounts.

13   Bloom and Holder, in Jelinek, ed., *Women's Autobiography,* p. 207.

14   Cf. George Whetstone's discussion of women's capacities in *The English Mirror* (London: I. Windet, 1586) with John Knox's denigration in *The First Blast of the Trumpet Against the Monstrous Regiment of Women* (1558; Philadelphia: Andrew Steuart, 1766). This debate focused on the question of Elizabeth I's rule.

15   *The Works of Hannah More* (New York: Harper and Brothers, 1854), I, 367. The edition I cite throughout this chapter is a popular nineteenth-century collection of More's work, the "first complete American edition." More's view was considered enlightened in its day.

16   Although Hartley's work itself contains no discussion of gender and intellectual capacity, it could have been used to draw such conclusions by anyone who assumed the physiological inferiority of women.

17   Harriet Martineau, "Female Writers of Practical Divinity, No. II, Mrs. More and Mrs. Barbauld," *Monthly Repository,* 17 (1822), 747.

18   Mary Kirby Gregg, *Leaflets from My Life: A Narrative Autobiography* (London: Simpkin, 1887).

19   Mary Cholmondeley, *Under One Roof: A Family Record* (London: J. Murray, 1918). That Cholmondeley was capable of thinking about her life both retrospectively and comprehensively is clear from a private account Elaine Showalter quotes in *A Literature of Their Own,* p. 72: "I was nothing, a plain silent country girl, an invalid no one cared a straw about . . . but a dull smouldering fire of passion seemed to be kindling in me . . . a slow fire to overcome all these

dreadful obstacles of illness and ugliness and incompetence." Showalter's source is not Cholmondeley herself, however, but Percy Lubbock's recollection of her words in *Mary Cholmondeley: A Sketch from Memory*. Of the three memoirs cited in this paragraph, Cholmondeley's is by far the best.

20 Mary Lisle, *Long, Long Ago: An Autobiography* (London: J. and C. Mozley, 1856).

21 Mrs. Oliphant expected her son Cecco, who was her literary executor, to provide the interpretation when he edited her manuscripts after her death. Cecco died before Mrs. Oliphant, however, and she was left to do the job which, in a typically feminine way, she had hoped her family would do. See my "Audience and the Autobiographer's Art: The *Autobiography* of Mrs. M. O. W. Oliphant," in Landow, ed., *Approaches to Victorian Autobiography*, pp. 158—74.

22 The notable exception is the Quaker sect, which allowed women to "divide the word" in its meetings and which, not coincidentally, also encouraged women to publish a Quaker form of spiritual autobiography, the private journal after the model of George Fox's.

23 Quoted by Frank Baker in "John Wesley and Sarah Crosby," *Proceedings of the Wesley Historical Society*, 27 (1949), 79. Wesley later changed his mind about some women preachers.

24 James Boswell, *Life of Samuel Johnson* (Oxford: Oxford Univ. Press, 1970), p. 327.

25 The accounts of Dinah Morris' preaching in *Adam Bede* draw, in part, on Eliot's knowledge of her own aunt's career. Elizabeth Evans was an itinerant Methodist preacher, well known for her clarity in Scripture doctrines and readiness in the Spirit. See Wesley F. Swift, "The Women Itinerant Preachers of Early Methodism," in *Proceedings of the Wesley Historical Society*, 28 (1951), 93.

26 *Jane Eyre*, ed. Richard J. Dunn (New York: Norton, 1971). All citations will be to this edition; both chapter and page numbers will be included in the text.

27 See Landow, *Victorian Types, Victorian Shadows*, pp. 97—100.

28 Martineau's account is not written completely in the form of a spiritual autobiography. Because she decided to prohibit the publication of her letters, she herself included large sections of literary memoirs (e.g., IV, i—ii), and she further instructed Maria Chapman, her editor, to add a third volume of "memorials" to the *Autobiography*.

29 Martineau and her sister Rachel were educated at Perry's academy due to a quirk of religious politics in Norwich. The Reverend Perry had converted to Unitarianism in 1813, when Harriet was eleven, and as a consequence of his conversion, he lost his Presbyterian congregation and the majority of his pupils. Along with other Unitarians, the Martineaus sent their children—sons and daughters both—to his school to help him through the financial crisis. Thus began the two years of "that delectable schooling" that Martineau looked back upon as one of the unalloyed pleasures of her life.

30   Harriet Martineau, trans., *The Positive Philosophy of Auguste Comte*, 2 vol. (London: John Chapman, 1853).

31   Ibid., I, 3.

32   Quoted in Webb, p. 83.

33   These sections of the *Autobiography* (III, iv; IV, ii—iv) are closer in form to memoirs than to spiritual autobiography, as are many sections in part VI, the final positivist phase.

34   Harriet Martineau, *Household Education* (London: Edward Moxon, 1849), esp. pp. 1—10.

35   William James, *The Varieties of Religious Experience* (New York: New American Library, 1958), pp. 198—99.

36   Ibid., p. 201.

37   Jean Starobinski, "The Style of Autobiography," in *Autobiography: Essays Theoretical and Critical*, ed. James Olney (Princeton: Princeton Univ. Press, 1980), p. 74.

38   Showalter, p. 13.

39   *Positive Philosophy*, II, 463.

40   Bunyan, *Grace Abounding*, sec. 44—45, and *Apologia pro Vita Sua*, ed. David J. DeLaura, p. 82.

41   *Confessions of Saint Augustine*, p. 13.

42   Webb, p. 71.

43   Charlotte Brontë, *Shirley*, ed. Herbert Rosengarten and Margaret Smith (Oxford: Clarendon Press, 1979), p. 371.

44   Quoted by Elizabeth Gaskell in *The Life of Charlotte Brontë*, ed. Alan Shelston (London: Penguin, 1975), p. 618, n. 6.

CHAPTER 6

1   In *British Autobiography: An Annotated Bibliography*, William Matthews includes the *Memoirs of the Life and Writings of Mr. William Whiston* (1743) in his index to accounts by scientists, thus suggesting it to be the first published scientific autobiography. Although Whiston engaged in astronomical studies and was the first Londoner to give scientific lectures with experiments, his autobiographical recollections contain very little of science—and only then to bolster the theological views with which he is primarily interested. Ferguson's account, published originally in *Select Mechanical Exercises* (1773), is more clearly the work of a scientist recording new discoveries.

2   James Ferguson, *A Short Account of the Life of James Ferguson, Written by Himself* (London: Hunt and Clarke, 1826), p. 3. This edition, based on the account in *Select Mechanical Exercises,* is the sixth volume in a series of autobiographies published by Hunt and Clarke during the 1820s.

3   Joseph Priestley, *Memoirs of the Rev. Dr. Joseph Priestley . . . Written by Himself* (London: C. Stower, 1809), and Richard Watson, *Anecdotes of the Life of Richard Watson . . . Written by Himself at Different Intervals* (London: T. Cadell and W. Davies, 1817). Watson experimented with salt solutions, and Priestley conducted experiments that led to the discovery of various gases, including nitrogen, nitrous oxide, carbonic oxide, and hydrochloric acid.

4   Robert Munro, *Autobiographical Sketch* (Glasgow: Maclehose, Jackson, 1921). Robert Munro (1835−1921) was an archaeologist and anitquarian whose primary work was *The Lake-Dwellings of Europe* (1890). Like Ferguson, Munro justified the publication of his memoirs in terms of the model that it provided for readers: "a description of the successful steps by which a country lad—without possessing any exceptional ability [and] without any social or financial backing, but solely through a determined will to conquer—attained to a position of some distinction in the scientific world, may be an inspiring object-lesson to others" (pp. 77−78).

5   Priestley, p. 26.

6   Charles Darwin, *The Autobiography of Charles Darwin, 1809−1882,* ed. Nora Barlow (New York: W. W. Norton, 1958), p. 21; Thomas Henry Huxley, *Autobiography and Selected Essays* (Boston: Houghton Mifflin, 1909), pp. 1−2.

7   Quoted from a public address by Evelyn Hopkinson, his mother, in *The Story of a Mid-Victorian Girl* (Cambridge: Cambridge Univ. Press, 1928), p. 65. This memoir is, in large part, about the engineering achievements of her husband, John Hopkinson.

8   See the quotations on speculation and generalization that Barlow assembles in the appendix, "Charles Darwin and His Grandfather," pp. 159−66.

9   Darwin, p. 119.

10 Ibid., pp. 21−28. After the initial segment of the *Autobiography,* Darwin is less original in his method, more predictable in his selection and organization of data. The accounts of Cambridge and the voyage of the *Beagle,* pp. 56−82, assume the conventional forms of memoir writing, as does the final section, "My Several Publications."

11 Ibid., p. 43.

12 See, for example, Munro, pp. 2−5, and Francis Galton, *Memories of My Life* (London: Methuen, 1908), pp. 13−21.

13 James Olney, *Metaphors of Self: The Meaning of Autobiography* (Princeton: Princeton Univ. Press, 1972), p. 183.

14 Darwin, p. 21.

15 See Nora Barlow's list of the passages Francis omitted in her edition of the *Autobiography,* pp. 244−45, and esp. Darwin's comment, "Nothing is more remarkable than the spread of skepticism or rationalism during the latter half of my life" (p. 95).

16 Olney, pp. 187−88, 196.

17   Olney's preference for psychological interpretation is clear in his praise of Jung's *Memories, Dreams, Reflections* as a complex autobiographical work and in his label of "autobiography simplex" for works that choose other hermeneutic systems (Fox's *Journal*, Darwin's *Autobiography*, Newman's *Apologia*, and Mill's *Autobiography*). While many twentieth-century readers share this preference, it is important, I think, to understand the very different assumptions of nineteenth-century autobiographers.

18   Martineau, *Autobiography*, II, 333–34.

19   Galton, pp. 1–12. The chapter is titled "Parentage."

20   Herbert Spencer, *An Autobiography* (New York: D. C. Appleton, 1904), I, vii, xi.

21   Ibid., I, 22. Chapter 1, "Extraction," uses family history to describe inherited characteristics; chapters 2 and 3 analyze his parents' and grandparents' hereditary contributions.

22   Ibid., I, 47.

23   Ibid., I, 89, 95.

24   Ibid., I, 86, 101, 106; II, 509–10.

25   Darwin, it should be noted, was extremely distrustful of Spencer's tendency to generalize and interpret too quickly. In an expurgated section of his autobiography, he comments that Spencer's "deductive manner of treating every subject is wholly opposed to my frame of mind." "His conclusions never convince me," Darwin added. "Over and over again I have said to myself, after reading one of his discussions,—'Here would be a fine subject for half-a-dozen years' work'" (pp. 108–09).

26   Ibid., pp. 23, 26, 79. The last statement was evidently too strong for Francis Darwin, who deleted it from the official version of the *Autobiography*.

27   Huxley, p. 4.

28   Galton, p. 288.

29   Munro, pp. 7–8, 77–78.

30   Huxley, p. 13.

31   Spencer, I, 171.

32   Ibid., II, 489–90.

33   Ibid., 492–503. Most readers will find in Spencer's discussion of his "underdeveloped thoracic viscera" an amusing rationalization for his lack of philanthropic activity.

34   Ibid., 538–40. See also his comment in the preface that "in the genesis of a system of thought the emotional nature is a large factor," I, vii.

35   According to Daniel F. Howard, Butler wrote the first volume of his autobiographical novel in 1873–74 and the second in 1878. See Howard's edition of *Ernest Pontifex or The Way of All Flesh* (London: Methuen, 1965), p. vi, which will be used for all citations in this chapter.

36   Spencer was not, of course, a literary figure, and his work did not attract the

attention it might have as literary autobiography. Butler was, in contrast, well known for his interests in both literary form and scientific theory, and thus his autobiographical novel had the greater possibility of suggesting a means of a generic reform.

37 See. R. A. Streatfeild's "Note" to *The Way of All Flesh* (London: Grant Richards, 1903), and Petronella Jacoba de Lange, *Samuel Butler: Critic and Philosopher* (1925; rpt. New York: Haskell House, 1966), pp. 92—93. On the relation between Butler's scientific theories and the novel, see also Claude T. Bissell, "A Study of *The Way of All Flesh*," in *Nineteenth-Century Studies*, ed. R. C. Bald et al. (Ithaca: Cornell Univ. Press, 1940).

38 Sigmund Freud, "Dostoevsky and Parricide," in *Dostoevsky: A Collection of Critical Essays*, ed. Rene Wellek (Englewood Cliffs, NJ: Prentice-Hall, 1962), p. 103.

39 Indeed, to paraphrase Malcolm Muggeridge, *The Way of All Flesh* was "engendered by a grudge and enlivened by hate" (see *The Earnest Atheist: A Study of Samuel Butler* [London: Eyre and Spottiswoode, 1936], p. xiii). Butler began the first section of the novel in 1873, immediately after a quarrel with his father in which Canon Butler accused his son of killing his mother with his disgraceful writing. The second section was completed in 1878, following another quarrel between Butler and his father. For an account of the genesis of the novel, see Howard, pp. v—vii.

40 One might also point to Butler's division of his ambivalent feelings about his own mother in his creation of the novel's two maternal figures: Christina and Alethea. Christina has usually been considered a portrait of Fanny Worsley, Butler's mother, and Aunt Alethea, a portrait of Eliza Mary Ann Savage, Butler's friend of over twenty years. Howard argues, however, that except for a few details in chapter 32, Alethea is "an idealized projection of his mother," with Christina retaining Mrs. Butler's unpleasant characteristics and Alethea exhibiting her attractive ones (see pp. viii—ix). If Howard is correct, then Butler has plotted the novel so that Ernest can defeat his father in the oedipal struggle, winning both Alethea's love and money.

41 Quoted by Arnold Silver, ed., *The Family Letters of Samuel Butler, 1841—1886* (Stanford: Stanford Univ. Press, 1962), p. 28.

42 Samuel Butler, *Life and Habit*, Shrewsbury ed. (London: Jonathan Cape, 1923), p. 64.

43 Ibid., p. 41.

44 Edmund Gosse, *Father and Son: A Study of Two Temperaments*, ed. James Hepburn (1907; London: Oxford Univ. Press, 1974), p. 5. All citations will be to this text, which is reprinted from the first impression of the original 1907 edition.

45 Although Gosse was ambivalent about the naturalism of Zola and his European contemporaries, the choice of a term such as "diagnosis" for *Father and Son*

suggests his attempt to identify the work with literary realism, which in "The Limits of Realism in Fiction" (see *Documents of Literary Realism,* ed. George J. Becker [Princeton: Princeton Univ. Press, 1963], pp. 384–93), he discusses in similarly scientific terms: "anatomy," "pathology," "clinical," and the like. This identification with literary realism implies a special claim to truth. In Gosse's view, the realistic movement sought to convey truth, "founded on and limited by actual experience," and to avoid "the romantic and rhetorical elements that novelists have so largely used to embroider the homespun fabric of experience."

46   These signals have produced a lively tradition of critical debate about the genre of *Father and Son.* Harold Nicolson started it innocently enough when he discussed the biographical innovations of the work and almost incidentally suggested that it contained "all the apparatus of Greek tragedy" (see *The Development of English Biography,* 3d ed. [London: Hogarth Press, 1948], p. 148). In "Tragedy in Gosse's *Father and Son*" (*English Literature in Transition,* 9 [1966], 137–44), Gosse's most recent critical biographer, James D. Woolf, followed out the suggestion, arguing that the Father is a "tragic hero," a Lear figure betrayed by his anger and angst to resist the natural order. Almost inevitably, another critic, R. Victoria Arana, countered Woolf and his predecessors, pointing out that the rhetorical emphasis of the book falls on the son's development and thus upon the autobiographical and comic elements (see her "Sir Edmund Gosse's *Father and Son*: Autobiography as Comedy," in *Genre,* 10 [1977], 63–76). Others have tried other generic possibilities intimated by Gosse: a "diagnosis," which borrows the detailed critical vocabulary of Matthew Arnold's Hebraism and Hellenism; a "document," which raises the classic problem of truth of experience versus truth of form and shows a scientific concern for facts; and a "fiction," a term which Gosse avoids in the preface, but which describes an alternative to the Word of God and explains the novelistic elements in the autobiography. On the Arnoldian diagnosis, see Anthony Arthur, "Gosse's *Father and Son*: Escape from 'The Prison of Puritanism,'" *Modern British Literature,* 3 (1978), 73–77, and Philip Dodd, "The Nature of Edmund Gosse's *Father and Son,*" *English Literature in Transition,* 22 (1979), 270–79; on the issue of fact versus fiction, see William J. Gracie, Jr., "Truth of Form in Edmund Gosse's *Father and Son,*" *Journal of Narrative Technique,* 4 (1974), 176–87, and Roger J. Porter, "Edmund Gosse's *Father and Son*: Between Form and Flexibility," *Journal of Narrative Technique,* 5 (1975), 174–95; and on the work as a "fiction," see Vivien and Robert Folkenflik, "Words and Language in *Father and Son,*" *Biography,* 2 (1979), 157–74.

These analyses all cite legitimate evidence in defense of a single generic category, but they are mistaken in their arguments against other generic possibilities. Gosse's text suggests a variety of generic forms. It does so because of the breakdown of a coherent biblical system of self-interpretation and the failure of another single model, scientific or otherwise, to assume its place.

47 See, e.g., Anna Shipton's memoir of Gosse's mother, *Tell Jesus: Recollections of Emily Gosse* (Philadelphia: Mrs. Jane Hamilton, 1868), which combines biographical materials about Mrs. Gosse with an autobiographical narrative about Shipton that incorporates many of the conventional motifs.

48 James Hepburn, "Religion, Science, and Philip Henry Gosse," *Contemporary Review*, 233 (1978), 196—97.

49 Here Edmund Gosse follows almost verbatim the description of his mother's death written by his father, Philip Henry Gosse, in *A Memorial of the Last Days of Earth of Emily Gosse* (London: James Nisbet, 1857), pp. 75 ff. On matters that deal with the love between mother and son, however, Edmund significantly revises his father's account, making maternal love stronger than marital or (to put it in psychoanalytic terms) revealing an unresolved oedipal conflict as the basis of the scene. When Emily learns of the fatal cancer, e.g., her husband remembers:

> To me the prospect was dark indeed; but to her death had no terrors. Our dear child she was able to leave *in the hands of that loving Lord,* for whom she had trained him from the earliest infancy, and to whose care she now, in the confidence of faith, committed him; but her loving heart deeply tasted the bitterness of the cup which she saw I should soon have to drink. (*Memorial,* pp. 52—53)

Edmund repeats the italicized phrase, but alters the focus of her concern:

> When it was quite certain that no alleviations and no medical care could prevent, or even any longer postpone the departure of my Mother, I believe that my future conduct became the object of her greatest and her most painful solicitude. She said to my Father that the worst trial of her faith came from the feeling that she was called upon to leave that child whom she had so carefully trained from his infancy for the peculiar service of the Lord, . . . [but] she was able, she said, to leave me 'in the hands of her loving Lord.' (38)

Although Gosse softens (perhaps guiltily) the insistence on his own priority with the phrase, "I believe," the account of his mother's death in chap. III consistently reduces his father to an inconsequential figure, as it makes the son the true object of Emily Gosse's affection.

50 Alex Preminger, Frank J. Warnke, and O. B. Hardison, Jr., eds., *Princeton Encyclopedia of Poetry and Poetics* (Princeton: Princeton Univ. Press, 1974), s.v. parody.

51 J. Hillis Miller, pp. 5—6, 14—15. Miller's comments follow from his translation of a passage in Deleuze's *Logique du sens* (Paris: Les Editions de Minuit, 1969), p. 302: "The first exactly defines the world of copies or of representa-

tions; it establishes the world as icon. The second, against the first, defines the world of simulacra. It presents the world itself as phantasm."

52 The first phrase is Edmund Gosse's in *Father and Son*, p. 97; the second, Philip Henry Gosse's in the preface to *Actinologia Britannica: A History of the British Sea-Anemones and Corals* (London: Van Voorst, 1860), p. viii.

53 See his letter of 4 March 1873 to his father, quoted in Evan Charteris, *The Life and Letters of Sir Edmund Gosse* (London: William Heinemann, 1931), p. 56: "For my own part, I cling to nothing so much as the Godhead of Christ. If Christ was man and no God, I am driven back into chaos. I can see no scheme of the world's history. Devoutly and firmly do I believe that Jesus Christ was perfect God and perfect man."

54 Samuel Butler, *Luck or Cunning?*, quoted by Frank Miller Turner, *Between Science and Religion: The Reaction to Scientific Naturalism in Late Victorian England* (New Haven: Yale Univ. Press, 1974), pp. 189—90.

55 Edmund Gosse, *Aspects and Impressions* (New York: Scribner's 1922), p. 60.

56 *Confessions of Saint Augustine*, pp. 151—52; Bunyan, sec. 264; Cowper, p. 83; Carlyle, p. 187.

57 Porter, pp. 188—89.

58 *Confessions of Saint Augustine*, p. 131.

59 This standard treatment of Gehazi comes from Scott, *The Holy Bible*, s.v. II Kings 5:20—25.

60 See n. 46 above.

61 Bunyan, sec. 140—41.

62 Folkenflik, pp. 157, 170.

63 See de Man's comments on "the gap separating the artist as an empirical subject from a fictional 'self,'" as well as his discussion of the "ontology of unmediated presence" in "The Rhetoric of Blindness: Jacques Derrida's Reading of Rousseau," in his *Blindness and Insight: Essays In the Rhetoric of Contemporary Criticism* (New York: Oxford Univ. Press, 1971), pp. 102—41.

64 Hans W. Frei's phrase in *The Eclipse of Biblical Narrative*, p. 3.

AFTERWORD

1 Bloom, p. 5.